Vol State 500K

VOL STATE 500K

A Journey Through Madness, Blurring the Lines of American Division

Nancy Barber

Ultreia Unlimited

This publication is designed to provide accurate and authoritative information in regard to the subject matter covered. It is sold with the understanding that neither the author nor the publisher is engaged in rendering legal, investment, accounting or other professional services. While the publisher and author have used their best efforts in preparing this book, they make no representations or warranties with respect to the accuracy or completeness of the contents of this book and specifically disclaim any implied warranties of merchantability or fitness for a particular purpose. No warranty may be created or extended by sales representatives or written sales materials. The advice and strategies contained herein may not be suitable for your situation. You should consult with a professional when appropriate. Neither the publisher nor the author shall be liable for any loss of profit or any other commercial damages, including but not limited to special, incidental, consequential, personal, or other damages.

ISBN: 979-8-9916509-0-8

Cover design by Kirk Marsh & Nancy Barber
Figure photo by Ray Krolewicz
Map illustration by Nancy Barber
Interior photos by Nancy Barber unless otherwise noted

First printed in the U.S.A. by Ultreia Unlimited

Contents

With love for Chris, who's made all the adventures more fun.

*"We are not enemies, but friends. We must not be enemies.
Though passion may have strained, it must not break our
bonds of affection. The mystic chords of memory, stretching
from every battlefield and patriot grave to every living heart
and hearthstone all over this broad land, will yet swell the
chorus of the Union, when again touched, as surely they will
be, by the better angels of our nature."*
Abraham Lincoln, First Inaugural Address, 1861

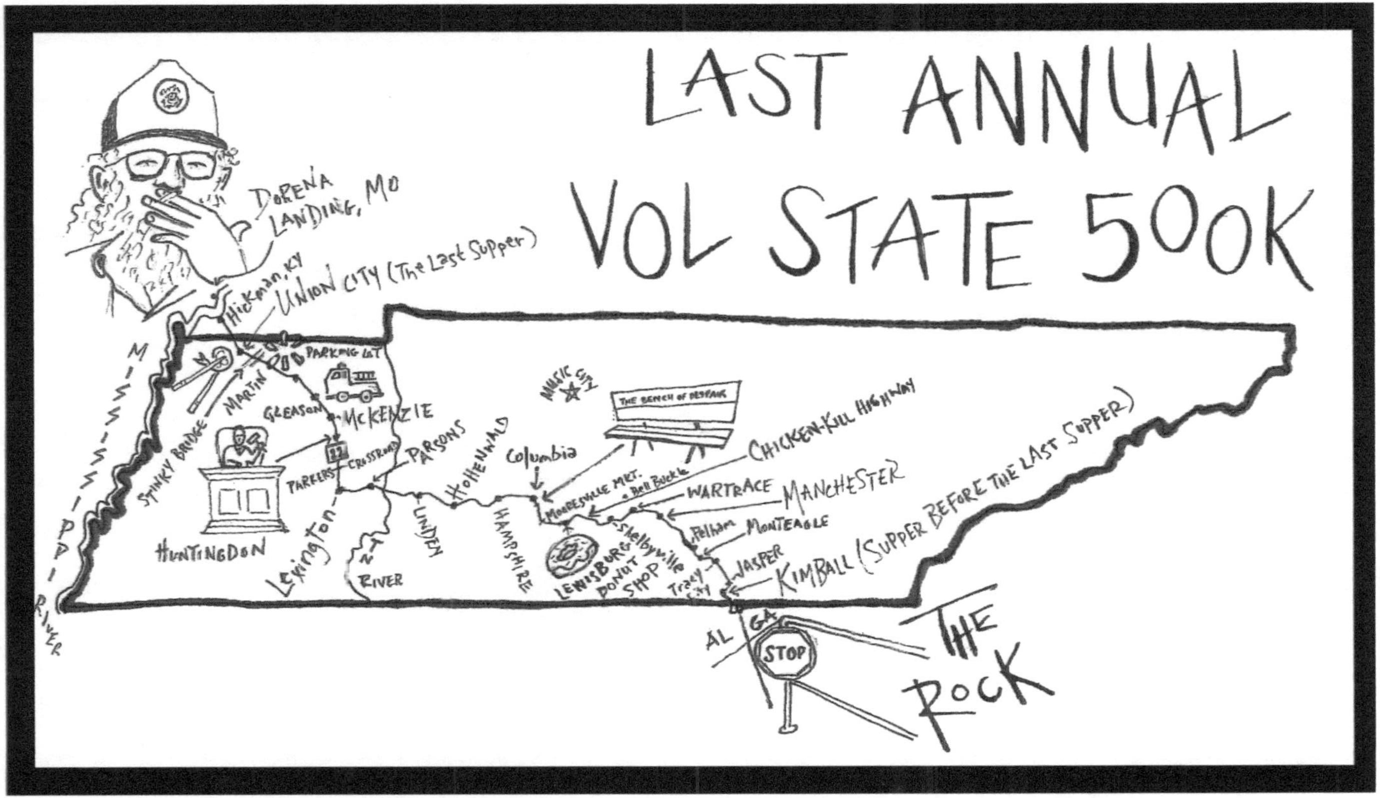

LAST ANNUAL
VOL STATE 500K
DoReNA LANDING, MO
Hickman, KY
UNION CITY (The Last Supper)
PARKING LoT
M
Martin
SPINKY BRIDGE
Gleason
McKENZIE
HuNTINGDON
Lexington
PARKERS CROSSROAD
PARSONS
LINDEN
N
River
HoHENWALD
HAMPSHIRE
Columbia
MUSIC CITY
THE BENCH OF DESPAIR
MooRESVILLE MKT.
Bell Buckle
CHICKEN-KILL HIGHWAY
WARTRACE
MANCHESTER
Pelham
MonTeagle
Shelbyville
LEWISBURG DONUT SHOP
Tracy City
JASPER
KIMBALL (SUPPER BEFORE THE LAST SUPPER)
AL   GA
STOP
THE ROCK
M—I—S—S—I—S—S—I—P—P—I— River

Introduction: How it came to pass....

*"Laz is not a race director. He's a poet. He's an artist.
And races are his medium and runners are his paints.
He writes these 12-hour updates, and they're just brilliant.
There's all this drama in there, and we're just his raw materials."*
—Bob Hearn, King of the Road, Queen of the South,
(*The Adventure Jogger* podcast)

A vacation without a car... or any common sense

When I arrive at London-Gatwick Airport at noon for my 2 pm flight, the Norse Atlantic Airlines gate area looks like a refugee camp with a line that takes up every inch of space in an intricate labyrinth, then spills out around the corner in back, and way down the terminal. Norse—new, I know, but cheap—doesn't issue boarding passes online, so every passenger has to wait in line for one of them. Three hours I stand in this line, long past my flight's supposed departure time, now delayed, listening to the budding but likely short-lived romance of two globetrotting work-from-anywhere types. She's been in Lisbon for the last six months. He's been in Sydney until the most recent stint in London. Like me, they're both Americans used to living abroad, and they're both heading home.

Why in the hell am I doing this? I've been perseverating on this mantra for almost a year. Leaving behind my civil partner Chris and a lovely summer in England for most of July, I'll start with a week acclimatizing to the miserable Florida heat and humidity, then drive up to Tennessee for the start of the Last Annual Vol State Race (a.k.a. LAVS or Vol State or even Vole Stare). The plan is to walk 314 miles in 10 days across Tennessee and bits of four other states, then spend five days recuperating before I fly back to London.

What in the world is attractive about a 500K unsupported walk up and down Tennessee hills in the melting July humidity with 119 other folks, most of whom will speed off at the start, and I'll never see again? Why would I want to spend ten days wandering through 17 counties that all voted for Donald Trump in large numbers . . . *twice*, in 2016 and 2020. And they'll probably vote for him again in 2024.

It's the Bible Belt of the South. I'll be eating convenience-store cuisine, walking just this side of heat stroke, hoping to catch four hours sleep a day, including naps on benches and concrete floors. Why would I consider repeatedly hiking all night on Tennessee backroads, searching for discreet places to pee, dodging rednecks and hallucinations? Why, as Race Director Lazarus Lake so eloquently puts it, would I want to spend ten days learning to "live like a stray dog"? This is not my weather. These are not my people. I'm not even sure if this is my country anymore. *Why in the hell am I doing this?*

Maybe it's the hillbilly. . . .

At least part of the reason is a self-proclaimed "old hillbilly who lives in the woods" of Tennessee, whose trucker's hat disguises balding white curly hair that he sometimes wears in a rat tail. A scraggly white beard falls down his face and chin to the front of a white button-down shirt just above a modest pot belly and a pair of old jeans. He doesn't look like an ultrarunning guru. If we traded the clothes for a red-velvet-with-white-trim suit, he could easily pass for a homeless Santa Claus. If we traded his clothes for a tunic, sandals, and some beads, he might be mistaken for an Eastern spiritual teacher—until he opened his mouth and a Southern drawl jumped out.

His mother named him Gary Cantrell, but his *nom de plume* is Lazarus Lake, and most folks call him Laz. Some folks still call him Gary, but it seems almost an affectation—a signal that they're in the inner circle of the cult. Did I mention the cult? Laz is the cult guru who creates performance art under the guise of ultra races. First, he crafts his idea for a race and what sort of transcendent (and horrific) experience he wants to shape for the participants—each of his eight races is different—then he uses his poetry and charm to so whip people into a frenzy about the adventure that they sign up—sometimes even beg—for a bit part in his artistic, sadistic madness.

People, I say. Me, I mean.

Then again, maybe I should blame it on Tony Webb Pest Control . . . .

It was really Tony Webb's fault. A year ago I had never heard of Vol State, but my pal Tony, who was my pest control guy ("Your web of protection") when I lived in DeLand, Florida, kept posting about it on Facebook. He was running the 2022 race. I should mention that when I say "running," I usually mean "walking." This is true for Tony and most other participants. Even Vol State record-holder Bob Hearn, who finished the race in three days and four hours in 2021, said that he walked over half of the race (albeit at 14-minute-per-mile walking splits). Nevertheless, the convention is to say that you "ran" Vol State even if you walked 100% of it at a pace much slower than Bob's. The good folks of Tennessee know better, though, and they often refer to Vol State participants as "them walkers."

So, Tony's FB posts about Vol State led me to research what it was, which led me to join the Last Annual Vol State 500K Road Race page on Facebook, which led me to a soap opera of race stories and a link to the tracker where I could follow individual participants' progress every 12 hours and read their agonizing and often funny comments. "Last Annual" is just one of the many ironic bits that Laz throws in to keep things "fun." Laz ran a version of Vol State with some friends in the 80's and then kept refining it over the years. LAVS has been run every year since 2006 on essentially the same course, and Laz has no plans for a *last* one.

Tony is a short, thin, handsome 62-year-old with shiny blue eyes and the enthusiasm and energy of a young boy. He's also an avid Trumper, which I generally overlook because he was so generous with his pest-control help and because he's a Cincinnati Reds fanatic from the Big Red Machine days when I, too, was a crazed fan. Tony had apparently been training for Vol State for a year and was busting to get started on the 2022 event with his trusty "Who Dey" doll, the Cincinnati Bengals mascot. They were set to traverse the 314 miles through five states from Dorena Landing, Missouri, to Castle Rock, Georgia.

All this five-state stuff is just more hype from Laz. It's essentially a race across Tennessee, but for more "fun," Laz throws in four other state bits.

To give you a little taste of the insanity, the group starts with a ferry ride across the Mississippi River from Hickman, KY, to Dorena Landing, MO. Then everyone gets off the ferry, walks up the bank, and stands behind a pole until Laz lights a cigarette to officially start the race. Then the group walks back onto the ferry, which crosses back over the river to what is the effective start of the race back in Hickman. After 11 Kentucky miles and a few hundred in Tennessee, the race ends with a short, steep hike through Alabama en route to Castle Rock near the top of Sand Mountain just inside the Georgia border.

Two days before the race started in 2022, Tony had posted on FB:

> *It is all I have thought about since signing up a year ago and was lucky enough haha to be chosen.*
> *Many people have asked me why? l think it's my Moby Dick....My Mount Doom...my pitch for the angels! Either way I'm here now and I say ynot (my name backwards).*

Ynot indeed! Tony's "haha" after being "lucky enough" is the typical paradoxical response for getting into Vol State, the quintessential "be careful what you wish for" event. Why would anyone want to do this race? As a native Floridian, I cherished a vampiric existence during the hot months. Stay in the AC as much as possible unless it's dark outside. Then you can roam with plenty of humidity but tolerable temps. This walking all day long sounded dreadful, but something else was also at play. "I'm alive," wrote Tony. "I feel like I'm 10 years old again!"

Chris and I had a great time cheering on Tony and Who Dey as they made their way across Tennessee with its scorching July temperatures through places I'd never heard of: Martin, Gleason, McKenzie, Huntingdon. . . .

We followed Tony's progress on the Vol State tracker, which posts new mileage checks for each racer at 7:30 Central Time, am and pm, which means that we were checking every 1:30 British Summer Time, am and pm. If I woke up in the middle of the night, the first thing I would do is check Tony's progress. And after all the chatter and photos on the Facebook page, I was soon checking out the progress of 73-year-old Terrie Wurzbacher, 65-year-old Diane Taylor, and 67-year-old John Price. The Vol State participants are not all so old. The first three 2022 finishers were in their forties, the next three in their thirties, and the following three in their forties. Still, it's not a young person's event. Only four 2022 finishers were in their twenties, and the first one, 23-year-old Addison

Hendricks, came in 11th place. I suspect that part of the draw of these journey races is that they reward the ability to suffer, and sometimes that kind of training takes decades.

In the first 24 hours, Tony had covered a phenomenal 45 miles; he made 67 miles in the first 36 hours. But then the bottom dropped out. After a quick four hours of sleep, he took a wrong turn out of the Heritage Inn in Huntingdon—no doubt due to fatigue—and ended up 10 miles down the road before he realized his mistake and had a come-to-Jesus moment on the side of the road. He described it as "one of the toughest days" of his life. He was "pacing back and forth like a wild animal in a cage" and had to decide what to do. But God told him to go back to the route and start again. "Then I was back with the angels," Tony explained.

Tony was speaking literally and not just metaphorically about being "back with the angels." Vol State is officially an unsupported race, especially for the 100 or so "screwed" runners who bring no help with them. About 20 "crewed" runners have one or more people in a car who make their way along the route with their runner to provide aid. The "road angels" are people who live or drive along the route and go out of their way to help the runners: think cold drinks, food, chairs, medical supplies, and more. So, although Laz provides no official support on the Vol State route (except a lift back to the finish line if you quit), unofficially, lots of people help out.

Walking 20 miles off course and staying in the race—knowing that he had another 247 miles to go and he'd lost all the extra miles he'd built up—was one of the most inspiring feats I'd seen in a long time. Tony's 36-hour check-in was 67 miles at the Heritage Inn. At his 48-hour check-in after walking the 20 miles off course, he was back at 67 miles, only four miles ahead of Oprah.

Yes, *that* Oprah. . . .

Vol State folks—participants, race administrators, and fans—talk obsessively about Oprah, which confused me for the first couple of days I followed Tony's 2022 progress. When you look at a Vol State tracking sheet, there she is, near the bottom, but higher up than virtually anyone who has dropped out. It's possible, though rare, for a person to drop out miles ahead of Oprah, and it may take one or more 12-hour check-ins for Oprah to catch up, but catch up she will if a person quits or if they're too slow. Oprah never stops, you see. And she never sleeps. She keeps her pace at 31.4 miles a day, which means 15 or 16 miles per 12-hour check-in. No participant has ever seen Oprah in person. Only Laz, Carl, and Jan—the Vol State administrative team—have seen her, and according to legend, Jan keeps her supplied with double-strength Vahdam chai tea and cornbread all along the course. Oprah supposedly walks in stiletto heels and an evening dress, a vision terrifying to every back-of-the-pack Vol State racer; according to legend, they can hear the sound of her heels—click click click.

Oprah is the mileage every Vol State participant needs to maintain along the route to make it to Castle Rock, Georgia, in 10 days. She's the compass that keeps Vol Staters on track when they want to sleep for seven hours in a motel instead of four, or they want to hang out longer with road angels in the shade of a comfortable tent or porch.

At the 36-hour check-in, Tony was a whopping 20 miles ahead of Oprah, but he paid the price when he turned the wrong way out of the Heritage Inn and gave Oprah 12 hours to move 16 miles closer to him while he wandered off course. Imagine what that would do for your resolve in a race when participants often balk at walking an extra half mile to a good motel because an extra mile roundtrip that doesn't get them closer to the Rock is more than they can bear. But bear it, Tony did, and he made it another 118 miles in four days before his back was so bad that he couldn't continue.

Tony bore it all till he got to the iconic Bench of Despair, an apple-red bench outside the old Glendale Market on Culleoka Highway near Columbia, Tennessee—a bench on which Vol State participants ritually sign their name with a Sharpie. Tony had seemed so upbeat on his Facebook page, and then suddenly, he was out. We were stunned and saddened. Tony explained on Facebook that another Vol Stater was taking Who Dey to the Rock.

So, Oprah passed my friend Tony, and by that time, I was thinking I might like to try this crazy race.

Maybe it's a late-in-life longing to fit in with the—well, not the popular kids, but . . .

Maybe this was just an extension of middle school psychology, and I wanted to be one of the cool kids or the rebel kids. There's certainly an element of that. I was following many of the participants in the 2022 race, and no matter how mangy, homely, and sleep-deprived they looked and sounded, they were definitely cool—if only because they were doing something I couldn't imagine doing.

Only I had been.

Imagining, I mean.

Or maybe it's just a last-ditch effort to figure out what the hell is going on in my country

I've heard it before: if you don't like the U.S., why don't you get out? First of all, it's not that easy. Most countries don't really want us. Second, it's not that I don't like America. I love America. I just don't like what's happened to it. I'm embarrassed by America these days. Like most Americans from the right and the left, I think the country's gone off the rails.

And let me take this moment to apologize to all the other "Americans" out there from other North and South American countries. I know that the U.S. usurped the name despite being just one of the countries on two American continents. I just don't have a better word for people who live in the U.S.A., and you know what I mean.

Although it's not easy to get out of the U.S., I've got a head start: I fell in love with an Englishman the summer before the country demonstrably lost its ever-loving mind by electing Donald Trump. I don't really have anything against Trump. He had a screwed-up childhood. I feel kind of sorry for the guy and sort of get why he turned into a lying, narcissistic, misogynistic, ignorant, jingoistic bully, cheat, and avowed sexual predator. I've met guys like him before. No big deal—as long as they're not your husband, your father, your boss, or your President. I just give them a wide berth. What I don't understand is the 74 million-plus Americans who voted for him . . . the SECOND time.

OK, let's be fair—I didn't understand the almost 63 million people who voted for him the first time either . . . not at all. Election night 2016, I stormed off for a walk on the beach at midnight—furious, uncomprehending, trying to align my brain with what had just happened. Chris followed me gingerly at 20 paces, knowing better than to try to talk to me but making sure no harm came to me by partying Trump supporters or myself. I had good friends and family members I love dearly who voted for Trump. How was this possible? And that wasn't the worst of it: they didn't just vote for him—they *supported* him! They somehow looked past his self-involved, brutal, anti-democratic, anti-Christian spirit. They didn't think he was dangerous. They weren't embarrassed to be American with him as our President. Who were these people? What had happened to my country?

Listen, I'm a left-leaning Independent who doesn't want to be associated with the Republican or Democratic parties. I get the attraction to government outsiders. Most politicians on both sides of the aisle are majorly problematic—it goes with the power of the job. But Trump is beyond the pale, even within the sleazy field of politics. I'd be rich if I had a penny for every discussion I've had with liberals and occasionally conservatives in the last eight years, the theme of which was, "What do they see in this guy? How does such a reprehensible human capture the imagination of so many? How does he manage to bewitch them?"

When I've asked Trump supporters what they like best about him, a number of them told me, "I like him because he tells the truth, and he does what he says he's going to do. He's a great businessman." I'd just look at them bug-eyed. What was there to say?

For a big chunk of the country, Donald Trump is like being in love—he's never very far from their thoughts. They want to say his name and talk about him whenever they can. He invades their dreams. They imagine what they'd say to him if they got the chance.

For another chunk of the country, Donald Trump is like being in love—*only the opposite*. But still, he's never very far from their thoughts. They want to say his name and talk about him whenever they can. He invades their dreams. They imagine what they'd say to him if they got the chance.

He's energized almost all of us—one way or the other.

Stanford sociologist Robb Willer in his Ted Talk compares U.S. polarization to a zombie apocalypse movie: "There're people wandering around in packs, not thinking for themselves, seized by this mob mentality, trying to spread their disease and destroy society." But the catch is that each side thinks they're the good guys, "and all this hate and polarization, it's being propagated by the other people." *You're the zombies! No, YOU'RE the zombies!* I fear this American zombie movie will end in tears.

So, my home base has been Rochester, Kent, for six years now, and I hope we'll soon move to a forever home in Falmouth, Cornwall, my happy place. I don't understand what has happened to the America I knew and loved, but I don't feel the need to stay put and try to change it. You might say I'm lazy or want to take the easy way out. You might be r ight.

But that wouldn't explain my fascination with Vol State.

Maybe it's the hillbilly's poetry....

As I've said, Lazarus Lake is not really a hillbilly. Sure, he looks like one, and he sounds like one if you stop at the Southern dialect and don't listen to what he's saying. But one of the coolest things about this race is that Laz writes a poem/update about every 12 hours during Vol State. It's Laz's version of a check-in. His post-script to the 2022 Vol State includes the following:

> *we were made to struggle.*
> *we were made to face challenges*
> *we were made to make great journeys.*
>
> .
>
> *for 314 miles life was simple*
> *reduced to the search for water, food, and shelter*
> *and reduced to the need to move.*
>
> .
>
> *[...]*
> *along the way they cleansed their souls*
> *they found freedom on the open road*
> *they found purpose in the goal*
>
> .
>
> *and on the way to the rock*
> *they found themselves.*

Oh, heck yeah! Could it be true—a chance to find cleansing, freedom, purpose, myself? Put me in, Coach. I'm ready to play. Without the poetry, I never would've found myself enduring an interminable line at Gatwick Airport, preparing to fly home to the States at the hottest time of the year. I never would've signed up for Vol State. I never would've been planning to make myself as vulnerable as I've ever been on a walk through 17 counties that voted for Donald Trump by big numbers . . . twice, and probably would a third time.

I signed up for the Vol State lottery in August 2022. No one knows how Laz actually works the lottery, but let's just say it doesn't follow Marquess of Queensbury rules. I figured I had a better shot because I was applying from Great Britain, and indeed, on August 8, 2022, I got an email that said,

> **UltraSignup** Vol State - 500K Screwed - Registration Invitation
> Congratulations you have been selected to participate in the 2023 Vol State!
> Please use the link below to confirm OR decline your entry. You must respond immediately!
> <u>Confirm or decline using this link</u>

I confirmed my entry, sent in my $500, and soon got a confirmation email from Laz with a "special note" (highlighted in orange):

> congratulations.... i think.
> you have just punched your ticket to run in the last annual vol state road race, 2023.
> in case you did not already know, there is a facebook group where you can learn more about what you have just signed up for.
>
> should this knowledge convince you that you have made a huge mistake, you will be able to withdraw by simply notifying me with an e-mail. a refund will be issued in accordance with our refund policy.
>
> should you have the intestinal fortitude to stick with your entry,
> and step on that ferry next july,
> be prepared for an experience you will never forget
> (no matter how hard you might try)
>
> looking forward to seeing you next july,
> in the vacation without a car!
> laz

So, that's the best I can explain how I ended up in an interminable line at Gatwick Airport, leaving the good life behind to walk in the sweltering Southern heat in my home country.

Chapter 1

MY NEW WANNABE CULT

what do you get if you finish?
the answer:
a sticker....
it isn't even a fancy sticker.
just a white football with "314" on it.
but it is much more than just a sticker.
it marks you as a member of a unique family.
it signifies that you boarded that ferry.
that you walked and ran an irrational distance
finally arriving at the rock powered only by your own two feet.
--Lazarus Lake

What could be more American than starting at a China Buffet . . . or two?

I walked into the China Buffet in Kimball, Tennessee, late, for what is affectionately known as the Supper Before the Last Supper. I'd started the day in DeLand, Florida, with a quick but brutal teeth cleaning by a pedantic dental hygienist I'll call Boris; then I drove for 11 hours with only two bathroom/gas stops. I knew I was in the general vicinity of the race when I passed a billboard in North Georgia that said, **"EVERY TONGUE WILL CONFESS / JESUS IS LORD / EVEN THE DEMOCRATS"** with the last word in red and a pitchfork after it.

Tuesday evening was busy in Kimball. The Vol State crew had packed all the tables in the large dining room off the main room, and the hostess told me I could sit at the corner booth that only had one diner.

Tony Webb, already surrounded by his tribe at another table, jumped up and came over to give me a hug. "You made it!"

"I did. Better late than never."

"Go over to the table in the back corner to pick up your t-shirt," he told me. "I'll come over to your table when I'm finished."

I walked past the long tables of runners, some of whom I recognized. There was the King of the Road, Bob Hearn. There was tiny Terrie Wurzbacher. There was the famous Lazarus Lake. I walked over to the tall guy in the back corner, who turned out to be Laz's heir apparent, Carl Laniak.

"Hi. I'm Nancy Barber. I was told to come by here to pick up a t-shirt."

"Are you registered for Vol State?" he asked.

"I sure hope so."

"Well, we've got brown with green or green with brown. What would you like?"

"I'll take the green with brown." The t-shirts had "Vol State 2023" over a silhouette of the state of Tennessee, which was created by all the participants' names. "Nancy Barber" was north of Knoxville. Cool.

I went out to the buffet and spooned up rice and various American-Chinese favorites: Gen Tso's Chicken, beef and broccoli, Kung Pao Chicken, and added an eggroll and some pseudo-sushi rolls for good measure.

I sat down in the corner booth and introduced myself to Steve Smalling, a mild-mannered Southern gentleman with white hair and a welcoming smile. "I'm not actually a runner," he told me. "I'm a road angel. My house is at 294."

A road angel's identity becomes the mile marker they're closest to in Vol State. Dorena Landing, Missouri, is 0 and Castle Rock, Georgia, is 314 (at least in theory; Laz miles are a little suspect at best). I had no doubt that a road-angel station at 294 would be very welcome.

Steve, a diehard University of Tennessee fan, had worked in finance and got transferred to Jasper. "I was hoping for interesting, eccentric people, and the next thing I knew, I ended up with Vol State coming through every year and a bunch of crazy people."

He's got great road angel stories: "There was this woman who was weaving her way down the road one morning, and I said, 'Come here. Do you need some water? What do you need?' and she said, 'I need sleep!' So she sat in a chair and fell right to sleep for 20 minutes. Then she woke up and was ready to go again."

And these, apparently, were my people for the next 11 days.

I almost quit before I started

My training had gone pretty well into February. I'd done a 100K overnight ultra in September, and I was up to back-to-back 20- and 15-mile days in Florida. I felt on track. Then my 26-year-old cousin Buck died tragically at the beginning of March, and that knocked the wind out of the entire family. Training for anything seemed trivial, and I slowed down a lot. Buck was a wild boy-man and a sweet boy-man, a crazy surfer, always looking for the next wave until he wasn't. Vol State seemed unbelievably trivial next to his death, but so did most everything else. Still, maybe it was fitting to do something wild and perhaps sweet, even if it was a land thing and not a water thing. I had a feeling Buck would approve.

I tried to ramp up my walking again in April because I had to get ready for my second training race, the London2Brighton 100K Ultra at the end of May. But then Chris and I both got Covid at the end of April, and then I got bronchitis, so I went into the London2Brighton race severely undertrained. I managed to finish it—ugly, slow, and beat up—and it gave me enough confidence to think I could try Vol State six weeks later.

During a last-ditch training effort in June, I had walked 51 miles in three days—not much by Vol State standards, but enough to make me colossally bored with walking. So bored that it made me wonder for the thousandth time why I was going to all this trouble to walk many more miles each day and be even more miserable and hot for ten days in the Southern U.S. I would be leaving Rochester, Kent, where the weather was beautiful in July, and leaving Chris to go make myself wretched on a Vol State mission.

So many folks are thrilled to finish the race, and I would be thrilled too—to stop having to walk 31.4 miles a day. But being a Vol State finisher? Getting the sticker? I couldn't quite wrap my head around the pride and joy in that. Who cares? Most of the world has never even heard of Vol State. I was still hoping, though, that there was something to this Vol State family thing people kept talking about. Back to the idea of belonging with the cool kids—if these kids were cool.

The idea that flipped the switch for me, however, was the thought of sitting around in Rochester's beautiful weather, reading the Vol State Facebook page, keeping an eye on the tracker to watch Tony's and other runners' progress, and reading Laz's 12-hour updates, all inciting intense FOMO. Finally, despite all the other reasons, that may be the ultimate explanation for why I decided to fly to this expensive, stupid event. How many ridiculous things have people done in the world because of the fear of missing out? Capitalism would never survive without FOMO, and Laz could never make a living as a race director.

A party where folks wear their mangled toenails like badges of honor

Addison Hendricks, now a 24-year-old veteran of Vol State and still the youngest person in the race so naturally the party planner, posted these details on the Vol State Facebook page:

> *The lavs 2023 Tuesday Social Hour is an absolute "GO."*
> *NOTE: This is a non-race coordinated, non-mandatory, and unsanctioned event. Having said that, members of the race team are welcome and, hopefully, will attend.*
> *TIME. Shortly after The Supper Before the Last Supper concludes.*
> *LOCATION: The Valley Inn (formerly known as the Super 8 for you veterans...) parking on the south end near the gazebo.*
> *LOGISTICS. There will be at least two coolers+ of adult beverages while supplies last, limited, first come-first serve seating.*
> *SOCIAL HOUR PARAMETERS. Social gathering, tall ultra tales, potential for tattoo comparisons, ride & convoy coordination.*
> *If you want to know more about this event, show up. Most of what happens at lavs stays at LAVS...*
> *Also we all know I'm a well known honey collector of local grown honey!!! If anyone would care to bring me a jar of their local grown honey I'd appreciate it And can repay with laughter and cold drinks.*

I checked into the Clarion Pointe, alternately known as "The Valley Inn" and formerly known as the Super 8. It's the unofficial race headquarters. A woman was drinking beer in the lobby and watching TV. "Are you in the race?" I asked, thinking she seemed especially laid back.

"The race to drink beer?" she said.

I shrugged. "Sounds good to me."

"No, I'm just hanging out," she told me.

The real party was in the back parking lot, near the gazebo. I dropped off my stuff in the room and, with some trepidation, decided I better wander down and try to make friends. I brought a brown bag with the honey I'd picked up for Addison at the Ace Hardware Store in Winter Garden. Tony was staying at another motel in town and wasn't coming to the party, so I was on my own. Forty people or so were milling around, talking to each other. It seemed like a cliquey group of old friends who were happy to see each other, many in sandals who wore their destroyed toenails like Vol State jackets or scout merit badges. Tattoos, too, told of miles conquered: Ironman symbols, The Blue Bridge, the Glendale Market—and 314 was just one of the trophy numbers. I opened a cooler and found a Corona. A guy sitting nearby had a boot on his right leg.

"Are you in the race with that?" I asked, incredulous.

"Yeah, I'm going to give it a try," he said.

"What happened?"

"I was doing 300 miles a month, but that was normal for me. I started having problems, but then I stepped into a hole and broke my foot. I've had the boot on for two and a half months, and I'm gonna see how far I can get." The guy's name was Jim Halsey, and he and his wife Vicky, both 62, were veterans of Vol State and many other ultra races. She had completed Laz's other big journey race, the Last Annual Heart of the South (HOTS), only a few weeks before.

The main party chat consisted of comparing notes on various ultra races, including Vol State, and the group seemed happy enough to welcome a newbie with fresh ears for their tales and open to their advice.

I met Regina Sooey, 52, and her partner Bill Page, 67, who live in Jacksonville. Regina's a whippet-thin real estate agent with the energy of an aerobics instructor on amphetamines. I'd been seeing her madcap training video posts on the Vol State Facebook page. She only entered the screwed waitlist on June 26, and she and Bill didn't both get into the race until July 2. Regina had quipped in a post, "If anyone has a good 12-day training plan, we are interested lolo."

"I've been looking forward to meeting you two," I told Regina. Clearly, they were veteran ultrarunners who were joking about training in the last two weeks before the event when most runners were tapering their mileage. Still, at the party, Regina seemed less ironic and more of an earnest eccentric. Bill, on the other hand, was quieter, more serious—a businessman who seemed worried. "This is the longest thing I've ever done," he said. "I'm in great shape for bicycling." He had spent plenty of time crewing for Regina and others in ultra races but participating in this one was another matter. Having crewed Vol State, he knew a lot more about what he'd signed up for than I did. This reminded me of what Tony had said earlier when he came over to sit with Steve and me at dinner: "I'm a little more scared this year than I was last year because I know what it's all about."

I would cherish my ignorance for a while longer.

I asked who Addison was, and Vicky pointed him out. I walked over to give the garrulous, young redhead his honey. "This is for you. I didn't know if you wanted the comb, but...."

"Where's it from?" he asked.

"Umatilla, Florida."

He took it out of the brown paper bag and unscrewed the top. "The comb is OK, and I'll still buy them with combs because it's already done, but it's the bees' home, and they have to build it back." He stuck his finger in and tested it. "This is dark honey."

"Oh." I was being schooled as a honey gift bearer?

The guy next to me said, "That's the good kind with a comb."

"I don't know," I said. "He was just telling me that it's the bees' home, and they'll have to rebuild."

"But you can chew on the waxy comb," said the guy.

I nodded. There was that.

Bob Hearn, the 57-year-old King of the Road, having crushed the Vol State course record in 2021, was standing next to Addison. Bob's short hair was bleached blond (I'd seen pictures of it blue and pink), and he had a close-cropped goatee. He's tall and rangy, a good-looking guy who seems a bit self-conscious. It must be tough to be a genius *and* a world-class athlete among mere mortals, but Bob manages it with much graciousness and goodwill. "I would've brought you some from California," Bob told Addison, "but when I left, I didn't know if I was going to do Vol State."

"You mean you decided en route?" I asked. Clearly, Bob was a special case, and Laz would let him in the race anytime he decided.

"Well, I was already at a family reunion in Tennessee, so I didn't have far to go."

"So, what's your Plan A, B, and C?" I asked him. I'd heard him on a podcast describe his multi-layered planning for races.

"I don't know. I'll see where I am at later in the race and make a decision then. It's going to be hotter this year."

Not what I wanted to hear. What Bob didn't mention was that he had also just won Laz's June journey race HOTS, which this year went 347 miles from Fig, North Carolina, to Castle Rock, Georgia. He did it in four days and eight hours, and, as tradition dictates, became Queen of the South, the designation cemented by the first winner of the inaugural 2020 HOTS, Canadian Bev Anderson-Abbs. The HOTS route changes every year, and the participants don't find out the course until the night before the race. HOTS makes Vol State look sensible.

"Your enlightenment story from Vol State is one of the reasons I'm here," I told Bob, but the conversation got diverted.

Addison started grilling Bob about not liking beer: "You're from California, that's why."

"Actually, a lot of people in California drink beer. If I throw a back-yard BBQ, most people will be drinking beer."

"I think of California people as being wine people," Addison explained, and then started grilling Bob about what kind of wine he likes ("Red.") And what sort. ("Bordeaux and Northern Italian, Nebbiolo.") And what temperature it should be served at. ("Room. Well, room temperature was actually cellar temperature, and that's about 60 degrees.") And how big his wine cellar is. ("I don't have a wine cellar.")

I wasn't going to wade into this conversation. I decided that a Corona and a half was enough, and I should get some sleep. By the time I hit the queen-sized bed, I was totally exhausted. Four hours of "automatic cocktail party mode" and 11 hours of driving had swamped me, but each time I got sucked toward the Land of Nod, my brain took off again with a million Vol State details. *It's your second-to-last night of real sleep. Don't blow it!* I finally nodded off about 2 am My alarm went off at 5:30. Might as well get an early start on the sleep deprivation.

OK, I forgot about Bob Hearn's Enlightenment Story as motivation for this insanity

So, yes, these ultra racers are a different breed, and I'm not at all sure I belong, but the two overnight races I did (with lots of supported aid stations along the way) helped prep me for that part of the Vol State. Walking through the night is a surreal experience, and I knew I needed to try it ahead of time. The 2022 South Coast 100K Challenge had me hiking in the middle of the night through the wilds of England. Well, "wilds" may be a stretch—"rural areas" is closer: farms, sheep, and such. Things happen to you in the middle of the night when you've been walking for 20+ hours. I wore a chest lamp for these races, which meant I could see a little circle of light wherever I pointed my torso, and not much else unless it was lit. Not much is lit in rural England in the middle of the night. Your mind plays weird tricks.

For example, in that first overnight 100K, at about 4 am, I was hiking through more rolling English farmlands, past many more sheep, over more stiles, and I suddenly came to a road, and there was a big-screen TV next to it playing a game show. At least, that's what it looked like to me. In consensus reality—the version most of us would agree on if we weren't sleep-deprived and starved of sensory data—the big-screen TV was actually one of those mirrors by the side of the road that help drivers see around blind turns. Not really a hallucination as such (we'll come back to the distinction later), but a distorted reality because my brain was so fatigued.

This brings us back to Bob Hearn, the King of the Road who holds the Vol State course records for fastest completion. In 2021 he ran it about eight hours faster *screwed* than he ran it *crewed* in 2020. Bob apparently won the gene lottery and has other claims to fame: at Burning Man, he's won the 50K naked ultra race multiple times, and he and his wife both play trumpet in the Blackrock Philharmonic. Besides his physical and musical prowess, Bob's also brilliant: he has a PhD from MIT in Theoretical Computer Science and Artificial Intelligence, post-doc work in neurology, and a keen interest in astrophysics. Oh, and he does math art (picture a Spirograph set in the hands of Obi-Wan Kenobi) and he's a leader in a field of international puzzling that I don't begin to understand; it includes lots of spiky models held together by magnets and math. Before I came on this ridiculous trip, I listened to lots of podcast interviews with Bob. Here's what he had to say on *The Adventure Jogger* about the sensory deprivation an ultrarunner often experiences at night:

> I was thinking of minds as antennas that tune into differ-
> ent realities. If there's not enough sensory data coming in,
> there's not enough reality to lock onto, so your brain is
> just trying to find the model that matches best what it's
> getting, and there are all the other alternative realities out
> there that you're tuning into.

Hence the big-screen TV in rural England.

But Bob didn't just talk about *that* sort of altered reality. He also talked about his "enlightenment" experience during Vol State 2021:

My brain's notion of self at the moment has broadened, and I'm not so much identifying with this body. I'm identifying with the whole race and everybody along it and everything that's going on. The notion of the critical importance of where I am along the course at a particular time being the defining variable—that just seemed a little strange because why should I pick that out? Reality is so much more than that, so it got harder and harder for me to keep track of my goals. I was looking at my Garmin, and it's like, OK, I know, sort of, I'm supposed to keep this pace field in this range, but why exactly is that and what exactly does it mean?

It's this pushing through "knowing" to "not knowing" that's intensely interesting to me. Bob also talked about the lingering effects of Vol State after the race, when he felt more compassionate and in tune with the people around him. And, because he's Bob, on the podcast *Miles with Marty*, he tried to explain the science of it all:

> There's this brain mode called the Default Mode Network—there's all these different brain regions that interconnect in different ways with different patterns, and the Default Mode Network is kind of shutting down things that it thinks are not relevant. It will sort of control what filters into consciousness.

This makes sense. The DMN enables us to screen out pesky, irrelevant stimuli and focus on the task at hand. The interesting part happens, though, when the DMN starts breaking down, which Bob explains it can do for advanced meditators or LSD users or even gifted daydreamers.

> Brain imaging studies show that the Default Mode Network shuts down and that enables much more free associations; it enables random thoughts and perceptions to filter up much higher into awareness and broader connections between brain regions that don't normally connect to occur.

And what does this have to do with ultrarunning? Bob says that a version of this can happen with the crazy effort of an ultra: "You sort of exhaust that brain function, and your default mode sort of gives up, and again you're able to access these same kinds of awareness that you can in those other contexts."

Yep, this is just the sort of woo-woo stuff that attracts me to extreme experiences. Before Vol State, I had done one-fifth of the distance in about 28 hours. Now I was setting out to be sleep-deprived for over ten days and 500K. Psychedelics might be an easier way of melting my Default Mode Network, but at least Vol State was legal—except for maybe the trespassing stuff.

Laz's night-before-the-last-night update prompted a text from my mother

Laz started the updates early, and in his Super-before-the-Last-Supper update, he muses about whether it is better to be a virgin or a veteran getting ready to start Vol State. This is what he says about the virgins:

> *314 miles is not child's play*
> *daily temperatures in triple digits is no laughing matter.*
> *having the sky ripped apart by violent thunderstorms*
> *with no recourse but to hunker down and keep moving*
> *is a nightmare not a dream.*
> *their imaginations fill with the unthinkable.*
> *and the reality will be worse.*
> *ahead of them are horrors they do not yet even conceive.*
> *horrors with which,*
> *in 3 days they will be intimate acquaintances.*
> *yes, the virgins do not fully comprehend what is coming.*
> *and they do not know if they can pass the test.*

After reading the update, my mother texted: "You know you can quit and come home. I know I'm not supposed to say that, but I'm your mother."

The top 10 things that scare me about Vol State

Because the lottery for Vol State was almost a year in advance, the catastrophizing part of my brain had plenty of nights to wake me up at 3 am for a chat about its concerns, which were, in order of importance,

1. **The heat**. I grew up in Florida, but I hate exercising in hot weather, and the heat index at Vol State regularly tops 100 F. I have no idea what it will do to me. I overheard Jan, the Meat-Wagon Lady, telling the story about a woman from Texas who drove all the way to Kimball and then decided it was too hot, so turned around and drove home. Makes some sense. I'd spent the summer months in Europe for years, and I only had eight days to get acclimated to the kind of heat that smothers the Southern U.S. in July. I started my final training walks at 2 pm in the Florida heat, and I also practiced sitting on towels in my car with the windows rolled up. I'd emerge after an hour, looking like I'd been thrown in the pool with my clothes on by my Uncle Jerry, famous for such mischief. I tried out various long-sleeve sun hoodies in Florida. The one I chose was too warm and didn't breathe as much as I would've liked, but I'd had enough skin cancers to know I needed protection. I also paid $55 for a Six Moons Design Silver Shadow Carbon Ultralight (6.8 oz.) Travel Umbrella with silver on the outside to reflect the sun and black on the inside to pretend it's not as bright as it is outside. It's supposed to be 10 degrees cooler underneath it. I was skeptical, but even a few degrees would be worth the investment.

2. **The traffic.** Traffic is the most likely way to get killed on Vol State. To my knowledge, no one has died so far on any of Laz's journey runs, but one New York City woman, Kim McCoy, was struck by a car in Alabama during the 2020 HOTS race and ended up having her right leg amputated. She was a Vol State veteran. So was Rebecca Gartrell, who ran Vol State in 2018 and was tragically killed in a hit-and-run accident in 2021 while she was attempting a solo journey run across Texas. The cars, pick-ups, and semi-trucks are no joke, and Laz isn't super safety-conscious when he designs a course. The roads with big shoulders are great, but many LAVS roads have no shoulder and lots of blind turns. When you're sleepy, it's easy to get careless.

3. **Blisters**. I've had plenty of blisters in my hiking life, but mostly, I've conquered the problem with the help of Injinji toe socks. Vol State is another animal entirely, though, partly because of the camber of the road—you're always walking toward traffic, so the road is slanted to your left for water run-off, putting consistent pressure on the left sides of your feet. (People suggest training on roads before the race to get used to the camber. That's a great suggestion . . . which I did not take.) Also, lots more sweat and walking in the rain will increase the chances of blisters in this race. I read a race report from Chris Haas after the 2022 Vol State. He basically hobbled up Castle Rock without much skin on the bottom of his feet. He included gory photos of his feet that haunt me to this day.

4. **Dehydration.** I'm not stupid. (Well, maybe the jury's still out.) I know I'm supposed to keep drinking in the heat. I shouldn't get dehydrated, but things can sneak up on you. You can miscalculate how far it is to the next water stop. You can try to minimize the extra water weight in your pack. Your electrolytes can get out of whack because you don't drink enough Gatorade. Things happen even when you think you're conscientious.

5. **Thunderstorms.** I've been in a lot of thunderstorms in my day, and I'm pretty good with them, but the part that scares me the most is getting my feet soaking wet and having no way to dry my shoes. I've got three extra pairs of socks, excessive by Vol State standards, but I'm willing to carry the extra weight if regular changing into dry socks can help with #3 above. But if the shoes are totally soaked . . . ? I also brought along Bedrock hiking sandals, which I bought a week before the race. They can help in a pinch, but I haven't properly broken them in enough for long-distance walking.

6. **Shelbyville**. This is the town all the veterans tell tales about. *Walk through Shelbyville if you can. But whatever you do, don't stop at The Magnolia Motel. Unclean rooms, bedbugs, tweakers.* This place has the worst reputation of any motel on the Vol State route.

7. **Chiggers.** As a Southerner, I'm well acquainted with the pernicious redbugs. I still have PTSD from the time in high school

when I was working at a YMCA Day Camp in Central Florida and hid in the bushes during a counselor hide-and-seek. By the next day, I was scratching all over my body and painting clear nail polish on scores of chigger bites. Chiggers are what keep Vol State runners from just sleeping in fields along the course. I can't even imagine trying to finish this race in the heat with an army of chiggers embedded in my body.

8. **Smoke from Canadian wildfires**. We have been reading about the wildfires for weeks as the smoke has crept farther and farther south of the border. I've got asthma, and the thought of hiking through smoke for days on end is incomprehensible and could be a deal breaker.

9. **Deranged Redneck Trump supporters**. I could just say *deranged rednecks*, I suppose, but Trumpers have become the boogiemen of modern sensible America. While it's true that most Trumpers are not deranged rednecks, the ones who are . . . a scary bunch. They were scary before they were Trump supporters, but they've become more emboldened, more unhinged since his presidency. Hence more dangerous.

10. **Convenience store food**. I'm a foodie and an omnivore. I'll eat almost anything as long as it's good. Making a steady diet of gas station food sounds daunting. If I'm sleepy and hungry enough, though, maybe it won't matter.

The bus ride from hell

After 3.5 hours of solid sleep at the Clarion Pointe, I showered and changed into my thrift-store khaki shorts and pink V-neck t-shirt. I didn't want to wear race clothes the day before the race, and my suitcase would be locked up in my car. These would be my throw-away clothes.

I headed down to the small, generic breakfast room off the lobby and checked out the offerings. I settled on yogurt and a banana, then looked around for a place to sit.

"You can sit here," a clean-cut, grey-haired guy said. "I won't bite."

"At least not this early in the race," I quipped. "Later on, who knows?"

The guy was Glenn Kasper, a 60-year-old UPS pilot from Mississippi. He'd tried Vol State before but hadn't finished. I sat across from a 58-year-old Sunderland A.F.C. fan from Durham, England, named Nigel Simpson, who was one of two Englishmen entered in the race. On the other side of me, Ed Masuoka, a 71-year-old retired NASA employee, tried to help Nigel with his GPX map. I still hadn't figured out how to get the GPX route map for the race from my phone onto my Garmin Forerunner 955, a Christmas-present watch that's like wearing a Ferrari on my wrist, but there was still time. Jim Halsey limped into the breakfast room, looking very serious. In truth, everyone seemed more serious than I would've liked at this point.

The drive from the Clarion Pointe to the parking field down from Castle Rock was a 14-mile lights-on funeral procession. Still, the scene across the Shelby A. Rhinehart Memorial Bridge, better known to Vol Staters as the Blue Bridge (Mile 303 of the race), gave some hope: low clouds over Guntersville Lake with the sun just peaking up across the water. Gorgeous. With any luck, there would be lots of beautiful scenery along the route.

Laz had already warned us by email that the buses would leave precisely at 7 am, and nobody wanted to be late:

> *at 0700 if you are parked and have your ass in a seat on the*
> *bus*
> *your life will be good!*
> *if you are running up castle rock road trying to get to the bus*
> *you will be really distressed*
> *and we will feel really bad for you....*
> *as the buses drive away and leave you!*

I parked my car in the mowed fields across from the corn fields, grabbed my packed running vest, and walked up the road toward the buses. Along the way, I met a tall, ropey guy from Reno named Ken Zemach. Ken was a 54-year-old veteran ultrarunner but a first-time Vol Stater. He never runs a race more than once. "I can do three 100s a year till I'm 70," Ken told me, "and I still won't get all the races I want to do in." He is much more ambitious than I—not a hard race to win among these folks.

Tony sat next to me on the bus that would take us the entire length of the route, backwards. "This is batshit crazy," I told him, "and it's all your fault." He just laughed.

The Halseys (or the *Halsi* as they call themselves—one of the great journey-race power couples) sat behind us and occasionally threw in tidbits of wisdom: good places to eat, stretches to watch out for traffic, road-angel tents (some already up), possible places to sleep or get a shower, and places to avoid. I found it overwhelming, but I managed to make a few notes.

"Most people quit in the first two days," Jim told me. "You feel the worst on the second day. Your muscles are sore; the heat is bad."

"You gotta get to the point where your muscles know that this is your life," added Vicky.

This is my life. . . .

I turned around in my seat to ask something I'd been wondering about for a while: "Are there donation boxes set up at the road-angel stations so we can pay for the stuff we're taking?"

"Nope," said Jim. "It's all free. They do it out of the goodness of their heart." *Amazing. Why do they spend all this money?*

Some folks might appreciate a chance to check out the route backward, but not me. For one thing, I get car sick on windy backroads, so I felt lousy most of the day. For another, the fastest route to Union City, TN, where we were staying for the night, should've taken a little over four hours, but following the Vol State route, including having a picnic lunch in Columbia and two bathroom breaks along the way, took over 10 hours. And finally, I think the bus route is all part of Laz messing with our minds. He wants to scare us—about many things—and he often succeeds. Me? I do better starting major trips stupid. I have been serially underprepared for every journey I've ever taken. It keeps things fresh.

For lunch, we stopped at a park pavilion near Columbia, Tennessee. In line for a sub, sides, cookies, and iced tea, I met Steven Godfrey, the second Englishman runner. Steven is a 58-year-old absolute beast from Manchester. I don't know what he does for a living, but he travels all over the world doing crazy triathlons—races like the double Ironman. But this was his first Laz race.

"I've never done anything like this," he confessed, but I was sure he was prepared, and his resumé, like so many others, made me feel decidedly ill-prepared. In our brief discussion, it turned out that Steven has a place in Clermont, Florida, home to the National Training Center, an iconic triathlon Mecca, and, coincidently, the town right next to Winter Garden, where my mother lives and where I'd been heat-acclimating. "I flew into Chattanooga," explained Steven, "but I've got to figure out a way back to Clermont. I wasn't sure when I'd finish."

"Well, I'm driving back, and if you want to wait around till the back-of-the-packers come in on Day 10, I'd be happy to give you a ride. My plan is to finish the race under the cutoff time, spend the night at the

Clarion Pointe, and then drive back to Winter Garden in one go."

"That would be great," said Steven. He seemed unbothered by the days of waiting he might have to do. It could be nice to have another driver. I didn't expect that one good night's sleep would totally revive me after ten days of sleep deprivation.

Sandwich and potato salad in hand, I sat next to Jessica LaBelle, one of the two Jessicas I'd followed in the HOTS race. Two Jessicas and one Alexis had raced together, and it looked like they were having so much fun on Facebook. The truth was much grimmer, which I found out while Jessica was explaining to Vicky how tough it had been when Alexis's blisters had gotten so bad. Alexis was supposed to do the triple crown of Last Annual journey races that summer—HOTS, Vol State, and the inaugural Last Annual Third Circle of Hell, the granddaddy of all of Laz's journey races, which would be held in August. Finishing all three was called the "Salute to Insanity." But Alexis's blisters were so nasty at HOTS (a doctor had subsequently cut the roof off his blisters—audible gasps of horror all around the picnic table) that he was skipping Vol State but still planning to do the 3COH. She was worried about Alexis, and I was starting to get the feeling that the Facebook side of these races—like most of social media—painted a curated reality that was far from the real thing.

When I saw Bob Hearn standing alone in the middle of the pavilion, I decided I would ask him about his enthusiasm for Squirrel's Nut Butter, which I'd bought but hadn't ever used on my feet. It's pretty much standard that Vol State participants lube up their feet with Desitin, Body Glide, Vaseline, Squirrel's Nut Butter, or some such product. Bob wrote on Facebook about how great SNB is for feet and any other places that need chafing protection, and that was enough for me to buy it. But I didn't really know how it was supposed to work. Bob confirmed that he lathered it all over his feet each time he took off his shoes during the race. "What about the tape on your feet?" I asked.

"I don't really tape my feet unless I need it," he said. I guessed it didn't matter about the tape, which was already protecting the skin. Bob remembered that I had been talking to him last night about his enlightenment story, and we got cut off. "You were saying that it was one of the reasons you were here. You read about it?"

"Actually, I listened to podcasts of you and of Laz. It's weird. I feel like I know you guys, but I don't really. And you don't know me at all."

"You probably know me better than some of my friends do."

"Have you had this sort of enlightenment experience at other events?" I asked. "The Six Days in France, for example?"

"Yes, to a certain extent."

"Has it happened more often since it happened at Vol St?"

"No, it's actually been less often. Maybe because the novelty has worn off."

"I want to get to the rock," I said, "and I plan to slowly, but that's not the interesting part to me." He nodded knowingly, but it was time to leave the picnic. Folks were heading out. We wished each other good luck and walked back to separate buses.

Chapter 2

GOD AND COUNTRY

*"We build all manner of walls and fences around ourselves and then we
wonder why we feel so alone. We don't trust each other as much because
we don't take the time to know each other. And in that space between us,
politicians and algorithms teach us to caricature each other, and troll each
other, and fear each other. But here's the good news […] all across America
in big cities and small towns, away from all the noise, the ties that bind us
together are still there."*
--The 44th President of the United States

**The Last Supper, where we pick up our American flags at
yet another Chinese buffet**

At the end of the excruciating bus ride, my Laz-appointed roommate for the night—Michelle Chauvin, a 57-year-old nurse practitioner and mother of six from St. Louis—and I dropped off our packs
at the Quality Inn in Union City, Tennessee. We had about an hour
to rest before heading back to the bus for the trip down the road to
the China Buffet, larger than the one in Kimball, Tennessee, but very
familiar. The Vol State contingent was herded into the far part of the
dining room. I sat across from Tony, who sat next to 37-year-old Tara
Watson from Lewisburg, Tennessee, a town that was actually *on* the
route. I quizzed her about restaurants in Lewisburg, naively assuming
that if I could find good restaurants all along the way, the journey would
be made more palatable. Tara was mostly quiet and seemed above it all.
I mistook her reserve for ultrarunning confidence and insouciance.

Laz didn't actually require you to eat at the China Buffet (again), but
he did require you to be there for the briefing and to check in and pick

up your American flag.

During the briefing, Laz lectured, he cajoled, he berated:

- *You gotta take care of yourself. If you have an emergency—a medical emergency, a person-giving-you-trouble emergency, call 911. Me and Carl and Jan are not first responders, we're not police, and we're probably not that close because we'll be spread over probably 200 miles by the end of the race, so if you've got a real emergency, immediate emergency, call the person who's closest and can do you the most good. If you require medical attention, seek it.*

He also gave a lot of general, common-sense admonitions that participants have obviously messed up in the past:

- *Do not leave any trash. Good, nobody said, "What about in trash cans?" Cause I had a smart-ass remark to that, which is related to where I was going to suggest that they put it.*

- *Do not remove your shoes in any place that has food. I can't believe I have to tell you that, but do not remove your shoes in any place that has food.*

- *At the Clarion, pick up a tracker and head for the Rock. If you want to leave some stuff there, get a room and leave it there. If you want to sit down and rest, get a room.*

- *Do not sit on their good lobby furniture with your nasty self because you can't tell you're nasty, but to the rest of the world, you're nastier than you can imagine.*

- *Have some sense. One, do not go into someone's house, even though these people are wonderful who want to help us. We've had people go into houses where I've felt like I was in—what's your show, Sandra? Criminal Minds. What in the hell? Do not invite strangers to meet you out in the darkest part of the road in the middle of the night on social media, and then call me and say, "There's a really creepy guy out here." "Oh, where'd he come from?" "Oh, I met him on Facebook." Ahhhhhhh!*

You get the drift. Laz doesn't worry about treating us like wayward children. Presumably, he's had enough wayward adults in his races that he feels entitled. And the reasonable among us just figure he's talking to someone else.

Laz-issued stars and stripes

Truly, there were so many wonderful reasons *not* to do Vol State. Among them was the American flag Laz required us to wear instead of a race number. Why did I have to pin an American flag to my backpack? To show that I'm not a terrorist? To make Republicans believe I'm one of them? Because Laz says so? This requirement grated on me. I didn't always feel resistance to the flag. I used to wear it on clothes and pledge allegiance to it every morning.

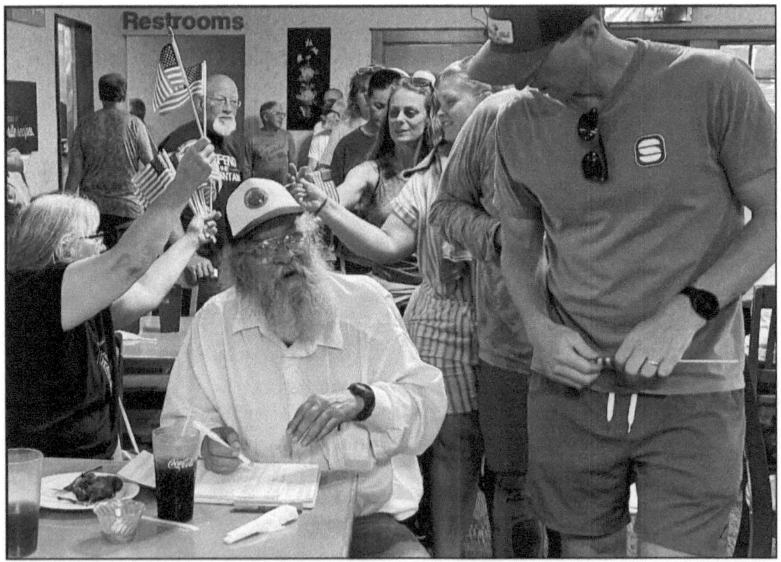

Laz and his wife Sandra check off runners and hand out flags at the Last Supper.

It's just that Trump managed to drag the flag into the culture wars. These days, if somebody's flying it outside their house, they're usually Republican. Because Democrats don't care about the flag? No, because the flag as a symbol has gotten usurped by the ultra-conservatives who want to return to an America where white male straight supremacy rules and we're all "good Christians." I wouldn't mind as much wearing an American flag in an international race or even in a domestic race in a blue state, but in Tennessee, it signifies too many things I can't cotton to. Yet here I'll be, marching through the Tennessee back roads with an American flag on my backpack.

I recently finished Amanda Ripley's book *High Conflict: Why we get trapped and how we get out*, where Ripley explains that high conflict is

> what happens when discord distills into a good-versus-evil kind of feud, the kind with an *us* and a *them*. In this state, the brain behaves differently. We feel increasingly certain of our own superiority, and everything we do to try to end the conflict usually makes it worse. Eventually, we can start to mimic the behavior of our adversaries, harming what we hold most dear.

This sounds exactly like something that could happen to me, maybe already has, and it made me want to join Vol State even more. Rural Tennessee, away from the Smokey Mountains, is about the last place I'd like to spend a miserably difficult ten days of walking. All those Trumpers, evangelical Christians, sexist, racist, gun-toting homophobes! How's that for gross, reductive generalization? Sounds like someone in high conflict.

On the other hand, my family is Southern—my mom from small-town Kentucky; my dad from rural Georgia. My roots are in the South, and I admire much about it—the hospitality, the politeness, the slow pace, the BBQ, jazz and country music, Jimmy Buffett, Mardi Gras, the colorful colloquialisms—even as I'm appalled by so much.

It's not unlike the Catholic Church I grew up in. I still love parts of the Mass—the mysticism, the rhythm and repetition of the liturgy, the stained glass, the community of the eucharist, the chiming bells, the wafting incense, the feeling of belonging. Despite the spiritual depth of a more progressive Pope Francis, I still don't like the church's stance on women or gay people. And how could I look the other way when I found out about widespread pedophilia and its executive coverups? When I found out what the church did to mothers and babies in Ireland? What they did to Indigenous children in North America? Could I belong to a church that's both anti-choice *and* anti-contraception?

And finally, could I be a Christian in a country where White Christians overwhelmingly supported Donald Trump, a country where Christian Nationalism has made such deep inroads? This isn't Jesus's fault. Christian Nationalism is to Jesus Christ as barium swallows are to bears . . . or swallows. It's an inversion of Jesus's message. Apparently,

I found myself in "high conflict" with both the South and conservative Christianity.

Ripley shows healthier ways to deal with conflict as she chronicles example after example of ways that certain people in high conflict "rehumanized and recategorized their opponents, and they revived curiosity and wonder, even as they continued to fight for what they knew was right." Easier said than done.

I confess to not having spent a lot of effort trying to "recategorize" the Trumpers of the world. The truth is that I'm slowly moving out of the U.S. I spend most of my time in England or Ireland with my English civil partner, Chris. (The U.K. finally gave heterosexuals the option to choose civil partnerships instead of marriage in 2019, and we did.) I would be spending the fall semester directing Stetson University's Global Gateways Program in Dublin and spring semester teaching on campus in Florida. If not for a job I much enjoy, I probably would've emigrated from the U.S. altogether. I haven't always felt this way, though.

In the summer of 1999, I rode my bicycle solo across America. I started in Yorktown, Virginia, and ended up in Seaside, Oregon. I was on the TransAmerica trail until Bardstown, Kentucky, where my mom grew up, and then I went due north to Indianapolis to attend two nights of a Billy Graham crusade.

I wasn't a Graham fan, but I was curious about all things American, and he'd certainly had a lot of influence. I pitched a tent at the Indianapolis Fairgrounds and rode city buses filled with poor people back and forth to the Indianapolis Dome. I was so curious and filled with wonder at Graham's hypnotic voice calling me down from the rafters of the Dome to commit my life to Jesus that I finally understood Graham's appeal. This sort of evangelical Christianity wasn't my journey, but I could see why so many would take it.

I wanted to explore my country, and I wanted to do it in the historical way of the Colonial settlers—East to West, unfortunately against the prevailing winds and without enough discerning attention to what that colonization entailed for the Indigenous people already settled on the land.

Everywhere I went that summer, the recurring refrain was, "Aren't you afraid?" Afraid of bicycling across my own country? It's true we have an inordinately violent culture by advanced-economy-country standards, but we also seem strangely attached to our fear. We wallow in it. Bojan Louis, a Native American, writes in his essay "Fear to Forget and Fear to Forgive,"

We're afraid of Black people, Muslims, Mexicans, China, Russia, North Korea, the Middle East, Africa, Cuba, greasy food and being fat, being too skinny, being wrong, being right or righteous, being accused of being politically incorrect or correct, of teenagers (especially Black teenagers, teenagers of color), of bees or lack of bees, of not enough people liking our status updates, of reading and critical thought, of not reading enough or of what we read, of thinking for ourselves, of understanding.

The U.S. certainly doesn't have a lock on fear, but as a culture, we seem to like being afraid. It makes us think we're on our toes, ready for anything. We have this convoluted notion that fear keeps us safe. Look around at all the bad things that happen to people who are fearful, as well as to people who are not. I see no safety in fear. Life is only safe in small snippets. Might as well enjoy them while they last and keep fear at bay when possible.

On the bicycle trip, sometimes I was uncomfortable because of the community around me— the stray dogs in rural Virginia, the hollows of the Kentucky Appalachians, the White-person fear of Native Americans in South Dakota—but mostly, America felt friendly and expansive. People were curious about my trip, surprised that I had found so many other good people (besides them). And I did. I found lots of great people, more than you can imagine, on the backroads of this country.

That was before 9/11 shook the country to its core; before the subprime mortgage crisis; before Obama's two-term Presidency exacerbated the country's racism and polarization; before Trump doubled down on the racism and polarization; before Covid added to the culture wars; before the murder of George Floyd and the subsequent BLM protests; before the "Big Lie" and the insurrection of Jan. 6; before the Supreme Court swerved right. The last summer of the Millennium seemed a simpler time. A lot has happened to change my view of the United States I rode through that summer and enjoyed so much. I feel like the bicycle trip was a journey of innocence (no doubt combined with ignorance), and Vol State is a journey of experience, culturally and historically, if not physically.

Maybe it was time to wander through the U.S. again and see what it's like on the ground in Trump Country. Maybe I can learn to "rehumanize and recategorize" Trumpers with "revived curiosity and wonder," as

Ripley says is possible. Some deeply American Vol-State absurdity might be good for me.

I understand the oozing privilege of this race—from the $500 entry and the ability to afford a hotel room when I need one (as long as I can walk to it, although Jan will drive me if I want to quit) to my privilege as a White person walking through rural Tennessee. A few Black people have completed Vol State—Frederick F. Davis III has the veteran number V17: the 17th person to complete Vol State—but no Black participants were registered in 2023, and I haven't met any of the ones who finished in years past. A single Black runner or walker, especially a male, would need an extra pump of courage to run along Tennessee backroads in the middle of the night . . . or the middle of the day for that matter.

But I don't only have the privilege of having some money and being White; I'm also an *old* White *woman*, which commands still extra privilege. People always focus on the vulnerability of women, and there's no question women *are* vulnerable. But people don't spend enough time considering how women are also protected. Normal, good people worry about women traveling alone. We're also generally unthreatening, so people aren't scared of us, which makes them even more willing to help when they're worried about us. And at 59 years old, I'm less vulnerable because I'm less alluring. Saggy skin has its privileges.

Maybe it was time to reevaluate America's high conflict and the trouble our fear has led to by walking on America's roads instead of reading about the country in the news. In Laz's post at the start of the 2022 Vol State, he writes about paying the price

> *to discover the real America.*
> *one where unexpected angels are there when you need them*
> *most.*
> *one where we lift each other up*
> *instead of tearing each other down.*

He ends that inspirational post with another high-flying view of America:

> *for 10 days in July there will be no divisions of race, religion,*
> *money, or politics.*
> *just the "walkers"*
> *and the angels whose support they depend on*

with one common goal . . .

to get those "walkers" to the rock.

for 10 days in July
america will show what it can be.
america will be what it really is.

So, I'm going to survey another slice of America, almost a quarter of a century after the last time on a bike. This time slower, warier, and along a shorter swath. Unlike 1999, I'm more afraid of the U.S. and for the U.S. where the culture wars have reached an unprecedented crescendo.

I lost my best friend of almost four decades to the culture wars—because we couldn't talk about it . . . because we couldn't *not* talk about it.

On the other hand, I *haven't* lost my family, most of whom ride for the opposing cavalry, because we almost never mention the war. Since 2021, I've had the world's cutest great-nephew, who has given us all the best distraction from high conflict. A week before heading to Vol State, I met my brand-new great-niece, who will surely do her part to distract us and keep us filled with curiosity and wonder.

I don't know if the U.S. as we know it will survive another Trump presidency, but while we're still a representative democracy, I'll wear the American flag, regardless of its current connotations, for a ten-day exploration of my country's Southern backroads.

Veteran advice to virgin Vol Staters

The Vol State veterans tend to be less grumpy about race advice than Laz, probably because they don't have his responsibilities. One veteran posted this on Facebook a couple of days before the race:

You virgins are about to have the time of your life.
Recommendations/thoughts:
1. Listen to the veterans on the bus.
2. Don't miss the split going to Hohenwald (veer right).
3. Don't miss the turn after leaving Wartrace (go left at the fake well).
4. Desitin is your friend.
5. You're gonna make new friends.

6. Men, don't be afraid to wear a maxi-pad, they work.
7. If you go too hard on day 1, then later is gonna suck.
8. The course navigation IS NOT difficult (stop worrying).
9. If a kid offers you a water, take it, unless he has a banjo
in his hand.
10. Cherish the journey. You will realize you can do any-
thing.

Back at the Quality Inn, my roommate Michelle, a Vol State veteran, had more good advice. She and I chatted about foot care, jog bras, and road angels, and we each set an alarm for the next morning. The bus would leave at 6:15 am.

Fix Your Feet

When I awoke at 5 am on Day 1 of the Last Annual Vol State Race, I went entirely into present mode. The last thing to do at a time like this is to think about what's ahead for the next ten days or the cool breezes and outdoor fire pit I was missing in my English back garden. The motel room was quiet as Michelle and I went about our pre-race chores. I pulled on my Ron Hill black lycra shorts, which have a pocket on the left thigh for my phone and a zippered pocket in the back for my credit card and cash. Then I traded my thrift store t-shirt for my comfy Coobie bra and my Willit light blue, long-sleeve sun hoodie.

Next on the list of things to do was fix my feet. I wasn't sure how this taping was going to work because I was way out of my depth. I'd tried taping my feet in recent training, but where would I get a chance to walk 31 miles a day in sweltering heat and humidity *before* Vol State to see if I'd done things right? Why would I *want* that chance? Besides, I was tapering my training by the time I got to Florida. I would just give the tape and Squirrel's Nut Butter my best shot.

In the time leading up to the race, I'd kept Jeff Bezos happy with lots of random purchases, thinking that if I could just buy the *perfect* gear and first-aid stuff, I would have a serious leg up on finishing. The Vol State Facebook page has no end of suggestions for which kinesiology tape to buy, which shirt, which underwear, which running vest. The advice goes on and on, but it's not consistent, so you have to figure out who you're going to trust and do further research yourself. Early on, I decided I'd trust two people: Bob Hearn, not only because he's a journey-running superstar, but because he's an analytical freak of nature, and I was sure that he had done all the product research in the field that I had no chance to do. But Bob is an elite runner who finishes these races between three and four days. I'm a proletarian walker who hopes to finish within the 10-day cut-off, so I needed another source of wisdom who knew more about people like me.

Enter Jan Redmond Walker, the Meat-Wagon Lady. Six-ty-one-year-old Jan looks like an aging beauty queen who's put on a few pounds, toughened up a lot, and adopted a down-to-earth wardrobe: Columbia fishing shirts, shorts, and Bedrock sandals with Injinji toe socks. She's an ultra-racing coach who finished Vol State in 2013 and did a transcontinental walk from Oceanside, California, to Ocean City, Maryland, in 2016. These days at Vol State, she's famous for being the person who drives up and down the Vol State route, checking on runners and picking up quitters. She's a sort of boogie woman, mythically associated with Satan—a temptress who will try to lure runners into her van, thereby ending their Vol State quest. (No Vol State runner can enter any vehicle other than a law enforcement vehicle and be able to continue the race. If you get picked up by the police, you still have to get back to where you were picked up in order to continue. Even crewed runners cannot sit in their crew vehicle.)

The truth about Jan, as opposed to the myth, is that she's an expert on foot care and most anything else related to ultrarunning, and she *wants* people to finish. She's seen scores of back-of-the-pack walkers and knows what they need. When she recommended something on Facebook, like Leukotape K for taping your feet, I bought it. Now, I just had to figure out how best to use it all.

If Vol State has a corporate mascot, it's the Dollar General (DG to runners). If Vol State has an animal mascot, it's the armadillo (usually the deceased version). And if Vol State has a bible, it's *Fixing Your Feet: Injury Prevention and Treatment for Athletes*, by John Vonhof. Fear made me devour the book, whose first edition came out in 1997 and whose seventh edition came out in 2021. It's the gold standard of feet know-how for ultrarunners. It covers everything you need to know *before* a long race: shoes, socks, orthotics, lubes, powders, tape, lacing options, etc. And it includes everything you need to know *after* your feet go south and make you wish, yet again, that you'd never signed up for this stupid race.

The problem with fixing your feet for preventative purposes is that everyone's different, and what one pair of feet needs can be dramatically different from another. *Fixing Your Feet* can't help you with trial and error. I thought about where I'd gotten blisters in the past. I wrapped the piggies who "had none" on both feet because they tended to rub in the old days before my Injinji toe socks, and I knew I wanted to tape the balls of my feet because the endless asphalt was going to pound the hell out of them. What else? I wasn't sure. Heels? Other toes? I went with the two toes and balls of the feet for opening day and would see what happened. Then I lathered each foot with Squirrel's Nut Butter and slid it into its respective Injinji toe sock, which reminded me of the rainbow toe socks we wore in junior high—except made with more advanced textiles. They keep the toes from rubbing together. Then I laced up my royal blue Hoka Bondis, bought one size too big to accommodate future swelling.

When I finished packing my Solomon 12L running vest, which is SO much more comfortable than a conventional backpack, it was heaving with stuff: an extra pair of shorts; a short-sleeve shirt for nighttime walking; two extra pairs of ExOfficio breathable, moisture-wicking, anti-odor underwear; three extra pairs of socks; a lightweight running jacket; foot-care first-aid products; and, heaviest and bulkiest of all, tech stuff—I had a plug-in charger for multiple leads, including my phone, my watch, my earbuds, and my chest lamp, all of which had different connectors. Thank you, Silicon Valley! I had unbroken-in Bedrock hiking sandals hanging from the outside bungees and a quiver lashed to bungees for my collapsible hiking poles and fancy umbrella. I looked every bit the newbie I was with too much shit. Everything was in plastic bags because anything that wasn't would get wet.

They were calling for storms that morning, which would be a great way to get things going.

Laz had said in his final email,

> *carl and i have ordered up 70-74 degree temperatures for*
> *thursday*
> *with overcast skies*
> *and a gentle breeze...*
> *if it is 100 degrees with 95% humidity under a blazing sun*
> *and the only wind is what blasts you from passing trucks*
> *that is on jan.*

It sounded like he got the part about the overcast skies right. And yes, even his emails come in poetic form without capital letters or much punctuation. I suspect, like his accent and scraggly beard, the lower-case letters are supposed to lull you into initially thinking he's not that smart or he's just lazy. Both would be egregious misjudgments.

Already, this is not nearly as much fun as I thought it would be . . . .

The Quality Inn breakfast room doubled as the lobby and was heaving with racers in shorts, running shoes, hydration vests, floppy hats, and, oddly, lots of Columbia fishing shirts. I didn't get that at first, but the shirts offer UV protection, ventilation, and flexibility in how you wear them. Not many folks were talking. At the waffle maker, I asked a worried-looking guy named Gary how he was doing, and he said he'd left a bag on the bus on the way back from the China Buffet that had a bunch of important stuff in it. He hoped it was still there.

I sat down with a couple of veterans and introduced myself. They didn't have much to say. Maybe I'd been fooled by all the shenanigans on Facebook, fooled by Laz's nonsense leading up to the race, fooled by the sheer wackiness of the race itself—I was certain it would be a fun bunch and a hoot of a time until the real suffering started. Then I assumed it would be a different kind of fun. I've always enjoyed what I call "communities of pain." This can be anything from a long-distance race to getting ready for a hurricane to being stuck in a stormy airport. I don't think the pain is fun, but I like the leveling, the openness, and the connections that happen to strangers when they're all dealing with some version of the same pain. I mentioned this in a class one day, and a Mexican-American student held up his hand: "Don't you think that's a privileged position to be in because you haven't had that much real pain like poor people have a lot of the time?"

"Uh, yep, I do think that, now that you mentioned it." The buzz surrounding communities of pain is refreshing for me because it's novel. The worst communities of.pain I've experienced have centered on loved ones who've died.. Then again, I remember hearing about poor Dubliners moved from their squalid tenement housing to nicer digs in the suburbs; they liked the new living conditions but were sad to lose their communities. You hear soldiers talk about the same thing when they've return from war. They don't miss the war necessarily, but they miss the close ties with their platoon. One of the many real tragedies of COVID was that beyond the virus, so much of the pain came from the lack of community. I'll cop to being a privileged person who likes the occasional community of pain that isn't too terrible. Not many people want to be poor, sick, in combat, or in a natural disaster, but the communities that ensue from those painful experiences can be powerfully intimate.

As Americans, we're taught to value independence. Gated communities are the opposite of communities of pain. They're communities of privilege with plenty of fences and space between houses, keeping neighbors as well as outsiders at arm's length.

Consciously or unconsciously, I suspect lots of ultra runners crave the community that develops because of so much self-inflicted pain. Early morning on July 13th, the rest of the community of pain and I piled on the buses again for the last time. The subdued, nervous energy allowed for some quiet, anxious chatter, but at this point most people weren't communing; they were in their own little zone, no doubt trying to psych themselves up for what was ahead.

"The most beautiful town on the Mississippi River"

Mark Twain actually said this about Hickman, Kentucky, where the bus let us off at the desolate ferry landing. I love Twain for his spot-on wisdom about life, much of which still holds up well over a century later. I assume he was telling the truth as he knew it about Hickman, but the town clearly hasn't held up well under the pressures of the Industrial Revolution, two world wars, and a transition to the electronic culture. Many buildings were derelict, and most of the rest were tired. The freshest thing in the town was a mural of Mark Twain on the side of a building in the downtown area, and, to be fair, the Fulton County Courthouse with its Flemish Gables was still grand looking. Mostly Hickman seemed as dreary as the day. The morning was grey and overcast, with an ominous dark sky to the northwest. They were calling for storms. Would my feet get soaked right off the bat, thereby giving me the best chance to get the most blisters for the longest time?

The runners filed off the bus and lined up for the ferry. "The roundtrip ferry ride has increased 500% in the past year," Carl had announced the night before. "It's been $2 roundtrip for 20 years, and now it's $10 per roundtrip. Cash only. They'll be there to collect it in the morning." And so they were.

Although the morning had been subdued, even gloomy so far, the ferry ride itself, especially on the way to Missouri, was more convivial. The river air, the novelty of an old-timey ferry ride, and the fact that we were all as clean and fresh as we would be for a long time seemed to hit the runners simultaneously. This was it. No turning back. We weren't really interested in the Mississippi River. We just wanted to get to the other side after the 36 hours of pre-race anxiety. It was time to start.

The Vol Staters file onto the ferry in Hickman, KY.

At one point I was standing by the diminutive 74-year-old Terrie Wurzbacher. She was talking with Bob Hearn, who wore what looked like boxer briefs and a cut-off shirt that just protected his chest and shoulders from his running vest. "I hope your Default Mode Network dissolves quickly, and you can just float through the rest of the race," I told him.

He smiled.

The sprinkling rain had already begun, and our cult leader Lazurus Lake, occasionally called "The Most High Evil One," was at the head of the ferry, posing for selfies under an umbrella with his adoring disciples. His thinning, long white hair spread out from under a Big Bear's Backyard Ultra hat. Backyard ultras are last-runner-standing loop races, a format that Laz originated in his backyard. They've now spread all over the world; this hat was from a race in Žilina, Slovakia. He was also wearing his signature white button-down shirt, a baggy pair of jeans, and a blue-and-black Vol State jacket with his name and time on it—available to all finishers for $80. His disciples were mostly, but not always, adoring; there was a playful, love-hate relationship with the guy—kind of like your stern father who was practically impossible to please or impress, yet you couldn't keep yourself from trying. (*Dear Dr. Freud....*)

Tony and I took turns taking pictures of each other. He and Who Dey were pumped for the adventure to come.

Who Dey and his runner Tony Webb are all smiles on the ferry.

The rain stopped just as the ferry got to Missouri.

We all disembarked on that side of the river and walked up the bank about 100 feet. A bunch of men made a beeline for the trees to relieve themselves. Everyone eventually made sure they were behind a random pole, which is strictly a formality, given that there wasn't any way to get ahead in the race since we would all be walking back down to the ferry for the return crossing. Legend has it that a guy named Ray Baum swam the Mississippi to start Vol State . . . twice. I was fine with the ferry.

Laz prepares to light the start of Vol State.

I squatted down in the front row of the 120 of us, hoping to get a picture of Laz lighting his cigarette to start the race. I used to think that the cigarette start was just part of the absurd irony Laz brings to his endeavors, but Laz smokes—a lot—and the lighting makes literal sense besides being ironic. Laz gave a little speech: "Remember, the earliest quit was at the Tennessee border. Fifteen seconds . . . " He had the cigarette in his mouth. We waited for him to light the flame and breathe in the nicotine. Amazing with Laz's serious habit that he's been running and walking unbelievable distances for decades. The man is a walking paradox.

Smartphone cameras were ready. He lit the cigarette, blew out smoke, and yelled, "You're off! Don't get behind now. You'll never make it up." Much hooting and clapping ensued. Then the runners walked back down the hill to the ferry. The 2023 Last Annual Vol State Race had officially begun.

Chapter 3

WHERE MADNESS MEETS ASPHALT

"Everybody's got a plan until they step off that ferry."
--Lazarus Lake

Do my shoes even work?

*D*o *horses feel this way when they're crammed into the starting gates?*
The Vol State runners were raring to go as we slowly headed back
southeast across the Mississippi River. The race had started, but the ferry
engines were doing all the work. I had my first minor panic attack when I
thought my shoes might not work. My feet were cramping just standing
around. I kept pulling my toes up and pointing them, but the arches
of my feet kept cramping. I had tried my new Hoka Bondis out for a
five-mile walk, and they worked fine. I'd trained in the same shoes, just a
size smaller. But I recognized the problem. I'd had it with a pair of Altra
Olympus shoes I bought in Florida and tried out in England. They were
intentionally a size too big, and I was hoping to use them for the race,
but I kept cramping, and my feet just wouldn't adjust to them.

This couldn't be happening with my new Hokas. I sat down on the
ferry deck and took off each shoe, slid my orthotic (made for my foot
size, not for a shoe that was a size bigger) back toward the heel, and
tried to hold down the orthotic as I slid my foot back in. I stood up,
and everything felt better. There was hope. Where would I have found
another pair of shoes in Hickman, Kentucky?

No one seemed in too much hurry to get to the front of the ferry, and
the veterans near me were quite talkative. Diane Taylor, who was often

among the last Vol State finishers, chatted with Sherry Meador, who was draped in an American flag and had the longest active streak of Vol State finishes.

The ferry docked, and the runners and walkers poured onto the street.

Vol Staters head off the ferry a second time in Hickman.

We quickly became a giant, raggedy snake of humans with American flags on their packs, heading through downtown Hickman. At one point, I was walking with Gary Ferguson, the guy I'd talked to over waffles who had lost his bag. "Did you find it?" I asked.

"Yes, it was right on the bus. Are you going to stay walking at this pace the whole time?"

"Uh, I doubt it, but I really have no idea." He soon walked ahead.

I saw Terrie Wurzbacher and figured it was time to introduce myself. Terrie is 4'11", a retired Army and Navy doctor from New York, and an unlikely veteran of four Vol State finishes after her first race DNF (Did Not Finish). She's a tough little woman with a no-nonsense Yankee/military air.

"Hi, Terrie. I'm Nancy. I read your book in preparation for Vol State, and it helped a lot." Terrie wrote a book called *It's Not About the Miles,* which chronicles her Vol State experiences, especially the 2021 race when she was crewed by "The Warden," another runner who had already dropped out of the race.

"I'm glad to hear that. I'm worried about the stairs up ahead," she fretted. "I'm not sure I'm going to make it."

"Sounds like you could use some of the positivity from your book," I said. Her worry seemed funny so early in the race, but Laz had added the stairs up to the county courthouse in Hickman just for sadistic purposes as near as I could tell—they were supposed to be steep and long but not daunting for a four-time Vol State finisher. "I'm sure you'll be fine. What's your next project?"

She talked about her new book, *From Tipping Point to Turning Point: A Journey to Self-Awareness,* due out later in the year. This woman had weathered a lot over the decades.

I walked on. Hickman introduced us to the Laz method of getting from point A to point B: You walk past Cumberland St., turn right a block later on Kentucky St., make your next right on Jackson St., then turn left on Cumberland St. I didn't know why, but I was sure Laz had a good reason. *Really? Why are you so sure? Maybe he doesn't want us to walk past L and L Fine Jewelry Design? Maybe he wants us to have a better view of the post office?* Usually, the weird routes had something to do with a county courthouse, which Laz races were determined to pass by, but why this extra block? *Why* started too many questions I kept circling back to, but it was better not to ask at all. Too many *whys* are rabbit holes into the speculative warren of Lazarus Lake's mind, from which I typically returned to daylight empty-handed. I only knew that if I missed the extra block and took that first right onto Cumberland, I would be disqualified.

In HOTS, just a month before Vol State, Chris Kane had figured out after the fact that he had made a wrong turn someplace and missed a small bit of the course. He turned himself in at the end of the race and got disqualified; in the process, he became a legendary symbol of integrity.

In that same race, Bob Hearn spaced out and walked along the main drag of Morristown, Tennessee, instead of on the odd, elevated sidewalks above his head as instructed by the race director. Bob, leading the pack by a lot, somehow figured it out five miles after Morristown and checked with Carl and Laz. He explained that he'd gone through Morristown by the correct route but on the ground. Did he have to go back and run the elevated sidewalks? Yes, he did. That was a 10-mile round-trip error, unbelievably disheartening in a 347-mile race. But Bob did it and still won by over 27 hours. Between these mishaps and Tony's at last year's Vol State, I was suitably spooked and so obsessively checked the route map on my Garmin watch that was strapped over the wrist of my sun-hoodie.

The steps up the cliff to the courthouse were steep but fine. Laz sat at the top of them with a check sheet to see who had made it the first 3+ miles. "I'm Nancy," I said.

"Last name?" said Laz, like some unshaven drill sergeant.

"Barber." He checked me off. I waited to take a picture of Terrie, who huffed to the top of the steps without much problem.

At one point, I caught up with 64-year-old William Cooper, a tall, resolute, retired military officer with a toothy smile. I introduced myself. "You're from Elizabethtown, right?" I said. "All my mom's relatives are from Bardstown," which was 25 miles way.

"Then you know about the five unsolved murders there?"

"Ugh, no." Apparently, the murders go back to 2013 and involve a police officer, a mother and her daughter, and a girl and her father.

"Part of the Cornbread Mafia?" I wondered aloud.

"Could be."

"Interesting. I'm gonna have to find out more about that."

I did wonder why my relatives hadn't mentioned the murders, but Bardstown is known as the Bourbon Capital of the World, and *USA Today* once called it the "Most Beautiful Small Town in America." There were other things to talk about in Bardstown, including family gossip. I stopped to take pictures of derelict buildings, and William walked on.

A little over 4 miles in, I stopped at a Marathon Station. I stood patiently in the long line of Vol Staters waiting for the bathroom. While I was standing next to the iced tea casks—sweetened and unsweetened—a guy with a scraggly, grey beard walked over. "Y'all be careful on that stretch to Union City," he told me. "There ain't much shoulder, and them cars just fly down that road."

I nodded and said, "Thanks, we will."

He poured a swallow of sweet tea into his Styrofoam cup and tasted it. "Sometimes they switch 'em," he explained; he didn't want to get back to his truck and find out he had unsweetened iced tea instead.

"Good to know," I told him.

After my turn in line, I got a Gatorade and a ham biscuit from the heated box by the counter. As far as gas station food goes, biscuits aren't a terrible option in the Deep South. I sat at a table with Diane, the 65-year-old veteran from Knoxville, who had done Vol State lots of times and often finished near last. She was a notorious lollygagger, which meant I would probably like her. Rumor has it that Laz was hopping mad at her one year when she stopped to get her hair done in Monteagle, 40 miles before the Rock, thereby making Laz have to wait longer for her at the finish.

"You know any place good to eat in Union City?" I asked her.

"I'm heading to Scott's Grill. They do a good burger."

Another Vol State guy came up to the table. "Where'd you say?"

"Scott's Grill," I told him. "All the cool kids will be there." He nodded.

The old guy with the sweet tea didn't lie. The Union City Highway stretch was miserable. The cars, pickups, and semis whipped by, and there were about four inches of asphalt to the left of the white line, then usually a dip down into a ditch, so it wasn't just that you didn't have much shoulder, it was that you didn't have any place to go beyond the shoulder without risking a twisted ankle and a tumble.

Fortunately, I've been blessed with a poor imagination when it comes to vehicular-pedestrian homicides, so I just stayed as far to the left side as I could and paid close attention to the oncoming traffic. I was only going to dive into the ditch if it looked like I was about to get smashed. Thankfully, the cars were mostly courteous, and they had seen enough Vol Staters ahead of me to know they shouldn't be texting and driving on this stretch. The only real problems happened when I could hear a car coming behind me and see one coming my way. Clearly, Tennessee drivers didn't want to hit a pedestrian, but I didn't want to test them with Hobson's choice of hitting a pedestrian or colliding head-on with another car. Sometimes, I would just stop and carefully brace my left foot down the slope, ready to dive while I watched the oncoming car. It made for slow, tense progress.

About nine miles into this thing, just before the Tennessee border, two women pulled over to ask me where we had started.

"Ugh, Dorena Landing, Missouri. We took the ferry."

"No, REALLY?" The driver was amazed that we had started nine miles ago.

I couldn't resist adding, "And we're heading to NW Georgia."

"OHHHHH, well, God bless you!" she said, smiling, and drove on. Lord knows what she and her friend had to say about all these lunatics on the road.

At some point in the long slog to Union City, I came across Terrie Wurzbacher again. She must have passed me when I was eating a ham biscuit at the Marathon station. As I came up behind her, I said, "Gosh, I thought I was signing up for Laz's sidewalk journey race. I didn't know

I was going to be dodging cars all along the way."

"Did you really?" she asked.

"No. I'm just kidding. But this barely existent shoulder isn't much fun."

"That's for sure. And I hate the rumble strips."

She was right about them. The rumble strips are great for alerting cars that their tires are heading for a ditch, but the deep grooves make the surface bumpy and uncomfortable for walkers. Also, the slight camber to the left was bound to play havoc. Over many miles, I didn't know how my body would react. Now I understood why a lot of folks trained on real roads. I figured that dodging traffic was only worth it during the actual race, so I put my training miles in on dedicated trails and paths where I definitely would not be run over.

I passed a sign in front of a church that said, **"BE SURE YOUR SIN WILL FIND YOU OUT."** Perhaps it already had, and that's why I was in this race.

Up ahead, I could see William Cooper. I was intensely envious of the bulbous ferrules he had on the end of his hiking poles. Somehow, I had managed to forget the extra rubber tips I had brought from England for my hiking poles, *sticks* in hiker speak. I remembered this morning on the ferry when I took them out of my quiver. The metal tips had worn through the tips I had, which meant I would click-click-click-click ad nauseam as the sticks hit the asphalt. William had the biggest rubber spheres I'd ever seen on the bottom of his sticks.

When I caught up with him, I said, "I'd hoped to be able to sneak up on people, but it'll never happen with these metal tips on my poles."

"Actually, I didn't hear you anyway," he said.

"You've got some great tips. I'm hoping to find some in Union City."

"You could also duct tape something to the poles if you don't find any," he suggested. William was a Vol State and HOTS veteran, and he was signed up for next month's Circle of Hell too. These folks are gluttons for punishment! "Even an old piece of tire would work."

Vol Staters are almost invariably helpful to rookies. There's none of that frat-house let's-be-assholes-to-the-newbies mentality. The veterans generally love to mentor and coach. They've been schooled in hell and are generous with the lessons they've learned. Tim Hardy, a veteran who had to back out of the race before it started this year, held a Zoom webinar in the spring, where he and other old-timers gave advice to the Vol State virgins, and then had a Q & A session. The experts don't always agree, of course. Hiking sticks, for example, are a source of much controversy. The anti-stick folks claim that they're just two more things to keep up with and add to the weight of your pack when you aren't using them. The pro-stick contingency says that the poles help with balance, camber, and speed, and prevent sausage fingers, the swelling in the hands that many walkers get swinging their arms by their sides for so long. I'm a big fan of sticks from way back for all those reasons, but damn, that constant clicking got on my nerves. I wasn't ready to try William's solution just yet, but I told him I would keep it in mind. How hard could it be to find ferrules in West Tennessee?

Upon meeting my first road angel

Fifteen miles into the race, just after the I-69 overpass, I came up to the aptly named Interstate 69 Motorsports, which apparently specializes in the planet's coolest four-wheelers. Who knew that you could pay $30,000 for a four-wheeler ATV? (Lots of folks in Tennessee, I'm guessing.) As I got near the dealership, I saw a tent in the parking lot, and a smiling woman walked toward me with a bottle of water. Ice cold water. Ahhhhh, so this was a road angel stop, not a promo tent for the dealership. "We've got chairs in the shade, and inside, you can use the bathroom if you want."

I thanked her profusely and took a long drink of one of the best waters I'd ever tasted. I passed a sign that said, **"Welcome Vol State Racers!! ANGEL STATION *Water * Shade *Clean bathrooms. Good luck to all racers!"** How great is that?

A bathroom sounded perfect. When I opened the dealership door, the air-conditioned wall hit me and reminded me of how most people in the South deal with July. I was tempted to sit in the lobby for the rest of the afternoon, but I headed for the restrooms instead. A little chalkboard at the sink said, "Welcome Vol State Racers! Good luck!!" It almost made me cry. Really. I'd heard about the road angels, but this was my first encounter.

I'd made a pact with myself before the race that I would always take something from any road angel who offered it. My reasons were three-fold: (1) I would never want to discourage another person's generous impulses. It could make them feel rejected and dampen their enthusiasm for helping someone else down the road. (2) I know that it feels good to give something to somebody who really needs it. (3) I knew that people wanted to feel part of this race, to feel part of the adventure, and the road angels *were* a major part of this adventure.

Soon, William, Robert George (48), and a woman named Michele

Radcliff (46) were all hanging out at the picnic table under the tent. Nobody was really speaking. It was a bit awkward.

"What's the best thing about living in this area?" I asked one of the road angels.

"Well," she thought about it. "One thing is we have a great lake made by an earthquake not far from here, and folks go swimming and boating on it." Reelfoot Lake State Park was 26 miles west of Union City. The lake apparently sprung up from a series of earthquakes along the New Madrid fault in the winter of 1811-1812. What must've been a tragedy for the folks living in the area eventually turned into a recreational boon for northwest Tennesseans. As the Taoists remind us, it's hard to say what's good or bad. Surely, a hot lunch at Scott's Grill would be good, though, and it couldn't be that far away.

When some more Vol Staters came by the station, I decided it was time to head into Union City proper... along sidewalks! I could give up worrying about cars for a bit.

Where the waitress calls you "Sweetie"

When I got to Scott's Grill on the main drag in town, William was already there, seated at a four-top with his stuff spread out on another seat. We acknowledged each other, but it didn't look like he wanted company. Another table of Vol Staters was finishing up their lunch, so I took a table in the middle of the restaurant. Sitting down in the AC, ready for a burger and fries seemed heavenly. The waitress called me "sweetie" and treated me like a regular. The couple at the next table, who turned out to be Labrador breeders, had figured out something was going on from all the sweaty folks with backpacks, so they started asking me questions: *Where are you going? How long will it take? Where do you sleep? What are you raising money for?* That last question always puzzles me. How did doing crazy stuff become so tightly associated with charity?

A quick search on my iPhone told me that the six-day footraces in the late 1800s had significant cash prizes (and also plenty of betting) as competitors did laps around a track to see who could finish the most in six days. For a while, it was the most popular sport in the country with as many as 70,000 spectators turning out for an event. One 1879 six-day race saw the winner take home over $20,000, a purse equivalent to over $600,000 in today's money.

The early dance marathons in the 20s and 30s similarly offered cash prizes to individuals. More endurance madness for prize money!

I'm not sure what changed, but contemporary dance marathons are almost always fundraisers. TRON at Penn State, for example, raises literally millions of dollars for Four Diamonds, a childhood cancer charity. The Leukemia Society's Team in Training Program started training runners to do marathons in 1988. In return, the runners would raise money for the charity. When I did 100K Ultra Challenges in the UK, I saw lots of race bibs with various charities typed under the person's first name. One guy told me that the thought of the charity he was raising money for was what kept him going through the night.

Me, I just paid the entry fee myself for the Ultra Challenges, and I didn't get the discount I could've gotten if I had partnered with a charity and raised money for them. I know so many charities do great work, and I'm happy they've found endurance events to help them make money. Personally, though, I get embarrassed asking people for money. I WANT to do crazy endurance races. Why should someone pay money to a charity so I can do it? That's just me, though. And it's most people running Vol State.

I also got grilled with the same questions by three generations of women who were eating with a baby boy who was the fourth generation. I had started this race thinking I would ask questions of folks all along the way, but here on Day 1, I realized that much of my time would go to *answering* questions, and they were going to be the same questions, over and over. Maybe that's why the Vol State racers kind of kept to themselves. William and the other Vol Staters were gone. Three Vol State women had just arrived and took a table in the far back corner.

Occasionally, people didn't ask questions; these were usually the folks who wanted to tell me their stories, often traumatic ones. Maybe they identified with the misery we were going through, walking so far in such a short time. Or maybe they were happy to talk to anyone who would listen.

An old guy stopped me as I got my pack on to leave the diner. "There was this E7," he told me. "I was in the Army. I had an E7 under me, a girl who could carry a 120-lb rucksack and hike seven or eight miles." I told him this was certainly impressive, which led him to tell me about something that had happened to his leg. I don't know if it was a military injury or not, but he'd had nine surgeries. "They told me I wouldn't walk, and I am walking. And now my wife's gotten sick, and I'm telling her that she can walk. But she's got cancer. We just come back from the doctor today, and she got a good report. The cancer is shrinking. But she still can't get out of bed, and she can't walk. She can barely just get to her wheelchair."

I told him how sorry I was and wished him and his wife good luck. Human resilience seems to be a recurring theme on this journey. I wondered if the woman would ever walk again. I was grateful that I still could.

Time to head back into the heat. Any hint of gray skies had lifted, and the sun was at full strength by the time I left the diner.

When I passed a gas station, I saw Tara from The Last Supper in her braids and peach fishing shirt sitting beside one of the pumps in the shade. She didn't look happy. "How's it going?" I asked.

"OK. I just bought these shoes from a thrift store. My sandals were cutting up my feet, and I had to get something else."

"Ugh. That sounds miserable."

"Now I'm trying to figure out where to get supplies to patch up my blisters."

I looked down the road. "I'm gonna stop at the Walgreens I can see a few blocks away. I'm looking for Gatorade, but they'll have all sorts of first aid stuff."

"Good idea. I'll do that."

I walked a little farther and came across another road angel tent in front of an accounting firm. It had big neon yellow signs: **"WELCOME VOL STATE RUNNERS" "GO VOL STATE RUNNERS GOOD LUCK!"** I said hi to the woman who was running it. She offered me cold water and snacks, and I took a couple of mini candy bars she had on the table. I talked to her for a few minutes, and when I told her I was from England and Florida, she asked me my name.

"Nancy."

"What's your last name?"

"Barber."

"Oh, somebody was looking for you this morning. This lady came by and was asking if we'd see you."

"Was her name Pamela?"

"Yeah, I think it might've been."

It must've been my Aunt Fran's first cousin Pam, who lives in Union City. My 81-year-old aunt is among my inspirations for an adventure-filled life. She and my Uncle Dan have traveled all over the world. She grew up in West Tennessee and wasn't getting to travel much these days, so she'd become semi-obsessed with the race. She encouraged lots of the runners on the Vol State Facebook page and occasionally admonished Laz when she thought he was being too tough on us. She'd bubbled on about the race to her cousin, who was apparently on the lookout for me. Sweet to hear.

314 miles in sandals?

I walked on to the Walgreens, looking for Gatorade. Inside, I met up with Tara again. She asked if I knew the best stuff to get for blisters. Up to this point, I'd thought Tara was an ultra-racing veteran. First of all, she seemed reserved at the Last Supper, like this was old hat. Second, I figured only veterans wore sandals in a race like this.

Initially, I was shocked that *anyone* wore sandals in a 314-mile race. Apparently, it's an offshoot of the barefoot runner movement, made famous by Christopher McDougall in his 2009 book *Born to Run*. He wasn't so much suggesting that modern folks run barefoot but that they run in minimalist shoes. For a while, I tried running in a pair of Merrell minimalist shoes—picture thick ballet slippers. It cured some of my chronic injury areas and replaced them with others. I couldn't stick with it long enough to know whether it could ultimately work or not, but only this year—coinciding with my reading of *Born to Run 2*, I had decided to give it another shot with Altra Escalantes, basically a running shoe with some support but zero-drop and lots of room in the toe box, the opposite of running in the cloud-like Hokas or Asics Gel-Nimbuses I was used to. I was only running in my Altras, though, not walking, and I was gradually building up the distance. I didn't even think about shoes without ultra cushioning for Vol State with all the pounding on sizzling asphalt. Still, a small minority of participants do the race in Luna, Bedrock, or Teva sandals, and they swear by them. In fact, that's why I'd bought a pair of Bedrock sandals to carry on my pack in case something went terribly wrong with my Hokas. Unfortunately, I didn't realize how long it took to break them in, so I wasn't sure how much good they would do, but maybe with Injinji toe socks, I could manage in them for a while.

But I digress. Starting off the race in sandals was part of why I thought Tara had done a lot of ultras before. Apparently, I was wrong. All veterans would know more than I did about how to treat blisters. I'd forgotten much of what I'd read in *Fixing Your Feet*. Mostly, I became fixated on what it had to say about not getting blisters in the first place—an optimist's way of reading. For Tara, I pointed out some of the first-aid remedies on the Walgreens shelf: cushions, ointments, hydrocolloid bandages. "Here's basically what you need," I told her, "but which ones work the best I haven't the slightest idea."

"I'll figure it out. Thanks."

When I went to pick up Gatorade, I found out they only had quart-sized bottles. I didn't want to carry one of those, too bulky and heavy. There would be someplace else with smaller versions down the road.

The Walgreens air conditioning was bliss, but it would never get me to Georgia. I headed back into the heat and called Chris on WhatsApp. I kept one earbud in to talk with him and used the other ear to listen to cars. I was passing a Marathon station, where I should've gone in to buy a Gatorade, but I got distracted by a close-cropped bearded guy in an SUV who pulled up next to me, rolled down his window, and asked, "What are you guys doing?"

I gave him the spiel, and he said, "My name's Paul Tinker. I own a bunch of radio stations in the area. Can I interview you?"

The next thing I knew, he'd whipped out his iPhone and was asking me about the race. Chris got to listen in on the whole exchange. Here's the transcript:

Paul Tinker: *"Now ma'am, you can tell me your name, or you don't want to—it doesn't make any difference, but what I'd like to know is why all the people walking around through West Tennessee?"*

Me: *"Well, we're on a race called the Last Annual Vol State Road Race, and it goes from Dorena Landing, Missouri, to Castle Rock, GA. It's 500 kilometers; it's 314 miles. We're not raising money for anything. We're just out doing something silly and fun and hopefully having a good time and suffering along the way and trying to stay out of the way of cars. So that's what's going on."*

Paul Tinker: *"Where are you from, and what do you do for a living?"*

Me: *"I teach at Stetson University in Florida. I'm from Florida, and I live halftime in England."*

Paul Tinker: *"Goodness gracious alive! So how many people are walking?"*

Me: *"About 120. The front group is running. There's a group that's running that will finish in less than four days and the rest of the gang has till ten days. We have to finish in ten days, or the race is over."*

Paul Tinker: *"Now what about gear? What do you have in your hand and pocket and shoulder pads?"*

Me: [I'm not sure why I ignored this question. Like a good politician, I suppose I wanted to sneak in what I wanted to talk about.] *"There are all these wonderful road angels along the way. Tennessee has just been awesome! People from Tennessee are great. They've known about the race. The race has been going on, I think since 2006. It's the same route every year, so people who live on the route, businesses have opened up with coolers* *of cold water and food and seats, everything."*

Paul Tinker: [And like any good journalist, he just rephrased the question.] *"So, what do you carry with you? That looks like an umbrella."*

Me: *"I've got an umbrella, hiking sticks, I've got water. I've got a change of clothes. I've got electronic stuff. Oh, and I've got a lot of foot care stuff for taking care of my feet."*

Paul Tinker: *"So, will you be able to walk in these shoes for the entire distance?"*

Me: *"I hope so, but I've got some sandals on my pack."*

Paul Tinker: *"I see those. Where do you spend the night?"*

Me: *"Wherever. Motels, Gleason's Fire Station opens up and lets us crash in there. Some people are walking through the night, running through the night, just depends on how fast they are and how sleepy they are."*

Paul Tinker: *"It's a little dangerous walking, is it not?"*

Me: *"It could be. The cars are the biggest danger. Just trying to stay out of the way of them is the biggest problem."*

Paul Tinker: *"I'm always going to ask the tough questions, but where do you go to the restroom?"*

Me: *"Uh, so far, gas stations, there was a road angel stop at the motorsports place that sells four-wheelers, and they let us use their bathrooms. I had a great lunch today at Scott's Grill. I used their bathroom. So, wherever."*

Paul Tinker: *"And change of clothes and shower and so forth. Where will you get that done?"*

Me: *"Maybe Gleason. That's probably the next stop."* [Boy was that ambitious!]

Paul Tinker: *"And then from that, how many miles a day do you think you'll walk?"*

Me: *"I don't know. I've got to walk 31 a day to finish in less than ten days, and I hope I'll walk more than that, at least in the beginning."*

Paul Tinker: *"Had any close calls or any interesting things, people interviewing you such as we're doing?"*

Me: *"No, you're the most interesting guy I've met so far today, so uh... No, it's early in the race, and we've got a long way to go."*

Paul Tinker: *"And I want to follow that by saying, you told me you are an educator. What do you teach?"*

Me: *"I teach writing, English at Stetson University in DeLand, Florida."*

Paul Tinker: *"We're familiar with Stetson. Yes, we are. And if there is one thing you would like to tell the people here in Tennessee that—something you've found interesting besides a lot of hospitality, what would it be?"*

Me: [Naw, I still want to talk about hospitality.] *"We're just really grateful for the people of Tennessee, not just for putting up with us but taking really really good care of us. So, we're happy to be here, and people have been great."*
Paul Tinker: *"Well, good luck, and God bless you."*
Me: *"Thank you very much."*

When the interview ended, he asked, "Is there anything at all I can get for you?"

"No, I'm good. The only thing I'm looking for is tips for my hiking poles."

"Can I have 30 seconds?" he asked. I was hoping maybe he had the tips in his vehicle. "Can I have your hand?" I gave him my hand, and he prayed to Jesus for my safe journey and food and shelter and all the things I would need and good health. It was sort of sweet. I wish he'd added the part about the hiking pole tips. He gave me his card and told me to text him with the race website and tell him how things were going. He said he'd send me a copy of the interview. And he did.

Chapter 4

BLURRING THE LINES

"When we apply compassion to people who disagree with us, the borders can soften. Compassion and love in this cruel world are the best resistance."
--George Saunders

Compassion . . . even to Trumpers?

At the Tampa Association of Writers & Writing Programs (AWP) Conference in 2018, George Saunders gave the keynote speech. Despite the giant ballroom of spectators, I really thought he was talking only to me. Like so many people, I was struggling with the turn our country had taken with the 2016 election of Donald J. Trump as President. I was still hopping mad. It had pulled the proverbial yoga mat from under my feet and left me on my butt, destabilizing everything I'd ever thought about the U.S. I was a left-leaning Independent, who occasionally voted for Republicans, respected American Christians, and admired the advancements of American women. Even if we disagreed on plenty of issues, I believed, perhaps naively, in the unshakable American commitment to democracy. The ascendence of Trump and the abhorrent values he represents shattered everything I thought I knew about America, especially about Christians, women, and the Republican establishment. My beliefs fractured into tiny colorful pieces, exploded by a Mardi Gras confetti canon on a street named Desire.

Like the good Buddhist he is, George Saunders often talks about compassion, and his AWP keynote was no different. "Everybody in this world is on a continuum with us. There's no such thing as 'the other.' The other is us on a different day."

I wasn't sure about that. Trump had shown me. You supported him, or you didn't. It wasn't a continuum. I would never support Trump on a different day. But I knew Saunders was getting at something essential. Should compassion apply even to Trump supporters? "Unfortunately, yes," advised Saunders. Sigh.

Just as his writing blurs the boundaries between high and low art, Saunders says it's important that we "soften the boundaries" between political oppositions in the country. The U.S. has no shortage of people escalating the rhetoric on both ends of the political spectrum. Anyone wanting to add to it can join the hordes. The media loves spouting venom, so it's hard to remember that the spectrum is a continuum and not two poles squaring off at one another.

Some little voice kept whispering that Saunders is right, and we're much more than Trump supporters and never-Trumpers. Maybe, just maybe, Vol State could be an experiential manifestation of the blurred continuum: an academic liberal with no protection, entirely vulnerable, walks through the heart of Trump Country with his supporters turning out in droves to help the libtard reach the Rock. What a weird vacation.

Lions and tigers and bears, oh, my!

The sun was a pizza oven as I walked out of Union City. It was going to be a long ten days.

At some point, I noticed two Vol State guys walking ahead of me, and one had an umbrella. Holy crap! I had forgotten that I had an umbrella for the sun. What an ingenious idea! I folded up my hiking sticks and traded them for the umbrella in my quiver—my fancy silver umbrella that reflected the sun back to itself: *Take that, you sunny sun!* The lightweight brolly surrounded my head with a cozy, black interior. I could almost fanaticize that I was somewhere else, not walking on a hot sidewalk in Western Tennessee. It didn't take 10 degrees off the temperature, but it was definitely an improvement.

I caught up with the two guys—Jerrod Richardson (47) from Tennessee and Carmel Weed (52) from Alabama—and I thanked Carmel for the umbrella reminder.

While I was stomping through 88-degree temps with a soaring heat index in Tennessee, Chris was in cool, breezy England, where the sun would be setting in a couple of hours, and he'd be under a roof—no need for umbrellas.

This umbrella was a lifesaver! (Photo by Lorraine Threlkeld)

Chris was great to talk to along the way when I was bored or miserable. I had warned him before the race, "No matter how whiny I get, no matter how exhausted or hurt, make sure you just listen and encourage me. Don't suggest I quit." He promised he wouldn't. Chris is mostly cheerful in real life and invariably cheerful when I'm doing something stupid and brutal. He was determined to support me from afar in this race. He followed exactly where I was on Google Earth and could tell me where the sidewalk would end and what kind of shoulder the road up ahead would have. He'd look up restaurants and motels in upcoming towns, and he'd listen sympathetically to my complaints. I couldn't ask for a better partner. He was the perfect non-crew crew from 4,000+ miles a way.

Twenty-one miles into the journey, I saw some folks in the distance, parked in the shade of an overpass. I wondered who they were. It didn't take long to make out the white beard. This must be Laz and the crew, taking names and making sure everyone was still alive. Sure enough, Laz, Carl, Laz's wife Sandra, and Jan, the Meat-Wagon Lady were all in folding chairs in the shade. Naresh Kumar was there taking pictures. I gave Laz both my names, which he checked off on his clipboard.

"We ran into a woman who's been looking for you," said Laz. "She couldn't figure out why we didn't know where you were. She was a little insistent." He and Carl started laughing. "I tried to ignore her, but she was persistent."

"She seemed to think that we should know a lot more than we do," said Carl.

"I've never met her," I tried to explain, "but she's my Aunt Fran's first cousin. Aunt Fran grew up in West Tennessee, and she's become obsessed with this race, so she's got her cousin Pam interested. It's all your fault," I told Laz. "It's those updates that hook people. My mother read your Supper-before-the-Last-Supper report and sent me a text that said, 'You can come home.'" He got a kick out of that. "My favorite reports this summer were about the bears during HOTS and the sad choices the runners had."

"Do you know people actually ditched their food because of that?" he said, chuckling. In his 12-hour update for the HOTS journey run just a month before Vol State, Laz had posted,

> *most of our heroes are going to have a long sleepless night.*
> *what sleep they do get will often be the sleep of a feral dog.*
> *where ever and when ever.*
> *sleeping beside the road in bear country can be fitful sleep.*
> *and sleeping beside the road in bear country with food in*
> *your pack could be a mistake!*
> *the road is a place of choices.*
> *if you don't carry food you may have no meal.*
> *carry food and you may become one!*

And Laz only laughed, that clown.

He's starting his next transcon walk on April 1st, 2024, which means that Carl will be heading up HOTS and Vol State next summer. Laz says that he'll take five months to do it. He'll be 70 in 2024, but he looks even older and obviously has the fitness of someone much younger. He last did a transcon in 2018, in his 65th year.

"I'm looking for the fun, slow people to hang out with," I told Laz.

"Well, don't stay with the people who dawdle," piped in Carl. "You gotta keep moving."

"But I'd like to find out about Tennessee. I wanna talk to people from Tennessee and see what they're all about." Carl just shook his head.

"I did like the sidewalks in Union City, Laz," I told him.

"And there are others!" he said, getting my hopes up. Maybe he was just messing with me.

This journey race was a crazy new experience for me. I'd done races before—marathons in NYC, DC, Chicago, New Orleans, and Clearwater as well as Ultra Challenges of 50-100K in the Lake District, London-2-Brighton, Windsor, and England's Southeast Coast—but besides the scenery during the races, the short time frame (4- 36 hours) afforded me plenty of opportunity to explore the area before and after the race. I like to pick races and journeys in places I haven't had a chance to check out. And the long-distance endurance journeys I've done—Georgia-Vermont on the Appalachian Trail, the transcon bicycle trip, a kayaking trip on the Intracoastal Waterway from Florida to South Carolina, four Caminos de Santiago, the European Peace Walk, the Tour de Mont Blanc, Hadrian's Wall Path, and the Saxon Shore Way—have all given me time along the way to chat with people, relax in cafes and pubs with locals and other travelers, all the while slowly absorbing a sense of place and people. That's the pace I like best. Get your hiking/bicycling/kayaking done for the day, then relax and hang out, swapping stories and gaining ne w insights.

Vol State, on the other hand, has an urgency about it that's both internal and external. My fellow racers, all the cool kids, were intense and driven—not just the folks like Bob Hearn who hoped to win the race, but the others too, who knew they wouldn't come close to winning. It was a goal-oriented group, concerned primarily with getting to the Rock as quickly as possible. Me, I just wanted to survey part of the South and beat Oprah. She'd give me plenty of external impetus to keep moving at a fair clip and not dawdle, as Carl warned. But ten days is a long time to keep only a race mentality without getting to know the local people and p laces.

"I hope you have plenty of water," Laz warned, "because there's nothing up ahead for miles."

Jan sat behind him and called me over with the crook of her finger. She whispered, "There's an outdoor store just a couple of miles up the road that has cold water, outdoor fans, and bathrooms."

Bad cop, good cop.

Carl Laniak, Laz Lake, Sandra Cantrell, and Jan Redmond Walker taking names at the Stinky Bridge.

What comes around goes around . . .

I walked on a little farther past Stinky Bridge, which gets its name from a nearby rendering plant, and still farther, I saw Terrie standing about twenty feet from the side of the road, bent over in a cornfield.

"Hey, Terrie. You OK?"

"No, I'm not," she said.

I walked over.

"I had a Sonic shake in Union City. I usually only drink part of it, but this time, I drank the whole thing. I had weight-loss surgery a while back, and there's this thing called dumping syndrome. If you ingest too much in your stomach, it just destroys your system." She'd tried lying down in the field, but that didn't help in this heat. She was having a hard time figuring out what to do. I asked if I could get her poles or her umbrella out of the pack, but she said that was too much trouble. I tried to get her water, but she said she couldn't drink it because of the stomach issues. I looked around. We were in the middle of nowhere, but Jan wasn't far away with the Meat Wagon. It didn't seem worth calling her just yet.

Finally, I said, "Look, I'll walk with you. I think the outfitter is only a mile or so up the road and you can get a rest there. I hear they have a fan and water." She decided to give it a try. She walked slowly and took breaks along the way. I tried to keep my umbrella over her to keep the sun off. In one hand, she was carrying a fanny pack, and I kept offering to take it for her. She said no a couple of times.

"It's like you say in your book, Terrie. You've got to know when to ask for help and when to take it." She finally let me carry the fanny pack. We stopped a few more times. The outfitters was a lot farther away than I expected, at least a mile and a half from where I found her. She thanked me profusely all along the way for helping her.

"It's no problem," I told her. "I feel like a redneck Mary Poppins." I was starting to understand how the Vol State family works. I figured that if Terrie could get to the outfitters, she'd have a chance to relax and cool down in case she could continue. And if she decided to quit, at least she'd be someplace comfortable while she waited for Jan to show up.

When we finally got to the Final Flight Outfitters' porch, they mercifully had a giant cooler with lots of water bottles on ice and an industrial fan blowing on a number of Vol Staters who were already there resting. We got Terrie some cold water, and she sat down in the blessed shade.

I rested too. My right calf was tight and sore. I tried to stretch it out and took advantage of the chance to take off my shoes and check my feet. I had my first blister on the outside of my left big toe, so I got that lanced and taped, and put more Squirrel's Nut Butter on my feet. I hated getting my hands all greasy with the foot goop, but the outfitters let us use their bathrooms, and I could wash up. I had been hoping they might sell some rubber tips for my poles, but no such luck among their mammoth inventory of guns, ammo, fishing and camping gear.

While I was there, Steven Godfrey, the British guy I had offered to drive back to Florida after the race, called me to tell me about the room he was vacating at a motel in Gleason. I was having a hard time understanding him on the phone, but it was an incredibly generous gesture. He said he'd leave the key card under the mat in front of his second-story room. He instructed me to go around to the back of the motel and climb the stairs by the vending machine so the cashier in the lobby wouldn't see me. This was all a lot to take in. I was talking in the parking lot, which was loud; Steven had a pronounced English accent; we had a poor connection; and I was trying to remember what he was saying as he spoke. Terrie, like a phoenix, walked over and tapped me on the arm to mouth, "Thank you again," as she headed back on the road, rejuvenated. It was the first time at Vol State that I had seen someone go from incredibly debilitated to relatively refreshed and back on the white line so quickly. It wouldn't be the last.

I told Steven I didn't know how long it would take me to get to Gleason that night, but I would sure try, and knowing I had a place to sleep would make it easier.

"I left a trashcan full of ice in case you want to soak your feet," he added.

Wow. I thanked Steven profusely and wrote down all the details I could remember on my phone. "Eco-lodge, Room 214, take back steps up by the vending machine." Gleason was about 25 miles away, and I had no idea how long it would take to cover that distance, but I stayed at the outfitters another half hour until they closed at 6 pm, and I figured I'd walk through the night and hope to get to Gleason by dawn.

Chapter 5

EVOLVING OR DEVOLVING?

"People when they have too much comfort—
music don't have the right intensity.
Even in life, if you're too comfortable, you don't evolve."
—Jon Batiste, American Symphony

What could be more American than throwing up in a Walmart parking lot?

Martin was the next town, about five and a half miles from the outfitters, and I could get some dinner there. I was refreshed when got back on the road, but in a couple of miles, I began to fade for the first time. I stopped by an unhumanned road-angel tent on the right side of the road and had a couple of pieces of candy. My stomach wasn't feeling so good. I wasn't sure why. I kept drinking water.

About then, the alarm on my phone went off. I had set it for repeating alarms at 7:25 am and pm because we had to check in with the Vol State tracker every 7:30. I was afraid I would walk right through the time.

The tracker is one of the most fun parts of Vol State. You see a running tally of people's progress, and you get a glimpse at their skewed world-view. The check-ins worked like this: you pull up the link on your phone, which is specific to you and already has your name on it. You put in the closest mileage marker and make a random comment, which gets added anonymously to the overall comments tab on the Excel tracker sheet.

In last year's race, the random comments had charmed me and given special insight into the warped minds of the racers. I was looking forward to glimpses of how my fellow racers were doing this year.

What to say? What to say?

> **12-Hour Tracker, comments in italics** (Thursday evening, July 13, 2023)
>
> Me: 26 miles-- *"I feel like a redneck Mary Poppins."* So, 26 miles in 12 hours wasn't great, but it was 10 miles ahead of Oprah, so there was that.
>
> The named mileage and anonymous comments pop up on the tracker as they're posted, so you can immediately see where you stand vis-à-vis the other runners (there were 10 people behind me at this point) and you can empathize with other competitors' comments.
>
> Anonymous: *"When a new runner asks you at 1pm today 'when does it cool off?' November. That's when."* I get that.
>
> Anonymous: *"Crewed runner (sitting in a chair in the shade) OH NO my ice cream is melting all over me. Screwed runner (me) Screams Internally."* Being a screwed runner is a little like being the kid at the prom in a hand-me-down dress from her sister and no date. The crewed runner gets pampered and fed by their crew. They get chairs and shade and whatever they want to eat and ICE CREAM anytime they want it. We screwed entrants are both jealous and contemptuous of the crewed runners, but only in our heads. We think how much easier it would be to cover 314 miles in 10 days with all that help. On the surface, though, we wave and say hello as we pass by their little picnics and hear them complain about their melting ice cream. We're all one big happy Vol State family.
>
> Sadly, Jim Halsey called it a race at 23 miles. I have no idea how he made it 23 on that foot. His wife Vicky went on, and she was up ahead in Martin. They're an amazing duo.

A little farther up, I saw a road angel station on the left side of the road: a hodgepodge of chairs, a cooler, and a massive fan under a big tree. Carmel and Jerrod were just leaving, and I was thrilled to sit down. The station was manned by two old guys who had been friends and neighbors for forty years. One lived in the house behind the station, two big pickup trucks in his driveway, and the other lived just down the road. I officially felt like crap, and I would've been happy to sit, enjoy their fan, and listen to their stories all night. One of the guys had worked on organs, and I think he was a pilot too. I'm not sure about the other guy. The organ guy had apparently traveled for his job and said that when he was in Munich, "all they could call us was hillbillies." He didn't like Germany at all.

These two friends had spent Vol State's opening day meeting people from all over and hanging out. They'd been there all afternoon.

Even though I was feeling bad—sort of nauseous—I somehow still thought I was going to Gleason to get a few hours sleep in Steven's motel room. Gleason was another 19 miles from Martin, and I wasn't quite to Martin. That didn't sound like fun, but I knew I had to press on if I had any chance. I thanked my new road-angel friends and said goodbye.

As I walked into Martin, I started feeling worse and worse. By now it was dark, and I was heading to Walmart, which was just to the left of the route, to get tips for my polls and carabiners. Maybe I'd feel better after a trip to the bathroom.

I didn't.

I wandered over to the sporting goods section and met two African-American teenagers in the fishing department. They asked about the race and one tried to help me find tips for my poles by looking up hiking poles on his phone's Walmart app. They couldn't have been kinder to me. It was only much later that I realized how bad I must've looked. They walked me over to the aisle where the camping stuff was and showed me the hiking poles. Unfortunately, Walmart didn't sell just the tips, and I wasn't yet willing to buy new hiking poles just to get $3 worth of rubber. The guys wished me luck. I kept finding angels everywhere, even ones who didn't know about the race.

I did find a couple of lightweight carabiners, which I would use to hang the sandals off the back of my pack more easily, but all in all, it was a disappointing shopping trip. I sat down on a bench just inside the entrance to Walmart. I would savor the air conditioning as long as possible. I looked up the Eco Lodge in Gleason. It turned out that there wasn't one. In fact, they didn't have any motels at all in Gleason. But they *did* have an *Econo* Lodge in Martin, and it was just around the corner. Surely, he must've said Econo Lodge. And could I have mistaken Martin for Gleason? What are the chances there would be two Econo Lodges so close together in the middle of nowhere, Tennessee? Maybe I *had* misunderstood. Steven must have been staying in Martin. There was one way to find out. I would make my way to room 214 and see if there was a key card under the mat. (I could, of course, have looked up Steven on the tracker to see where he had been at 7:30 pm, but I didn't think about that.)

This seemed like a minor miracle, but I didn't want to get my hopes up just yet. Outside in the parking lot, a woman asked me about all the walkers she'd seen. I explained about the race and told her I was tired.

"Where are you going to stay tonight?"

"I hope I'm staying at the Econo Lodge."

"Can I give you a ride there?" she offered.

"Thank you very much, but I'd get disqualified if I got into a car."

"I figured it was something like that," she said, wishing me good luck before driving off.

It was at precisely that point that I threw up in the middle of the Walmart parking lot. I looked around to see if anyone was watching. They didn't seem to be, so I hobbled for the grass between the parking lot and the road. Like a vomiting zombie, I threw up again on the way, and then I threw up again in the grass, and then I crossed the street and threw up a final time in the grass there. I felt a bit better after that, vomiting being the usual temporary cure for nausea. If only there were a key under the mat at the Econo Lodge.

I walked a block back to the official race route, then another block to where the Econo Lodge was set back behind an Advanced Auto Parts store and a Taco Bell. I went down the access road until I could see the vending machine at the end of the row of rooms. I hobbled over and climbed the stairs slowly, then made my way along the wrap-around walkway to the other side of the motel.

There was room 214. And it had a mat outside. I gingerly bent down and picked up the corner. Ahhhhh, the magical key card! Thank you, Steven Godfrey!

And so I slept while Oprah kept walking

In the luxurious motel room, Steven's queen-sized bed was rumpled from use, but mine was pristine. I ran a hot bath and tried to put my feet in the trashcan of ice. My feet and lower legs were covered with unsightly heat rash, bubbly red spots all over. I had seen it before, and the rash didn't hurt or itch, so I didn't worry about it. The ice was too painful on my feet, though. I knew it would be good for me, but I couldn't tough out any extra hurt at the moment. My calf was killing me, and although my stomach was much improved, it still didn't quite feel right. Nothing a sleep couldn't cure, I hoped.

I washed my shorts, underwear, and hoodie in the sink with the Econo Lodge's mini soap bar and draped them over the coat hangers. I sunk into the warm bath and promptly dozed off for a few minutes. I could've just stayed in the tub for the next few hours, but that didn't seem like the best use of my time, so I washed my hair, then headed to bed, making sure to prop my feet up on the extra pillows in hopes that the swelling would go down. My big-toe blister had filled up again with fluid, but I would deal with that when I awoke. I set my alarm for three am, five hours later, a decadent amount of sleep by Vol State standards. Still, I figured the disruption to my system warranted it. Truth be told, spending so *little* time in such extravagant surroundings seemed entirely wrong, but these were the exigencies Vol State and Oprah demanded. She was marching on while I stretched out and slept as soon as my head found the pillow.

The alarm went off too soon, but the sleep had changed things. My stomach still didn't feel right, but my calf was much improved, and the blister had drained on its own. I ate half a Payday bar I'd picked up along the way. It's an ultra racer's go-to candy bar because it's all peanuts and nougat, so it doesn't melt, but it gives you salt, protein, and sugar. It went down OK.

My hoodie still wasn't dry, and I didn't relish putting on a wet shirt first thing in the morning, so I used the motel blow dryer to help it along. The shirt worked great for lots of things: big pockets for stuff, a hood in case I got cold at night, and of course it kept the sun off my skin, but it wasn't as quick-dry as I would've liked. I should've washed it at home and hung it up to dry to see how long it took. I added a new Nexcare bandage to my toe because I'm paranoid about pulling the roof off a blister, and then I wrapped it with K-tape. The tape on the bottom of my foot was holding up OK, so I just left it. Somehow, it took me almost an hour to get back on the road. I'd have to get faster.

I followed the route through the downtown, past Martin's Coffee & Bakery, which sounded great but wasn't yet open. Past the Martin Public Library, which would be a wonderful place to while away the day in a cushy chair with a book. Before I'd left the Econo Lodge, I strapped on my chest light, which has a white beam in front with two different strengths and a red light on my back. It didn't matter much on the lighted sidewalks of Martin, but soon enough, I was on the outskirts of Martin, where it was dark and deserted. The light was a tiny tunnel of bright comfort.

A car would pass every once in a while, but mostly, I felt all alone. I have spent enough time in strange places on my own that this wasn't a big deal, but it would've been more fun to have some interesting company.

Still, there's something special about walking through strange towns in the dark. It's nearly verboten, first of all. Everyone would advise against it, especially for a single female. But it's peaceful and somehow empowering. I'm fortunate not to watch horror movies or read scary books, and I avoid them specifically for times like this when I'm alone in the dark and don't want frightening images to pop into my head. Greater Martin seemed benign, and I was happy enough to be walking, but my stomach still didn't feel great.

Soon, I got surprised by a little convenience store called JJ's Quick Stop—I hadn't seen it on the GPX—and it opened at 5 am. My lucky morning! I went in and headed for the drinks cooler. A couple of older guys were in the back at a big table. I suspected that a bunch of guys met there early most every morning like they do in diners and convenience stores all over America.

"Are you with them walkers?" one of the men asked.

I nodded.

They came up with all the standard questions about what was going on, where we were going, where we slept, where I was from, etc. When I told them I was from Florida but lived in England, one of the guys told me that his ancestors came from Herefordshire, and they had a big ole manor house in Rorston Village or something like that. The house had been turned into condos. I love how Southerners immediately try to make connections—my people to your people.

I picked up some Mombo candies and a Glacier Freeze Gatorade, and one of the guys in the back shouted to the cashier that whatever I bought was on him. The cashier made him come up and pay for my candy and Gatorade. Awfully sweet of the spontaneous road angel. I thanked him sincerely. I didn't need him to pay for my stuff, but I appreciated the gesture, and I knew by then that people wanted to feel a part of this race, to have "skin in the game."

The last thing I'd eaten before tossing my cookies at Walmart was a little candy at a road-angel stop. Once I threw up, I didn't feel like eating anything. I didn't feel like drinking much water either, but I did have half a Payday bar when I woke up, and I kept that down OK. Nothing much at JJ's had looked good to me. I drank the Gatorade back on the road, and pretty quickly, something switched inside me. I felt much better. It dawned on me that I'd had a Gatorade early yesterday and then never got one again after balking at the quart-sized ones at the Union City Walgreens. So that was the ticket. I'd had plenty of water but not enough electrolytes. I wouldn't let that happen again.

State Road 22 out of Martin was a perfect road to walk on—a big shoulder with plenty of space and not many cars so early in the morning. The sun was just rising, and that woke me up a bit. The whole biorhythm thing and the effect of light on our body and mind becomes a lot more understandable and important when you're wandering around outside during sunset and sunrise.

In the early light, I saw a couple of Styrofoam coolers in the grass beside the road. A biodome house was set back even further. I wondered if someone who lived there had written "Good luck! You got this!" on one of the coolers filled with water. Oddly, one packet of peanut butter crackers sat on top. I couldn't decide if I should take them or not. Maybe someone behind me would need them more. I wasn't even sure I really wanted the crackers, but I took them. I unwrapped and ate the first one. Wow! It was delicious. Plain old Ritz Peanut Butter Crackers. I ate another one and another, and in no time, I had devoured them all and suddenly felt *way* better. Why did I not know that I needed food? Why wasn't I hungry? Clearly, I needed salt too.

I knew there would be times when I'd want to thank road angels who weren't physically present. A lot of them leave guest books that you can write in, but some, like these, were just gifts with no way for them to know who benefitted. I'd brought little peel-off labels with me, so I wrote a quick note on one and stuck it to the Styrofoam: "This is fabulous. Thank you so much. Nancy."

The road angels at Vol State were crazy awesome, and I couldn't imagine wanting to do HOTS without road angels. This whole journey race thing was a weird, weird concept. The folks in the race were driven, generous, considerate, and kind. But they didn't yet seem to be MY people. A group up ahead was posting dancing Facebook videos—maybe *they* could be my people, but they were probably too fast for me. I'd seen no Vol State folks this morning. I was coming up on 34 miles and looking forward to taking a break at the Dresden Farmers Market at 40. It was early days. Maybe I'd find my people.

A little farther along SR 22, I saw a woman walking across the grass toward me. She stopped to chat. I think her name was Suzy—an attractive older woman with a grey bob cut, a lime green t-shirt, and a gentle smile. She asked me the usual questions about what I was doing, and I explained things. She was polite and well spoken. She could've been a retired doctor or doctor's wife. I asked if she lived in one of the houses nearby.

"I live in a shelter nearby," she told me. "I'm just out for a walk." Suzy was homeless and had found refuge in the shelter, which she quite liked and was grateful for. She seemed like so many other rural Tennessee folks: kind, Southern, friendly, but with a sad depth that she'd learned to live with and partially mask. I could imagine her as a teenager—beautiful, bouncy, bright. What had happened during her long life to land her in the shelter? I wondered if her teenage years seemed as near to her as mine did to me—just a blink of decades away.

She wished me luck, and we walked on in opposite directions. I was sorry there wasn't a café around. I would've liked to hear more of her story over a leisurely glass of sweet tea.

24-Hour Tracker, comments in italics (Friday morning, July 14, 2023)

Me: 38 miles--*"Never knew how much I loved Ritz peanut butter crackers."* Seven miles ahead of Oprah.

Not-So-Anonymous: *"Who Dey!"* Tony and "Who Dey" were still going strong. They were four miles ahead of me.

Anonymous: *"And the knee wins........probably tapping out."* It's always sad to see that someone is dropping. You wonder who it is. There but for the grace of God, go I.

Poor Tara Watson in her thrift-store shoes was in last place at 32 miles, just one mile ahead of Oprah.

Insanity is in the eye of the beholder

On the way into Dresden, a scruffy, middle-aged guy pulled up beside me on a quiet backroad. He was driving a pickup truck, hauling a home-made trailer with all sorts of mechanical junk in it. "What're y'all doing? Where're y'all walking?"

I gave him the whole spiel.

"What are y'all doing this for?"

"Hmmm," I said, "insanity?"

"Well, the government's insane," he shouted, a full 0-60 rant in a no time. "The government's totally insane, so it makes sense that y'all'd just be following along." I decided that he probably wasn't going to be a good buddy, and I certainly didn't want to make him any madder, not that I don't think the government is insane too. I was guessing, though, that we had different ideas about where the insanity lies. I smiled and shuffled a few steps like I was ready to go. He wished me luck and then peeled off.

On my way through Dresden, apropos of nothing, I suddenly had shooting pain in the top of my right foot, just under the laces. Veterans had warned me to loosen my laces a lot, but because I have such narrow heels, that meant I wouldn't be able to hold the heel tightly into my shoe, and I was worried about getting blisters from the up-and-down movement of my heel. Even the blisters seemed better than this tendon pain, though, so I loosened the laces a lot, which made the foot feel better. Now, my heel was flopping up and down. The pain reminded me that you never know what might cripple you and knock you out of this race. All is uncertainty—true of "real" life as well, but it somehow seemed more acute in Vol State life.

I lopped along to the Dresden Farmers Market, which veterans had been waxing lyrical about on Facebook and in the bus when we passed it before the race. Presumably, it's where the Farmers Market gets held, but for Vol State purposes, it's a big, covered pavilion with some coolers, chairs, and permanent bathrooms. Most of the goodies had been picked over, but I got some cold water and sat down for a while. A few other people from the Vol State bunch were there, some looking pretty rough, but nobody I knew except Carmel and Jarrod. The Dresden market seemed anticlimactic, and I was disappointed to find myself slipping into the mindset of one of those entitled, whiny Vol State people who doesn't appreciate whatever good things they come across in Middle of Nowhere, Tennessee. Like a lot of life, it was all about expectations. I needed an attitude adjustment. Gleason would help me with it. Everyone talked about how great the Gleason Fire Station was. I could get a shower and sleep there for a while.

I followed Evergreen Street out of Dresden, where it became Old State Highway 22. It was rural and boring, and it did nothing to help my mood. Tennessee has many beautiful sections, but this wasn't one of them. What in the world was I doing this stupid race for, anyway?

At one point I passed Carmel and Jarrod on the side of the road. They were a silhouette of a hill, lying on ground cloths with their feet facing each other and propped up on either side of some pipes sticking up out of the ground. A human tableau. It looked luxurious. I kept walking.

Thank you, anonymous road angels!

At 45 miles, still miserable, I saw a cooler next to a mailbox post up ahead. In my grumpy, ungrateful state, I thought, *A cooler with water is nice, but it would've been great if they had some chairs to sit in.* Then I saw a sign near the bottom of the cooler that said, "Enjoy cold water and/or our shade tree." *Shade tree!?*

I surveyed the front yard across the street from the cooler, and sure enough, there were two zero-gravity chairs under a big shade tree. *Oh, my sweet Jesus, thank you.* (Hang out in Tennessee long enough without enough sleep, and you start thinking like that.) I walked over and decided

I was going to take a proper break. I threw my pack and poles on one of the chairs, sat in the other, took off my shoes, and stretched the chair back until my feet were propped up. I figured I'd just close my eyes and pretend like I was somewhere else for a while. Heavenly.

I opened them about five minutes later and saw another Vol Stater heading my way—Michele Radcliff. I scrambled up to get my stuff out of the other chair so she could sit down. She flopped into the chair and said, "I think I'm tapped out."

I assumed she meant just tapped out and was going to take a break in the chair, but she meant tapped out for real.

"I'm just not meant for ultrarunning. I live in Hampshire, and I'm going to have my husband come get me."

"Are you sure you don't want to go to a hotel and just take a day to figure things out?"

"I'd have to walk 20 miles to get to a hotel. They're closing the Gleason Fire Station at noon today, and there's no place else until McKenzie." I didn't know it at the time, and math was starting to get difficult for me too, but we were only about 11 miles from McKenzie at 57.

I did recognize the problem with another number, though. "They're closing Gleason Fire Station at NOON? When so many people are still behind it?" I did a quick calculation. I wasn't sure I could make the three miles to Gleason by noon.

"That's what I heard."

It dawned on me that it was all well and good to take off a little time to find out what you want to do, but if you're in a spot where there's no place to take off time, then the decision gets a lot more dire.

"Here," she said, "take my notes on all the places along the way. It'll help you." She had four sheets of turn-by-turn directions, including highlighted spots with capital letters: "DO NOT MISS THIS TURN," as well as restaurants, gas stations, and a few road angel spots including their mile markers.

Just as I was thanking her, Jan pulled up in her silver van, the Meat Wagon. I wasn't sure if it was coincidence or if Michele had called her. A few other folks were in the van. "You got room for me?" Michele shouted.

"No," said Jan, all mean like.

"No, really," said Michele, suddenly out of the chair. "I'm going to call my husband and have him come get me. Legit."

Jan walked over and said, "What's the matter?"

"Well, I've got really bad blisters."

"Do you know how to take care of them?" said Jan.

"Jan knows how to take care of them!" I chimed in, hoping that Michele would follow her advice and stick it out.

"Did you put Desitin all around your foot?" asked Jan.

"Yeah, I did."

I left at that point, crossed the road in front of the van, and walked back to put a thank-you sticker on the cooler. Someone in the Meat Wagon said, "Wrong way."

"Thanks."

When I walked back by the van, Jan asked me how I was doing.

"Good! . . . Well," I shrugged, "good enough."

Jan nodded. I kept walking, and the Meat Wagon passed me, transporting all those runners back to the beautiful world of chairs and beds and air-conditioning. Heck, even the Meat Wagon itself was a beautiful world, except for the close quarters of so many smelly people. They'd find showers soon enough and smell civilized again.

I checked Laz's 24-hour update and zeroed in on this little gem:

the forecast starting by tonight;
explosive electrical storms with hail and damaging winds.,
god help the vol staters.

Great.

When I finally dragged myself to Gleason, I had to chuckle at my earlier idea that it could have an Eco Lodge or an Econo Lodge. It was a little village with a school and a few churches and stores. There was supposed to be a diner, but I didn't see it initially. I got to the Fire Station at noon. One big room with lots of firefighter coats and hats hanging up on two walls. The generous road angels had set up a couple of long tables with snacks and a cooler, and the concrete floor was strewn with lots of blow-up twin mattresses and pool floats. Two women were cleaning and packing up.

When I walked in, Terrie was chatting with Kim Montgomery, who runs the volunteer army of angels. "There's my guardian angel," Terrie said when she saw me.

I smiled. "Are you guys closing?" I asked the woman.

"We are. We've been here for over 24 hours straight, and we're exhausted. The fire chief said he'd let people stay on for a little while, though." Kim was still a part of the normal world. It was awfully sweet of her and her gang to crew this stop for so long. I'd seen photos on Facebook of all the racers they'd had sleeping here last night: a crowded, middle-aged slumber party.

I wasn't sure what "a little while" meant, but it didn't sound like the three-hour nap I was hoping for. My original plan had been to flip my days and nights so I could walk all night instead of in the heat of the day. "OK, thanks," I told Kim. "I'll just lie down for a few minutes." Dresden and Gleason made me ashamed of being so slow. We were only 48 miles into this event, but being a back-of-the-packer was definitely low status. Maybe I should've heeded Carl's warning. This is what happens to *dawdlers*.

I went to the back of the room, put my stuff down by an air mattress, and took off my shoes. I can't tell you how lovely it is to take off your shoes at Vol State. Sometimes it seems like too much trouble because you're only going to have to put them on again, but your feet immediately give little squeals of delight when you free them. I lay down for a few minutes on the velour mattress, but two women started deflating the air mattresses around me, so I took that as a sign. I got up and asked about the diner I'd heard about in town.

"Yeah, the Korner Kafe. It's just around the corner. They close at 1." It was 12:15. I figured that would be my best bet. A good meal, and then I'd trudge on eight miles to McKenzie and get a hotel room.

I gathered my stuff and walked back around the block to a little strip of shops. A guy out front with a long beard started talking to me. He told me he grew up in Antietam, on the battlefield. His father had been a nuclear submarine specialist, and his ex-wife worked for the Dept. of Energy and was in charge of a bunch of ex-Navy Seals, Green Berets, and Delta Force guys who were supposedly retired but officially unofficially broke into the nuclear sites as a way of testing security. I didn't totally understand that, but they apparently only did it when it was a code green—meaning no real threat. Hmmmm, this guy was fascinating, but I was hungry and tired, and standing wasn't helping anything. Besides telling me about his colorful life, he also asked the usual questions about Vol State, and I gave the usual answers.

Suddenly, I turned around, and there was Laz. An apparition. Like Mary suddenly appearing to little Yugoslavian kids. He was here to show me the way into the restaurant. "This is the guy you should be asking these questions to," I told Other Long Beard. "He's the impresario of this whole thing. The evil genius."

"I just did this trip and wanted to share it with my friends," Laz said.

"Yeah, he just wanted to spread the love around," I said.

So, I left Laz with Other Long Beard and went into the Korner Kafe—it was now 12:30, and the place was packed. The whiteboard announced a Country Fried Steak with Gravy special. That sounded great, but I would also be happy with a burger and fries. I went up to the counter separating the dining area from the kitchen where they were slammed—grilling, frying, and plating up—and the girl behind the counter told me, "We're not takin' any more food orders."

"No food of any kind?"

She shook her head.

I stayed calm. "Can I order a Diet Coke?" (I should've ordered a regular Coke for the calories, but I didn't like it.)

"Sure," she said. She took my money and poured me a Diet Coke. I sat down at the end of a table of Vol Staters. I can't even remember who was there; all I know is that each of them had a plate of food. I slurped my Diet Coke and almost started crying, but it would be too embarrassing in front of so many racers. Plus, Laz would soon finish talking to Other Long Beard and head into the diner. I couldn't let Laz see me cry.

Instead, I looked out the window and noticed for the first time that the sky was black. I checked the weather on my phone. "Storms continuing through 2 pm. Gusty winds and hail possible." Surely the fire chief wouldn't kick us out into that...would he?

I headed back to the fire station ten minutes later, and when I got there, Paul Heckert, a 69-year-old, longtime Vol State veteran, who was more comfortable playing the we-got-nothing-to-eat card than I, was telling Kim about getting cut out of lunch at the Korner Kafe. She looked stricken. "Well, there are peanut butter and jelly sandwiches and pizza over there."

I helped myself to a couple of cold slices of pizza because I hadn't had anything in 17 hours except a Payback bar, some peanut butter crackers, some Mombas, and Gatorade. As I mentioned earlier, I'm a foodie. I co-wrote a guidebook to Florida road food, and about half of my Stetson job is teaching a course called Writing about Food and Drink. I love pizza, but I'm a pizza snob, and a couple of days ago, I couldn't have imagined eating cold Little Ceasar's pizza leftover from the night before. This was no time to be discerning, though. Calories, not taste, were the order of the day, so I was grateful for what I could get.

People were still filing in, including Shenoa Creer, and I was sure no red-blooded American fire chief would kick Shenoa out into a storm, so I figured I was good there for a while. Shenoa is easily the most glamorous Vol State racer. She's 47, but you'd guess a lot younger. Tall and blonde, she looks like Adventure Barbie, and she brings fun changes of clothes that no one else would consider.

My weather app showed me the storm was moving in the same direction as the race. Once it blew through, I should be safe to walk the eight miles to McKenzie. I could get a motel room there or go on to Huntingdon, about ten more miles.

They'd deflated all the posh air mattresses, but there were still blow-up pool floats on the floor. And boy, they were great, too. I scored one of them next to Shenoa. This was her first year doing the race screwed, so she had to carry all her clothes. Her pack was noticeably bigger than anyone else's on the ferry. In the other Vol States, she'd always had a crew with plenty of outfits in the vehicle.

"How many times have you done this race?" I asked her.

"This is my seventh."

"Wow. Why do people do this more than once?" I asked. "I mean, I get the first time, but why keep doing it? So *many* people keep coming back."

She paused. "Well, it's a good question. For me, I come back to see my friends in the aid stations. I've made so many friends over the years, and we've really bonded. So, I guess that's probably the biggest reason, plus there's my streak. I've got a streak that I don't want to let go."

I nodded. Seven in a row of these babies was nothing to scoff at. I'd met a lot of nice people in the aid stations who'd been super helpful and kind, but I guess I hadn't bonded with any of them enough to want to come back to this misery.

"The other thing," said Shenoa, "is that getting to the Rock is such a great feeling. There's just nothing like it."

I nodded, but I was skeptical that I would feel that way. I had no doubt I'd be immensely relieved to get to the Rock, but great relief can come if you bang your toe with a hammer for a while and then stop. It'll feel really awesome not to be banging your toe with a hammer. I'd never much gotten excited about accomplishing long-distance endurance goals. Dipping my front bicycle wheel in the Pacific Ocean at Seaside, Oregon, was great because it meant that I didn't have to hike anymore, but it also meant that the adventure was over. It was bittersweet at best. Same with Santiago de Compostela in Spain. It was nice not to have to hike anymore for a while, but mostly, it was sad. I didn't even get a Compostela to mark the finish on that first Camino. I didn't *want* the adventure finished. I wouldn't buy one of Laz's famous Vol State jackets to mark the completion of this one either, but I'd take the sticker. I was skeptical that the Rock itself would mean that much to me, but the relief at stopping might be greater than for any endurance journey I'd ever done because this one was, so far, by far the most miserable with the fewest injections of fun.

I moved my pool float over to the station's big garage window so I could put my feet up on the ledge and watch the furious storm blow through, happy enough to be dry and horizontal on a long pillow of air.

Paul Heckert and Shenoa Creer catch some shuteye at the Gleason Fire Station.

Chapter 6

WHERE YOUR MUSCLES KNOW THAT THIS IS YOUR LIFE

"Genius is the infinite capacity for taking pains."
--Thomas Carlyle

Genius? (Eye roll)

If Thomas Carlyle had said "taking pain," Vol State racers would pretty much all be geniuses. But I'm living proof that that's not true, and I'm in good company. I think he had something else in mind, but we also take a lot of pains in preparing for and executing this mad journey race. Although in my case, probably not enough pains. It's best not to think about the pain or pains too much. Or the journey at large beyond the next town.

I was well into Day 2 as I walked out of Gleason and followed the corn fields and quiet backroads to McKenzie. On the way, I passed an angel tent on the left that had snacks, some chairs, and cold water, and it also had my new favorite treat: cold, wet towels! The thoughtful angels in the house behind had put out a cooler with ice in it and a raft of wash rags. You could pull one out, wash off a bit with the blessed cold rag, then throw it in a bag beside the cooler.

Sooooo great!

A road angel station with amazing cold, wet towels.

Back following the white line, I remembered something Laz had said, "Regardless of conditions, most of the drops are going to occur in the first two days. The whole race is mental." I hadn't yet thought about quitting. I couldn't imagine it without an injury, and it looked like I might make it the two days. But then, when I thought more about it, yes, I was on the second day of walking, but I was still some hours away from the 36-hour mark, much less the 48-hour mark. I needed to readjust myself to a full 24-hour clock instead of just thinking about a day from waking up to falling asleep. That was my old life. This was my Vol State life. Two days was still a long way away. I decided to focus on a decent hot meal in McKenzie.

I finally got into McKenzie about 5:00 pm on Saturday. There were two motels close to the route. The one that I wanted was full. The one that got all kinds of scary reviews was not. However, I had heard something about a farmers market aid station. Maybe that would work.

As I walked the route through town, I looked into some windows along the main drag and saw cots and Vol State racers before I saw the Farmers Market sign. They had turned the farmers market across from the McKenzie Fire Station into an aid station for us. Problem solved!

Inside, the place was like an emergency morgue with runners already comatose on some of the ten cots. A big bathroom had no shower but allowed us a chance to clean up. The angels had left food and drinks, and it was super quiet. Vol Staters' premium on sleep means they're especially considerate. I was simultaneously thankful for that and bored by the lot of them. This was part of the problem with this race. If people weren't walking or eating, they wanted to be sleeping, not having fun. A few runners talked quietly outside the market, but nobody seemed inclined to go farther into McKenzie for anything.

I got cleaned up as much as possible, changed clothes, and walked 600 yards up to Maria's Mexican Restaurant. I expected to see Vol State racers in the lively restaurant, but I was the only one. I ate too many chips with salsa, washed down with a delightful Negro Modelo, and caught up on the Vol State Facebook page while I waited for my chicken quesadilla. Life was wonderful! Why was I such a whiner?

36-Hour Tracker, comments in italics (Friday evening, July 14, 2023)

Me: 56 miles--*"Throwing up in a Walmart parking lot. It doesn't get more American than that."* Nine miles ahead of Oprah.

Anonymous: *"Ugh -- all these cars are going to drive by and say, 'What is that lady doing with her hand down her pants?!' I've worked so hard all my life to not be that lady."* I laughed at this comment, but I'm not exactly sure what she was doing with her hands down her pants—perhaps using a "She-Wee," the contraption that allows women to pee in the woods, or beside a road as the case may be. I didn't have one of those.

Anonymous: *"I was in too much pain to type this out this morning. Last night I was absolutely miserable trying to sleep on a picnic table. A homeless woman also sleeping in the park said 'I don't know your story but if I can help, let me know.'"*

After dinner, I only had to walk a couple hundred yards further to get to the Dairy Queen around the corner, where I spoiled myself with a

Heath Bar Blizzard with malt. *This must be heaven.*

No, it's Tennessee.

On the way back to the Farmers Market, I stopped by a convenience store and got a Payday Bar, a couple of bananas, and a Gatorade for the night walk. By the time I got to the market, my cot was in between Carmel's and Robert's. Carmel looked to be in decent shape, but Robert was nursing a nasty blister on his big toe.

The Farmers Market was still quiet. When I first lay down, all kinds of weird stuff was hurting—my lower back and shoulders, both calves, my right hip, and toes that didn't even have blisters on them. I took an Extra Strength Tylenol, which tamped down a bit of the pain. I tried to sleep on my cot, but besides the pain, I was freezing. The fans were on, and I think the place was air-conditioned. As much as I appreciated air conditioning on this trip, something about all this walking had whacked out my body's thermostat, so I was super cold. I put on my windbreaker with the hood up and curled into a modified fetal position inside a silk sleeping liner. It didn't occur to me to use my silver emergency Mylar blanket. That would've helped.

I felt like I was waking up every 15 minutes and trying to find a more comfortable position, but eventually, it was 11:30 pm—time to get back on the road.

I packed up and was on the Saturday night streets of McKenzie before midnight. I had another 10 miles to go to get to Huntingdon, where I was hoping to snag breakfast. Walking out of McKenzie, I saw a young woman in a too-tight short dress walking with purpose along Highland Drive, the Dairy Queen street. *What was her story?*

Farther along Old McKenzie Road, I saw a person up ahead, walking in the same direction I was. He had something hanging off him, but I couldn't tell if he was a drunk on his way home from the bar or a Vol State walker. As I got closer, I saw the red light on the back of his headlamp and decided he must be one of us. Local drunks don't pay that much attention to lighting themselves up for traffic.

It turned out it was Paul Heckert, my comrade-in-hunger from the Gleason Fire Station. I walked with Paul for a while. He was a pretty slow walker by this point but super engaging. He'd finished Vol State a bunch of times, and he'd not finished it a bunch of times. As we were chatting, he mentioned crewing for Terrie one year when he got out of the race early, and I suddenly realized I'd read about him in Terrie's book: "You're the Warden!"

He chuckled. "Most of what she says about me isn't true." He had coached her to the Rock in 2021 with lots of tough love. He's had plenty of coaching experience, being a retired physics and astronomy professor at Western Carolina University in Cullowee, NC, and having done lots of ultra races all over.

When I told him I'd walked to Maria's Mexican Restaurant for dinner, he chided "The first rule is that you never walk extra miles." That did seem to be the ethos of a Vol State runner. When I'd spent four months hiking on the Appalachian Trail, I'd sometimes walk a mile and a half off the trail just to get a cold Diet Coke. I'd certainly walk 600 yards for Maria's and another couple hundred more for a Dairy Queen Blizzard anytime at Vol State. At least I thought so at that point.

When we turned right onto State Rd 22, we were back with a big shoulder and a four-lane split highway. Somebody in a pick-up truck yelled, "WHERE ARE YOU?" out the window from across the highway but kept driving. Saturday night in Tennessee. *What did that even mean? Should I worry about where I was? Was he letting someone—us?—know he was looking for them? Was it just an existential yawp?* It *was* a bit ominous, but I was too tired to care. I'm generally blessed with not being scared in a strange place unless there's a real reason to be afraid, but Vol State helps with all that by adding the Oprah imperative and the overriding safety focus of not getting run over. That diffuses any free-floating fears.

Generally, Vol Staters and the road angels sidestep politics, but when I said I was from Florida, Paul asked me what I thought of Ron DeSantis. (In Europe, when I say I'm from the States, the first question is often, "And what do you think of Donald Trump?") People want to know where to place you before they start complaining.

Paul and I got to play the latest liberal parlor game: who would be more devastating for the country, DeSantis or Trump? I could make a case for either, but I was inclined toward DeSantis. He was just as brutal but smarter, more polished, and more of an ideologue. I could at least understand why right-wing people supported him. Fortunately, he doesn't have Trump's "charm."

It was nice to get to walk and chat with somebody, but I knew I was losing time, so when Paul said he was going to take a break on a guard rail, I decided to keep going.

I called Chris to help pass the time and pined for a breakfast in Huntingdon. I liked walking at night, but it was damn hot already, and it was supposed to get up to 95 today. I hoped to find a hotel room by midday.

At some point, I came across a simple folding chair and cooler. Ah-hhhhh, nothing like sitting by a state road in Tennessee in the middle of the night and drinking a cold bottle of water. The guest book said this angel stop was courtesy of the All-Star Café in Huntingdon. I couldn't wait to get there. I thanked them profusely.

Sleepover in the courtroom

It's a weird feeling, walking into a strange town at 4:15 am and making a beeline for the police station, but I had heard that the Huntingdon Police Department doubled as an aid station for Vol State. I walked in and went up to the window in the lobby, where a kind but official-sounding policewoman told me I could use the bathroom in the lobby and could rest in the courtroom, where there was some food and drink.

Tara, whose sandals had cut up her feet, was resting against the lobby wall with the thrift-store shoes beside her. At the 24-hour check-in, she'd been in last place with 32 miles, and Huntingdon was at 67 miles. She'd walked 35 miles in a little over 20 hours.

"Holy Gamoly!" I said to her. "You're flying!" (OK, I know, "flying" seems a bit much for 1.75 miles per hour, but Oprah does 1.3 miles per hour, so it's all relative. And this counts all the breaks along the way.)

"I just haven't been sleeping," she said, and I believed her. She'd turned into a walking machine. "I'm out here because it's cooler than in there." She pointed toward the courtroom.

It's an even weirder feeling, walking into a courtroom in the middle of the night to have a rest. To the right, a raised area for the judge and witnesses, plus whiteboards and a video monitor. In front of me, a long table where the lawyers and defendants sit, now loaded with breakfast bars and hot dogs and Ice-breaker mints. (Someone thoughtfully and rightfully concerned about our bad breath.) To the left, lots of chairs for folks to watch the court proceedings, now used as a place to store backpacks as Vol State racers sprawled out on the faux-wood floor. I saw Carmel and Jarrod and Ray Krolewicz, a 68-year-old legendary ultrarunner, although, for this race, he was walking with his girlfriend Casey Quaintance-Kramer (46) and being crewed.

I put my stuff down. I would only be there long enough for the All-Star Café to open. Chris had told me that it opened at 5 am, but I went back out and asked the dispatch woman to be sure.

"I think it opens at 6," she said," but ask that policeman over there. He'll know."

So, I walked over to a uniformed officer near the courtroom, who was talking to another man in plain clothes.

"Excuse me, sir. Could you tell me when the All-Star Café opens?"

"Sure. It opens at 6."

"Thanks very much."

I know Chris had found 5 am on the Internet, but I had confidence that a small-town, night-duty police officer would be way more in-the-know than Google. I figured I'd just rest for a while in the courtroom. I pulled out my ground cloth that folded up to the size of a super-thick credit card and laid it out near a fan. I set my alarm for 5:50 am, laid down on my back with my heels and calves up on a chair, and daydreamed of a big breakfast.

When I got to the All Star Café at 6:00 on the dot, I was hopping mad to see a bunch of people already in there and a sign on the door that said they open at 5. Had the police community run so far amok that you could no longer trust a small-town cop on night duty to know when the local breakfast place opened? I despaired for the country!

I walked in and sat down at a table catty corner from another Vol State runner, and I struck up a conversation with Joseph Dease (47), who had actually just quit the race as he approached Huntingdon. He was waiting for the Meat Wagon to swing by and pick him up. Joseph was a veteran of Vol State and HOTS and was meant to have joined two other veterans to do a special addition to Vol State. They were all going to fly into Nashville and start walking from the airport 186 miles to the start of the race in Hickman, KY, and then go on to do Vol State proper for a total of 500 miles. Unfortunately, one of the folks had to pull out for family reasons, and the other didn't get into the race off the waitlist, so Joseph had gone ahead with the Nashville-Hickman part of the trip solo and then developed a leg injury early in Vol State.

Joseph seemed like fun, so when he asked me how I was doing, I leveled with him: "The people on Vol State have been super kind and friendly enough to me, but they haven't been fun. They're intense, but they aren't having fun. I knew I was going to have to suffer a lot, but I thought I would have a good time along the way as well, but I'm not. I went to a Mexican restaurant by myself last night and had a beer. That's as fun as it's been."

"Your problem," said Joseph, "is that the fun people are more in the center of the pack. The front-of-the-pack folks act like they're fun, but they're not. They're just posing to mess with the other front runners. And the back-of-the-pack people aren't fun because they're really worried about finishing, and a lot of them are hurt. The middle of the pack is where you find people who are fit enough not to have to worry about finishing, but they're not fast enough to compete with the front of the pack. So, they're the folks who will actually go out for pizza and beer.

They get to have a good time. I start out fast, but once I figure out I can't hang with the elite runners, I hang back and have fun.

"Listen, there are three women ahead of you who are fun. Two of them are helicopter pilots. I just got a text from one of them, and they're at an aid station that's about nine miles from here. They're staying there for a while. You could probably catch them if you wanted."

That suggestion gave me renewed energy and purpose. I'd catch up with the middle of the pack and find some fun people. When I left the All-Star Café, it was bucketing down with rain, but I didn't care. I wasn't gonna be a dawdler anymore. I was going to catch the middle of the pack. I pulled out my emergency poncho from Walmart and my dual-purpose umbrella and hit the wet road.

48 -Hour Tracker, comments in italics (Saturday morning, July 15, 2023)

Me: 69 miles—*"How is it that a policeman who works the midnight shift in a small town could not know that the local breakfast joint opens at 5? He was certain it was 6. Nice guy otherwise."* Six miles ahead of Oprah. She's gaining on me.

Anonymous: *"Hellacious rain hit just after leaving Parkers Crossroad at 05 30 and followed me south for a good 90 minutes. Shoes and socks are fully hydrated. Now I know what it's like to be one of those waterlogged weather channel numbskulls reporting live from extreme weather events. "*

Anonymous: *"It's raining blisters."* I sure hope not.

The rain was pounding, but at least it was coming straight down, and my umbrella could keep a lot of it off my shoes. I didn't really mind walking in normal rain. It meant I could sing at the top of my lungs to my earbuds with my favorite playlist. I had a special Vol State playlist that had a bunch of songs I was determined to memorize—a number of Cornish sea shanties, plus "Always Look on the Bright Side of Life," "I Will Survive," and, of course, "Raindrops Keep Falling On My Head." Nobody could hear me because the rain was so loud.

Jan and other experts say that singing can lift the spirits when times are tough, which explains all the old working songs. Vol State should have it's own version of sea shanties.

My first rain walk.

In Laz's 48-hour update, he writes,

for the tail end of the pack
the battle has been joined;
a dozen runners see their existence on the road under threat.
there is no guarantee any of them will make it.
but it is certain that some will fail.

I was now the 13th "runner" from the bottom. At least there was that.

Outside of Huntingdon, I turned back onto SR-22 toward Clarksburg—a long straight shot with lots of rolling hills. I could see two Vol State people way ahead of me. Having just scanned the 48-hour tracker, I saw that Bill and Regina had also checked in at 69 miles, even though they'd checked in at 68 miles 12 hours before. That must be them. I walked faster.

Eventually, they stopped off at a road-angel stop in front of a house, with a few chairs and a cooler under a tree. I caught up with them there. Bill seemed to be having some trouble, but Regina looked as fresh and energetic as ever. They had spent the night at The Heritage Inn outside Huntingdon. "We just decided to sleep in," giggled Regina. "We stayed almost 12 hours." That sounded like heaven to me. The two had pushed so hard the first 36 hours that they were 12 hours ahead of me and many miles in front of Oprah, so they could afford it.

"Are you having fun?" she asked me.

"*Is* there really fun in this race? When do you guys have fun?"

"I think the fun is in the challenge," said Bill.

"I think the fun is in overcoming problems," said Regina, "like the one I had with my shoulder."

"Hmmmm," I said. "The Dairy Queen. That's what I think of as fun." (There was one up ahead at Parkers Crossroad, another nine miles.) Maybe this is the difference between me and other Vol Staters. I like the challenge; I like the problem-solving—but fun is definitely something different.

County pride and driver hospitality

Nine more miles on SR-22 seemed like forever. I stopped at a Clarksburg convenience store and ran into Michelle Chauvin and Tara again. Tara was buying snacks and cigarettes to support her habit—no doubt a Laz protégé! She had torn up the course after shredding her feet at the beginning and almost quitting. "You're just killin' it, Girl," I told her. She hadn't slept in 24 hours.

"I gotta get some rest and fix my feet," she told me.

"You definitely deserve some rest."

Michelle was generally well, but her bra strap was digging into her back, so she asked if I'd put some goo and gauze on it for her. We went outside and sat on a bench. I took a picture of the abrasions on her back so she could diagnose herself. An L-shaped wound looked particularly nasty. "You're the nurse practitioner," I said. "Just tell me what to do." She gave me some kind of ointment to put on and a gauze that would go over the chafed areas and under her bra strap. I hoped it would help.

I set off again with renewed kick, trying to reach the middle of the pack. That felt good-ish. I was hoping to put in a lot of miles, then rest at a Days Inn in Lexington, and get up in the middle of the night and walk through what was apparently a bad section between Parsons and Linden with not much shoulder and lots of crazy drivers with boat trailers going to and from the Tennessee River.

Mary Nienaber, a runner well ahead of me and clearly shaken, had just written on Facebook,

> *While I have some bars, I don't think Parsons wants us there. Even with no oncoming traffic and no shoulder they do not move. Several times I was by a guard rail, turned sideways, and prayed. Trucks with horse trailers and boat trailers especially!*

This post generated a raft of comments from kind road angels in the area, folks like Pam Moore Pratt:

> *I can assure you Parsons welcomes the runners. Our roads are so heavily traveled with people from other counties passing thru headed to the river etc. I'm sure there are rude people on the road. I'm sorry and I hope it doesn't give you a bad vibe about our small town.*

Even my Aunt Fran got into the discussion from Ft. Lauderdale:

> *Just reached out to the mayor of a town further west than your race route. And in hopes he might know officials near the river who could encourage some helpful hospitality!! Stay safe. Keep on keeping on!!"*

That made me chuckle. My aunt is great! And I loved the idea of a mayor who would call another mayor who would call....well, who? I guess the police are in charge of driver hospitality . . . What a lovely way to think of traffic cops!

Another resident seemed to think that Laz should be working on this:

> *You would think the promoters of this event would contact our County Mayor & our Sheriff prior to the event date to discuss what safety measures are needed from our authorities.*

When I first heard about this race, I too assumed that Laz would alert law enforcement all along the way to let them know about the race, but now that I'd met Laz, I was pretty sure that wasn't how it worked.

I'm guessing that for him, it would take some of the fun and adventure out of it if everybody knew what was going on. But with Vol State using the same route every year, lots of law enforcement knew what was happening anyway. I could only imagine what it was like for the HOTS runners going through new territory every year.

Well, I would have to cross the Parsons road when I got to it. In the meantime, I was closing in on the Dairy Queen, wondering if State Road 22 would ever end. According to my GPX, we wouldn't turn off it until Lexington, another 12 miles or so. At least SR-22 had a generous shoulder.

Far ahead of me, I noticed a person walking as if some invisible force were weighing down his right arm. I was catching up with him quickly and could see that his whole spine leaned to the right. *What was the matter with him?* As I got closer, I recognized him from behind—*It's Tony! But, oh, no—it's Tony. He looks terrible.*

Tony on the road to Parkers Crossroads.

"Tony!" I yelled. "What's going on, Man?"

He had messed up his back again. The camber of the road had gotten to him. This is what made him quit last year. "It's better than it was last night," he said. "I could hardly walk then."

"What are you going to do?"

"I'm going to check into the motel up here at Parkers Crossroad and sleep for a little bit, then get back up and go again. I was a little better after sleeping last night, but then it just got a lot worse before I saw you."

I had no idea what to tell him. "Look, I'm walking ahead and staying at the Days Inn in Lexington. I'll also put your name on the room in case you need a place to rest there. What about pain pills?"

He had ibuprofen.

I walked slowly with him the rest of the way to Parkers Crossroad, where I-40 crosses SR-22. I couldn't see how he could keep this up unless he got some help. We took a selfie in front of Subway that made us both look much happier than we were. Tony went in to get a sandwich to take to the motel, and I went to the Dairy Queen for my Heath Bar-with-a-shot-of malt Blizzard. I wished him the best.

I sat at a back table in the DQ, enjoying my Blizzard but worried about Tony. I texted Chris and Aunt Fran and told them about his problem. Chris suggested finding a chiropractor along the way, and Fran suggested crutches. I texted Tony with both ideas. Then I headed back out to walk as the day's heat intensified.

I passed by Michelle Chauvin on the I-40 bridge. She was moving pretty slowly, thanks to her back, and the whole thing was starting to seem sad and dire for too many people I liked.

Chapter 7

THE FASCINATION OF WHAT'S DIFFICULT

*"The fascination of what's difficult
Has dried the sap out of my veins and rent
Spontaneous joy and natural content
Out of my heart."*
—W. B. Yeats

Road angels extraordinaire

The heat was getting worse, and my attitude seemed directly connected to it. But then I saw a big road-angel stop up ahead on the left, and, as always, that brightened my world a bit. A guy with a long strawberry blond/gray beard welcomed me. He had a Tennessee Lady Volunteers National Championship shirt on and sunglasses both on his eyes and on his cap. His name was David Scott, and he was there with his brother Russell, who had a long auburn beard, a camouflage hat, and a t-shirt with a dog silhouette and the slogan "Straight Up—Southern" on it.

"What can I get for you?" asked David. "We've got cold drinks and bratwurst and plenty of snacks and first aid stuff. What do you need?"

"I'd love a Gatorade," I said.

"Just in that back cooler under the tent. How about a bratwurst?"

"Uh, sure."

"What you want on it?"

"Just mustard, please." Russell brought it to me.

A bunch of Vol State racers I'd seen but didn't know had already taken over the zero gravity chairs under the tent. I sat on one of the Tennessee-sized coolers outside the tent and enjoyed my cold Gatorade and warm bratwurst. "Thank you so much. This is just great! Why do you do all this?"

"Why not?" said David. "There's enough hate in this world. It's good to show a little love. If you listen to the news, you think there's hate everywhere, but there's a lot of good people in the world. We can't meet the kind of people we meet on this event. Ed Masouka worked for NASA. We don't have people around here who worked for NASA. Terrie—I just love meeting her."

He said he takes his vacation this week every year so he can help out the runners; he spends about $1000 on the set-up. They had two tents, although one got busted in the storm that morning, and two giant coolers—one with soft drinks, one with water and Gatorade. They had a cabinet with five different flavors of electrolyte power and all sorts of snacks, including my favorite: single-serving SPAM. Who knew something like that existed? It was perfect for Vol State racers who could stomach such things—not me!—but I was guessing that lots of hunters and campers also found it useful for on-the-go protein and salt.

I was unlacing my shoes and rubbing the tendons on the top of my foot. One of the racers, Chrissy Engh, said to me, "You know you can just not use the top couple of eyelets and tie your laces down further on your foot?"

I did not know that, but I would sure give it a try. "Thank you!" Why hadn't I thought of that? It would allow me to tie the shoes tighter while giving that tendon a break. Brilliant!

Most of the racers left, but I stayed chatting with the brothers for a while. David used to own the house just behind his aid station, but now he lived a little ways off but still uses the property. "I get about 3 hours sleep a night," he told me, "because I try to treat everybody the same way, from the first people coming through to the last people coming through. I'm always checking the tracker to see where people are and make sure I'm all set up for the last person coming through, even if they're behind Oprah." She even haunted the road angels.

These guys just made you feel good about humanity. I asked David what the best thing about living in this area was.

"You wanna know the truth?" he said. "This."

A little later, David would post on the Vol State Facebook site, "We are blessed to live on this course. We are vested [in] all runners and only want to share the love. Too much hate in this world!!! If we were running this race, we would want to be treated this way. Luke 6:31 DS." Luke 6:31

says, "Do to others as you would have them do to you." The Golden Rule. It's a tall order—impossible even—but when it comes to Vol State runners, I'd say that David and Russell exceed the imperative.

A delicious bratwurst, courtesy of road-angel brothers, David and Russell Scott.

David's earlier comment, "If you listen to the news, you think there's hate everywhere" reminded me of political and social psychologist Dannagal G. Young's Ted Talk "The psychological traits that shape your political beliefs." Young argues that society works best when it's filled with both people who worry about threats and prioritize order and safety as well as people who focus on innovation and exploration and are less threatened by the world around them. In other words, the U.S. needs the melding of both conservatives and liberals to make it thrive.

But these days, we're less interested in melding because our attention-driven society means that politicians and the media have vested interests in exploiting our differences, "to get us angry, to get our attention, to get clicks and turn us against one another," says Young. Controversy rules media—no conflict equals no interest, so they've got to keep stirring up the melting pot. We can argue about which news sources are more faithful to the truth, but even though I think the major left-leaning news sources are more factually correct, there's no doubt many of their stories are meant to whip me into a frenzy against "the others."

Politicians do a version of the same thing. And who is America's greatest divisive genius? Donald Trump. The U.S. has become increasingly more polarized since 1979, so we can't blame all this on Trump. But is he the coup de grâce? The one who finishes us off with his divisive superpowers?

Young goes on to explain that the most important part of our separate approaches to the world is that "these propensities are not absolute—they're not fixed." Some liberals are quite anxious about outside threats and some conservatives see the world as more gray, less black and white. We're not really one or the other. We have tendencies, preferences. The problem is that politicians and the media benefit when our differences are "reinforced" and even "weaponized."

Young ends her talk with two questions: "What if the real threat posed to society and democracy is not actually posed by the other side? What if the real danger is posed by political and media elites who try to get us to *think* that we'd be better off without the other side and who use these divisions for their own personal, financial, political benefit?"

And what if we could take David Scott's advice and quit watching the news long enough to realize how many good people there are on both sides of the political aisle? What if we could concoct experiences all across the country that would throw liberals and conservatives together in ways that would make us pay attention to our heightened humanity instead of our tribal divisions? Maybe this is Laz's real genius at Vol State.

On the power of broom handles

I'd have been happy staying at the Scott brothers' aid station for another ten hours or so, but I got back out moving again, and it wasn't too far before I saw a group of Vol State folks crowded around a van. In my semi-delirious state, I decided that the person in the van probably had popsicles because racers had been posting on FB that someone had been giving them out. Nobody had yet offered me a popsicle, but that sounded about as good as anything right then.

The Vol State group moved on, and as I got closer, I realized it was Jan in the Meat Wagon. Darn. I went up to the driver's side window and said, "Man, I thought you were here to give me a popsicle!"

"No, but I'll eat a popsicle in front of you," she mocked. "Or I might even eat an ice cream in front of you. Hmmm, now I kind of want an ice cream. I'm gonna have to go to the Dairy Queen."

"Well, I just had a Blizzard there, and it was damn fine." So we talked. She wanted to know how I was doing.

"Better today than yesterday, better yesterday than the first day."

"You'll just keep getting better and better."

"I somehow don't think so, but for now, it's OK. Have you had a bunch of business today?"

"Four people have quit today, but we've only had 11, and 20% is the usual number. I'd like it if we had 100% finish one year, but that would make Laz hopping mad." I knew about Laz's sadistic qualities, but I hadn't realized that Jan was so sweet. I weighed telling her about Tony. I didn't want to seem like a tattletale, but she really did seem to want to help people, and he certainly needed it.

"Well, Tony Webb is having a really hard time. He's walking like this." I did my best imitation of him walking bent over sideways.

"Does he have a stick? Poles?" she asked.

I shook my head.

"He needs a pole. Tell him to get one just from the Dollar General or somewhere. Tell him to get a broom and just use the handle as a stick. The closest Walmart is in Hohenwald."

"I thought there was one in Lexington," I said.

"There is, but it's not on the route."

I nodded. "I'll tell him."

"I'll check on him when I go up there," she said.

"Well actually he's at a motel back there at Parkers Crossroad, and I'm putting him on my motel room in Lexington so he's got a place to crash if he needs it up there."

She nodded.

"Why do people keep doing this race over and over?" I asked her.

"I wish I had a nickel for every time someone has said they were one-and-done and then came back to do Vol State. I'd have a big old jar of nickels!"

"Well, you're gonna lose your nickel on me," I said. "I don't have any idea why people would want to come back. I mean I'm having a fun time—No, I'm *not* having a fun time!—but I don't know why people would want to do it again. I keep asking folks."

"Well, I was one and done," she said, "and I never wanted to do it again."

"I don't know what Laz does to these people, whether he puts something in the water or sprinkles pixie dust on them at the Rock. But something weird happens to them."

"It does," she said. "You wait and see."

So, I'll wait and see, but I'm almost certain I ain't gonna want to do this again.

"You start thinking about it after the fact," Jan said, "and then you wanna do it. I had everybody tell me at HOTS, 'I'll never want to do HOTS again, never do HOTS, and then there they are with their finger on the button, waiting for August 1st to apply for another one."

Who knows? Maybe something will happen, but for now, I thought all these people were crazy. I was definitely not having enough fun to do it again. It has to be fun. Just the challenge, just an adventure? I could do that on my own. We would see. It was early, only day 3. I was happy to feel a little better today. And I was hoping that I could get myself and my clothes clean and catch a good snooze in Lexington. Just stopping for a while sounded heavenly.

The next six miles into Lexington seemed to get hotter and hotter, and I was totally wrecked by the time I arrived. I'd done 35 miles since before midnight, when I'd gotten some fitful sleep at the McKenzie Farmers Market.

Before I went to the Days Inn, I stopped by a nearby Dollar General and bought some clothes-washing tabs, a Heath bar, and a Starbucks vanilla latte, which, along with Gatorade, was becoming one of my go-to drinks. I rarely drank either in normal life. Something about the protein in the latte's milk, the caffeine, the sugar, and the cold temperature seemed to tick many of my body's boxes. On a trip like this, eating and drinking become more about what the body wants and less about what my foodie-pleasure mind wants—although the foodie-pleasure mind injects its limits, like single-serve SPAM.

60-Hour Tracker, comments in italics (Saturday evening, July 15, 2023)

Me: 91 miles----*"David and Russell Scott are the sweetest humans I've met in donkey's years. Lazarus Lake could learn a thing or two about how to pamper his runners from these guys!"* Twelve miles ahead of Oprah. I was opening a gap.

Anonymous: *"I'm blown away by the generosity and enthusiasm of the road angels. Vol State is their Thanksgiving, Christmas, Super-Bowl, and every other big celebration all rolled into one."*

Anonymous: *"It was yesterday, but then it was a while later, but that was still today, I think? I'm not really sure what day it was."*

I was toast by the time I got checked into the Days Inn in Lexington and made sure that Tony was on the reservation and could pick up a key if he wanted to. I hobbled up the stairs to the second-floor motel room and could barely shuffle around the room. My shoulders were killing me; my feet were crying in pain; my calves were hard as rocks; and below my pronounced Vol State tan (ankles to just above knees), the heat rash continued to rosy my feet.

I washed my clothes in the sink with proper liquid detergent, which I was hoping would work better than a tiny bar of motel facial soap. I rang the clothes out, then rolled them up in towels and gingerly stomped on the towels (thanks to a tip I had gotten from Michelle Chauvin). Then I hung them up.

Next was a long bath. I wondered if I should've taken a short shower so I had longer to sleep, but lying in that water felt so luxurious and made my muscles happy. I found myself taking cat naps there anyway. Finally, I got into bed and checked the FB page and tracker sheet—Tony was three miles before Lexington! I texted him to see how he was doing.

Sweet Jan had waited for him outside his motel and instructed him on what he needed to do. He found two broomsticks at the Dollar General to use as hiking poles, and that seemed to be working for him. He said he was planning to walk through Lexington, which was great. His back must be much better! He'd get some real hiking poles when he passed the next Walmart, but the broom handles had him back in business, and hopefully he'd finish this damn thing. It meant so much to him.

I don't know if it's physiologically possible, but it felt like I went immediately into deep sleep for four solid hours. I had no idea where I was when the alarm went off, but a sense of urgency despite the disorientation got me right out of bed. My predicament came back to me as I walked around the room, gathering my stuff. The Land of Nod is such a wonderful place to vacation, and then you wake up and remember Oprah is chasing you, and you have to leave a perfectly good, expensive motel room and go walking in the middle of the night in a strange city. The Days Inn cost $110. Fortunately, my generous mother and cousin Karen Gentry had both donated to the cause and earmarked hotel rooms. I didn't ask either of them, and I told them I was fine on my own, but they insisted. Nobody wants to think about their daughter or cousin sleeping rough in rural Tennessee, or anywhere for that matter.

I didn't relish getting back on the road, but I was totally amazed at how much the body can recover with four hours sleep. I didn't even eat properly last night. In Maslow's hierarchy, the bottom of the pyramid is physiological needs—basic human survival stuff like air, food, drink, shelter, clothing, warmth, sex, sleep. Except for sex, which I doubted any of the Vol State racers had the energy to be too concerned about, this lower band of needs was where we lived most of the race. But even within that lowest band, the body seemed to have its own hierarchy that shifted priorities as needed. Last night, the sleep need was definitely more fundamental than the food need. Pizza places were close to my motel, but I didn't care. I just wanted to be in a motel room. I also wanted to be clean—I don't remember Maslow talking about that. Eating could wait. I had picked up some potato chips from the last road-angel site, and that was enough of a dinner: salt and carbs. Before I left the room, I had the Starbucks drink and Heath bar that I had stuck in the fridge and peanut butter crackers from that last road-angel stop—more salt and carbs and protein—that seemed to be enough.

It still took me quite a while to get out of there. My clothes were mostly dry by the time I got up, so no time wasted blow drying my sun hoodie. (Thank you, Michelle!) I had to re-tape my feet. This time, I taped up my heels too. The camber was starting to take its toll on the right inside heel and the left little toe especially. The left-big-toe blister had finally stayed drained during what passes for overnight, so I just put another tape on it. I also put moleskin where I'm having trouble with the tendons at the top of my feet—where they meet the ankle, even though taking out the upper two eyelets and tying the laces farther down my foot had majorly helped. (Thank you, Chrissy!) By the time I taped up my feet and repacked, it was probably close to 1:45 am before I got out on the road. *Yep, I would have to get quicker at this.*

Lexington was a dark ghost town. So peaceful and quiet, and most folks never see it like that, especially not on foot. At the town's main intersection, the First United Methodist Church had an aid station with professionally printed signs: **"Welcome to Lexington!" "Lexington says: Good Luck Vol State Runners!!" "All the way to Castle Rock."** The route finally turned off SR-22, which we'd mostly followed since before Union City. We'd been traveling southeast since the ferry landing, but now we'd be moving due east on Hwy 412 for about 85 miles.

On the way out of Lexington, I passed the Creekside Farms Flea Market and Consignment, which had three metal cut-outs of Sasquatch by the road. The smallest was about as tall as me, the biggest about twice my size. Just the sort of images you want in your mind as you're walking in a world that's gone pitch black except for the little circle of light your chest lamp carves out of the darkness. Anything could be going on around me, and I might hear it, but I couldn't see it unless I turned to face it and it was within reach of the light.

Sasquatch triple vision

I assumed that Laz had arranged for the moon to be at its least helpful during the Vol State. The new moon was scheduled for July 17 and 18, 2023, right smack in the middle of the race for the slow folks battling

Oprah—just the kind of niggling detail Laz might consider.

The next stop was Pin Oak Elementary. A home-drawn poster taped to a DO NOT ENTER sign pole alerted me to the school: **"Welcome Runners! MI 98.75 *Cold Drinks Available*."** I felt like I'd been on the road forever, and I still wasn't even a third of the way to the Rock. The poster on the entrance to the school said,

"Welcome Y'all.
***Door is Open**
***Restrooms Open**
***Take A Break**
***Cold Drinks**
God Bless
+

Please Be Careful
Pin Oak Staff"

What a lovely bunch of folks in this state!

When I walked into the barely lit school, a woman was sitting with her back to me. She had long braids, and I was sure I knew who it was. "Hey, Tara," I said.

The woman turned around. Not Tara. "No, that's Terra," she said, pointing to another woman getting her stuff ready in the corner.

I went over and introduced myself. "Sorry, wrong Tara." Kendra Stallings (49) and Terra Turner (48) from Northwest Georgia were walking together and just getting ready to head out. I would have the place to myself. I set my alarm for 15 minutes and fell asleep immediately on a little kindergarten-sized mat with my feet and calves up on a metal folding chair. I didn't feel super tired at this point, yet I could pretty much sleep whenever and wherever I wanted. It was a cool party trick. Except there weren't any parties.

I picked up some Goldfish crackers and cold water, then headed back out in the dark. The subtle graying of the sky told me that dawn was looming and would soon give me a bit of a jolt, like a Monster energy drink from the universe.

I got to the next angel stop just after dawn-- a tent by the road in front of a Pentecostal Church with coolers, snacks, a fan, a portable chair, and two zero-gravity chairs. Who should be sitting there but my old pal Tony!

He looked good (by Vol State's admittedly low standards) and was much improved now that he had broom handles. He was still slower than usual but determined, and he'd been cranking out the miles. The broomsticks had made all the difference in keeping his back straight.

While we were there, a woman pulled up in an SUV and, still in her hair rollers, came over to check out the aid station. "Don't mind me," she said. "I didn't think anyone would be here this early."

We told her we were just grateful for all the help.

Funny, I thought. She didn't realize that Vol State has no early or late; racers are as likely to be at an aid station in the middle of the night as in the middle of the day. Normal time was just a memory. This reminded me of another of Laz's pet peeves: the 24-hour clock instead of am and pm. At the Last Supper he'd sneered, "You gotta be hard, but you gotta be smart. Fulfill your part. Check-ins....every 12 hours. 730 and 1930. If you can't understand 730 and 1930, I scorn you! The day has 24 hours. There aren't two half days with 12." Except that nowhere in the world does time seem more like two 12-hour half days than at Vol State, racing against Oprah. I was fine setting my repeating alarm to 7:25, am and pm.

Tony and I walked together for a bit; then I went on ahead. The world was waking up, and I was looking forward to a Hardee's biscuit in Parsons.

Before Parsons, I got to a mammoth aid station by the road. A gorgeous McMansion sat well behind it across a giant, just-mowed lawn. There were two tents and a lighthouse. No kidding. The first tent was also an advertisement for Ginger with Exit Realty, and the black-and-white striped lighthouse was about eight feet tall and, like the tents, cinched down by guy ropes. In daylight, the lighthouse looked like an odd prop, but I supposed it was lit at night, and instead of warning wayward Vol State racers, it beckoned them like a Siren. A sign outside the tent said, **"Welcome runners. If it doesn't challenge you, it won't change you. Good luck!"**

Kendra and Terra were just coming out of the larger main tent.

"They've got beer," Terra said.

"Really? A bit early, isn't it?"

"Naw, never too early at Vol State," she said. "We each had one."

I grinned. *Could these be the fun people I'd been looking for?*

I must say that beer was an excellent addition to an aid station—the first I'd come across—even if it was a little early in the morning for me. Inside, the tent had enough seats for a party, including zero gravity chairs and three padded lounge chairs with foot stools. Who in the world would risk padded chairs for sweaty, dirty racers? I looked in the coolers out of curiosity and didn't see any beer. I did, however, find a Tupperware container filled with homemade pasta salad, including all sorts of vegetables. Now, *that* was a boon! And there were paper plates and a serving spoon and plastic forks and napkins. You gotta like Southern hospitality! When was the last time I had a vegetable? Must've been at the Mexican restaurant in McKenzie. How long ago was that? It would've been grand to stay longer at the lighthouse angel stop, but I returned to the road. Oprah was training/brainwashing me.

Just up from the lighthouse station, an SUV pulled over ahead of me. A thin, attractive, blonde woman jumped out, and took my picture.

"Well, hey. I'm Pam Pratt. What's your name?"

"I'm Nancy."

"Can I get you anything?"

"Uh, maybe a water? Actually I just stopped at the aid station just back there," I pointed.

"Yeah, that's mine. I actually have two, but that's the first one. The other one's on the way to Linden."

"I had a great pasta salad."

"I make that every year. It's a big hit with the runners."

"It was delicious. And I heard there was beer, but I didn't see any."

"I got beer right here." She opened a cooler with lots of beer. "You want one?"

I smiled. "No thanks. It's a little early for me, but I would take one later, on the way to Linden."

"I'll make sure I got one there for ya."

"How did you end up doing all this?"

"Well, I got started in 2011. I met some runners, found out what it was all about, then ran down and got them some cold waters, came back, gave 'em out; then I ended up driving back and forth between Parsons and Hohenwald [pronounced *HORN-wall* by the locals]. And it just got bigger and bigger and bigger.

"Now I run two stations that are in front of my friends' houses. I live back from the route, but they live right on it."

I could imagine Pam being quite persuasive talking her friends into this.

"This is all so great, but why do you do all this?"

"I just love it."

"But why?"

"I just get to meet the most amazing people. I think you guys are so tough, amazing, courageous, and ... dumb."

I burst out laughing.

"I just don't know how you do it. I get sweaty and sticky and hot. I don't like it at all. I don't know how you do it. I just love doing this. It just blesses me so much."

Still, I didn't quite get it. I wasn't sure road angels knew why they were helping us anymore than we knew why we were racing, but it was a wonderful symbiotic relationship.

The lighthouse highlights Pam Pratt's pasta salad and beer!

I thanked Pam profusely, waved goodbye, and kept walking to Parsons. Not far up the road from Pam, another SUV was parked on the big shoulder facing me. A fit blonde in a bright yellow t-shirt jumped out when she saw me approach and walked over to me. "Here," she said, handing me a sausage biscuit from McDonalds. "It's still warm."

"Wow. Thank you so much." I peeled back the packaging and took a bite. Warm food was a special treat from road angels.

Mary Cruse walked with me to the back of her vehicle, where she had all kinds of stuff, including a big cooler with frozen water, Gatorade, and beer, plus snacks, bananas, and Wet Wipes. "You can have anything you want. What can I get for you?" She couldn't have been sweeter. These folks truly felt like angels who'd been beamed down from the Hallmark Channel—the guardian angels you'd always pined for but were never sure existed.

"Thank you. This sausage biscuit is totally hitting the spot," I said. "This is amazing. Why do you do all this?"

"Well, I gotta tell you my story," she said. "My granddaughter Emma was killed in a head-on collision in 2021. She was 14, and she and her dad used to drive up and down the road, giving things out to Vol State runners. That was one of their things. So, now I'm continuing on the tradition. It's my way of giving back and keeping on Emma's mission. Here, I want to give you this."

She handed me a little hard plastic sleeve with two silver infinity charms attached to it. Inside was a picture of beautiful Emma and the text "Our FOREVER Road Angel / Emma Elizabeth Cruse / #LLEC / Become A Light / For ALL To See." I had Mary pin it to the back of my pack.

She teared up as she told me the story, the grief still raw. "What do you do?" she asked in a far-off tone. "Do you take to the bed? Do you just drink every day? But my granddaughter wouldn't want me to do that. And today is my 50th Anniversary." She smiled.

"And you're out here with us?" I marveled.

"Well, we celebrated last night, so it's all OK. I like being out here with all of you."

Mary has two children, twins. Her son and his daughter Emma were so close—"went to Marvel movies together, did all kinds of stuff." Her 12-year-old grandson Ty is a big-time rodeo kid. He'd just won a short go in Oklahoma.

Mary is getting ready to work with children in difficult situations. She'd just gone through a course to prepare for her role. Clearly, she's a nurturer, someone who is always looking to give back. I'd bet big money she's a world-class grandmother.

Tony walked up while I was talking to Mary. She gave him an Emma memento to wear on his pack. I think he must've known the story from last year. He has strong feelings about God and where Emma is. In another life, Tony could've been a preacher.

"There's nothing you can do about it," he told Mary. "You've just got to understand that she's much happier. She's with God. Jesus is taking care of her. You just have to know that. But we miss her. We miss her." He looked off in the distance. "I think this race has angels all over the place. I see my parents here, my brother here, and they're angels."

Tony was right about all the angels. People like Mary and Pam were beginning to make me forget about all the polarization in the US. If you just judged the country by Vol State, you might think that Americans were the most generous people in the world to the downtrodden. At least to the voluntarily downtrodden. The angels were the best part of this race.

Mary Cruse on her 50th Anniversary.

Chapter 8

LAND OF THE FREE AND HOME OF THE BRAVE

> *"for 10 days in july the vol staters have nothing....*
> *except the freedom of the open road..*
> *but they have to earn it every day."*
> --Lazarus Lake, LAVS 2023

Freedom . . . right

Laz likes to talk about the "freedom of the open road." There's a kernel of truth to what the man says. Something mighty special takes hold of you when you eschew the creature comforts of American life—cars, thermostats, Nespresso machines, volumizing hair mousse, comfy chairs, knowing where the next toilet will be—and you take to the open road on a bodily-propelled journey from one point on the map to another a long way away. I'm semi-addicted to the openness and uncertainty of this kind of adventure, and the people and places I'll encounter along the way. Who knows what they'll be?

Freedom is as true a feeling as I know on the open road, but Laz's events are not exactly the open road. They're a precise route, so precise that if you deviate even by a little bit, you'll be disqualified.

Now, I'm not criticizing the precision of Laz's rules or routes or the integrity it takes to adhere to them to the letter. In fact, I'm fascinated by Laz's laws and the folks who subject themselves to them. (*Hello, mirror.*) I'm intrigued by the twists and turns on the road as these journey "runners" make their way across the American South. It just doesn't feel like freedom—not freedom in space and not freedom in time.

Which brings us to Oprah (or her inspirational doppelgangers in Laz's other two journey races: the Grim Reaper in HOTS and Cerberus in Third Circle of Hell). Oprah is definitely the most fun (and most lenient) of the three, but they all model strict distance-in-time limits during a race. Oprah is the taskmaster, the reason we back-of-the-pack participants are never really free. She's our consensus imaginary frenemy.

Someone like Bob Hearn has never concerned himself with Oprah because he's so fast, but he has his own spreadsheets, A, B, and C goals, and per-hour mileages he wants to keep up with. One might make the case that he has a lot more freedom when it comes to time, but the competition creates self-imposed pressure to hit mileage benchmarks so that he has a chance to win the race. The same is true for other elite runners and many middle-of-the-packers with specific goals. All that pressure curtails freedom. Vol State is a race; it's not quite the open road.

I'd also heard some of the Vol Staters talk about being out on the open road, relying only on oneself. It didn't feel like that to me. For whose adventure has this ever been true? We're always relying on other people: race staff, road builders, shop owners, cashiers, Facebook cheerleaders, Dairy Queen Blizzard makers—the list is endless. And at Vol State, we rely on a legion of angels. If there's anything I'm sure of in life, it's that I don't rely only on myself to survive—at least not for very long.

People really mean that we have to dig deep and bring our own mental and physical fortitude to finish any of these races. Other people can enhance that fortitude, help us, and inspire us, but we have to find something in ourselves that keeps us moving forward toward the ridiculous goal of the Rock.

The real open road is very different from a Laz journey race. In the race format, time and space limitations intrude on our freedom but give us something else: a game? a quest? a rite of passage? a purpose?

So, no, it's definitely not freedom except from our usual comforts and duties, but the limitations themselves unlock something extraordinary. If you're one of the lucky ones, you too can win the Vol State lottery and play Laz's game all the way to the Rock. Or you can DNF and try again next year. About 20% of the entrants DNF, but only a handful of DNFs try again the following year.

Vol State is less like the open road and more like some modern-day vision quest, a sacred rite of passage where one gets in touch with a guardian spirit, or at least a passel of road angels who often resemble guardian spirits.

It even reminds me a little of Emmanuel Carrère writing in *The Kingdom* about Moses leading his people into the desert:

Exiled in Egypt, the soul languished. Led by Moses into the desert, it learned thirst, patience, discouragement, rapture. And when it arrived in view of the Promised Land, it had to battle against—and brutally massacre—the tribes that had settled there. According to Philo these weren't real tribes, but evil passions that the soul had to subdue.

Exiled in a polarized U.S., the soul languishes. Led by Laz into Vol State, we were sure to be presented with the lessons of *thirst, patience,* and *discouragement,* and we hoped for *rapture.* Fortunately, there was no massacring of tribes, but we did have much time and space to battle against the *evil passions* in our own souls.

Just as medieval pilgrims suffered months of atonement through their difficult journeys to sacred places, are we somehow atoning for our American worship at the altar of comfort and convenience through our slog to the Rock?

At the beginning of day 4, the "open road" seemed less freedom, more anvil. Vol State was hammering on our addictions to creature comforts and spiraling division. Maybe, just maybe, it would remind us of the people we could be, the country we could be.

The dreaded Parsons-to-Linden highway

Pam had told me there were four more angel stops in Parsons and four more after the river. I wondered if all that hospitality would balance out the difficult road walk between Parsons and Linden.

Being a Vol State racer is a little like being a fish, and the road angels put out bait for us. They want to hook us into *their* place. Bait almost always includes cold water—we fish love cold anything. Chair bait is often a draw. Zero-gravity-chair bait, a luxury. A cot lure, well, almost irresistible if you've got any time to rest. Tent-shade bait is a godsend during the day. In theory, a tent could also help during a rain shower, but in practice, it may not be much help in a thunderstorm, when the tents have problems of their own. Porta-potty bait may garner the most appreciation of all, especially from the women. If the road angels come along in their car, it's like fishing from a boat, and they can use a GPX route map as a fish finder.

Laz tells newbie road angels that their efforts are a little like humming-bird feeders; put them out, and the hummingbird racers will find them. This is true, but it doesn't speak to the complexities and the art of luring if you want more Vol Staters for longer.

> **72-Hour Tracker, comments in italics** (Sunday morning, July 16, 2023)
>
> Me: 104 miles-- --*"Oprah—that dadgum woman doesn't sleep!"* She was 10 miles behind me.
>
> Anonymous: *"Ringing the bell. LAVS defeated me"*
>
> Anonymous: *"I kept looking at my watch this morning so that I wouldn't forget to check in, and it stubbornly insisted the time was 7:16. 8 miles later I figured out today is 7/16. Yay me! #OrientedX1 #Onlyknowmyname"*

The road out of Parsons on the way to the Tennessee River was a little like the road from Hickman, Kentucky, to Union City, Tennessee—i.e., virtually no shoulder, with rumble strips and a two-lane road with cars and trucks and boat trailers whipping along.

George Saunders once wrote that "empathy depends on how you spent your day." In normal life, I typically spend my day with motorists, not people walking on the side of the road. As a motorist, I feel that if I make sure I don't hit somebody on the side of the road, then I've done my job. But now that I was spending my days (and nights) with people walking on the side of the road, my empathies had shifted; I realized that showing the walker that you see them and you're getting out of the way early should also be part of a motorist's job. It helps with the walker's stress levels, which are likely on the high side, or why would they be walking on the road in the first place?

I ran into Kendra and Terra at one of the un-humanned aid tents just out of Parsons that had a cooler and a few chairs. I got a cold water.

"I was totally impressed that you two had a beer at that rest stop this morning," I told them. "I've only had one beer in the whole race, and that was at a Mexican restaurant."

"Oh, we'll take a beer any chance we get," said Terra.

These might be my people.

I walked single-file with Terra and Kendra for a while on the way to the Tennessee River. They work in different veterinary clinics in NW Georgia. They've done lots of races and hikes and did HOTS together the year before. They only stayed in two hotel rooms during that race, and they were trying to do Vol State without any. "You just waste too much time in hotel rooms," said Terra. She wasn't wrong. Gosh, did I love wasting time in hotel rooms!

They loved the HOTS race because the road-angel magic you came across was all spontaneous since the course hadn't been used before, and no one knew about it ahead of time. Some folks along the route would figure it out and then help because of impromptu goodness.

We talked about having fun in this race, and Terra said, "Well, you gotta have fun! Why wouldn't you have fun with all this?" *Uh, I could think of a few reasons.*

Kendra is a horse person and is renovating a big Southern house. She wants to hike the Camino de Santiago and is trying to talk her husband into it. They both have a sense of humor and didn't seem to take themselves too seriously, although they were obviously serious about finishing the race and ultra racing in general. Kendra was more reserved, and Terra was goofier, but they were good friends who did races together but didn't hang out much in normal life.

A special bond happens for people who do hard things together. That must be why so many Vol Staters talk about the Vol State Family. I enjoyed walking with them, but when we came to a gas station, I peeled off to get a Gatorade while they kept going.

Walking over the Tennessee River bridge, I saw normal people boating and having fun. It was ungodly hot and humid and absolutely still—no breeze at all except for the people flying along in boats with the wind in their hair. As usual during the day, I was walking with my umbrella, which helped a bit. Mostly, it was a great day for drinking cold beer in a boat speeding down the Tennessee River.

I stopped again after the river at a posh convenience store. They had all these already-made exotic flavors of milkshakes in a freezer cabinet. I picked up a Snickers and took it to the counter to pay. The cashier asked me if I knew what to do with the shake. I did not. "Well, you take off the top and put it in the machine over there and choose whether you want a thick, thin, or medium blended shake." That sounded like fun.

Terrie came in as I was crafting my shake, and we sat and talked for a while. We got into politics and were clearly in the same tribe, which included the usual incomprehension about what voters saw in Donald Trump. She was a fixture in the ultra-racing community, and I asked her if most ultra racers were liberal or conservative. She said that she guessed they were more liberal in general. That made sense but wasn't immediately apparent to me at Vol State, probably because Laz's races, especially the ones open to "ordinary" runners, skew more conservative than most ultra races by virtue of being mainly in Tennessee. This year, 22 Vol State racers (18%) were from Tennessee. Of the DNF's 6 of 26 (23%) were from Tennessee, suggesting that it's easier to try this race since you're close to home and also easier to drop out. As Laz points out in his 48-hour update,

> *the worst thing for your hopes of finishing seems to be a crew.*
> *crewed runners quit at twice the rate of those who are just*
> *abandoned alongside the road.*
> *the next biggest killer;*
> *the course passing near where you live.*
> *if you can just get in a car*
> *or make a call and have a ride in 5 minutes*
> *it will be awfully hard to finish this race.*

That made sense—30% of the crewed racers were from Tennessee, so there was plenty of crossover of crewed runners and runners who lived near the course. Just because the ultra racers were from Tennessee didn't mean they were conservative, of course, but I'm guessing that more of them would trend that way than the non-Southern ultra racers.

I didn't realize it, but the famous road-angel stop at Serenity Hill was a few miles past the river. A woman was outside on the road, taking my picture as I walked up. She welcomed me and asked about Terrie. I said she was just behind me. "Well, go quickly and sign her book. It's just on the table under the tent."

I did as I was told. She had a message by the book that directed all runners to sign Terrie's *It's Not About the Miles* book, the one where The Warden crews her to her third Vol State finish. Lorraine Threlkeld, the archangel of Serenity Hill, is an unabashed fan of Terrie and of Vol State in general. She was positively giddy with excitement, waiting to surprise Terrie. All those handwritten sentiments reminded me of how far behind the field I really was. I knew this from the tracking sheet, but it was different with the handwritten notes, a number of them penned days ago.

Terra and Kendra were sleeping in Lorraine's zero-gravity chairs. This aid station was legendary for good reason. Lorraine had gone to all sorts of trouble. She had a big tent with fans, medical supplies, lots of snacks, and coolers of water, Gatorade, and soda. I left the last zero-gravity chair for Terrie and sat down in a regular chair with a cold water.

When Terrie arrived, Lorraine was thrilled and gave her the royal treatment, ushering her into the shade of the tent and offering to get her anything at all. Terrie gets treated along the route like everyone's little old lost grandmother, but she has more of a tough, military, Yankee get-her-done attitude than any grandmother I've ever met. Scratch the surface, though, and she's a marshmallow. Although she seems uncomfortable with all the effusive fuss, she definitely likes it. Lorraine made a big deal of presenting the book to Terrie. I took pictures, and Kendra, Terra, and I clapped. Terrie thanked her but was initially more worried about having to carry the book.

"Don't worry," beamed Lorraine. "I'm going to mail it to you at the end of the race."

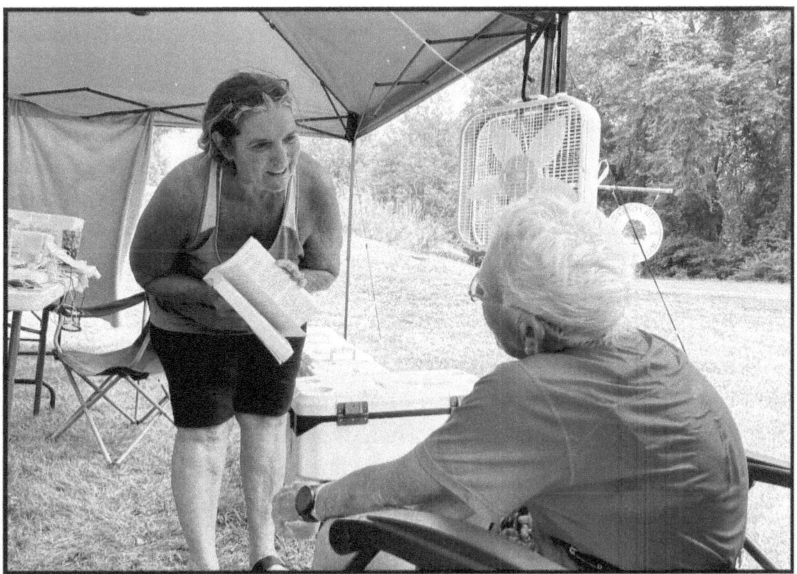

Lorraine Threlkeld presents Terrie with a copy of her book signed by all the Vol Staters.

Terrie didn't rest long at Serenity Hill before heading back out on the road, but later, she said that the book was "the coolest thing that's ever happened to me in my entire life."

When she left, I took her spot in the last zero-gravity chair and closed my eyes for a little while until Regina showed up at Serenity Hill. I asked where Bill was.

"He's coming up right behind me. You're going to give him that chair, right?" she said jokingly but not joking. I was going to give it to him anyway. Bill looked OK when he walked up but was apparently "on the struggle bus," as they say. He gladly took the comfy chair.

My priority was peeing. This is the biggest problem with most road-angel stops. There's all this cold liquid, which is so welcome but has the usual ramifications. I went over and whispered in Lorraine's ear, "I'm embarrassed to ask this, but would you mind if I went over and peed in your woods?"

"Oh, gosh, no," she laughed. "Why don't you just go behind my Ranger." Lorraine had probably heard it all. She had a Polaris Ranger four-wheeler parked behind the tent, and I gratefully slipped around the vehicle and took her up on the offer.

Beers and bras

By the time I thanked Lorraine profusely and left Serenity Hill, it wasn't quite as scorching as it had been when I arrived. I didn't have to walk far before I saw another aid station on the other side of the road. And there was Pam Pratt, whom I'd met that morning. So, this was her other angel stop.

"You want that beer?" she asked.

"Do I ever!"

She handed me an ice-cold can of Michelob Ultra, which in my normal life I might decline, but on Day 4 of Vol State, it tasted better than any beer I'd ever had. Three folks—mother, daughter, granddaughter—were just leaving the aid station to help Vol State racers from their car. They would drive up the route in one direction, spend the night in a motel, and then drive back the other way. Amazing.

Pam was sitting under a front yard tent with her friend Peggy Copous, who owned the house and was a tow-boat cook who'd worked on the Upper Mississippi River but was now on the Ohio River. Peggy was super sweet, too, but quieter. I could imagine her as the high-school sidekick to Pam, who's a consummate storyteller. Peggy would be the one who said, "Tell them the one about...." They were a great duo, super fun. Among other stories, Pam regaled us with the tale of Michelle Chauvin's bra. Apparently, Michelle had stopped off at Pam's first angel tent, the one with the lighthouse, and she was still having a lot of trouble with her bra digging into her back.

Pam explained, "Michelle and Shenoa come down there. Michelle's back's all chafed. She's got heat rash. So, 'You're going to have to take your bra off. We're gonna doctor this.' It was just salt dried on her and her bra. So, I pulled the plug on that big cooler, which is at the bottom, and I'm down there tryin' to wash the salt outta her bra. Then finally Shenoa said, 'Y'all gonna have to get that salt off her back,' so I'm given her back a bath, you know, scrubbin' her up with water.

"There she is—I made her take her bra off. I give her a beach towel and she kinda holds it over here. I pat her dry. We decide we're going to put the powder first. You know, dry it vs. the cream, the Desitin, or the Trail Toes. I washed the bra out, get all the salt. Mary comes over there. So Mary is pouring a bottle of water cause I got grass where the plug was down there. And I hang it up on that piece of wood where the fan was. So she gets out a different bra, and I said, 'You're not leaving right now, Michelle. You just sit here and let your back get some air.'"

Unbelievable! The story went on, including strategically placed Band-Aids, but in consideration of Michelle's modesty, I won't repeat all of it here. Pam and Mary got Michelle washed up and patched up enough to continue. I can only imagine how bad the chafing on her back was by that point. Apparently, Michelle ended up accidentally leaving the first bra in the tent, which Kara Teichroew kindly picked up shortly after to bring to Michelle, obviously paying no attention to Laz's grumpy update from the day before:

> *maybe it is just me.*
> *but i dont think any lost gear should ever be returned.*
> *if you cant keep track of your stuff when you have to carry*
> *everything you own with you*
> *then you dont deserve to have it!*
> *hots was a never ending stream of....*
>
> .
>
> *"oh no, i seem to have lost my drivers license and all my*
> *credit cards when i emptied every item out of my pack onto*
> *a traffic island"*
> *"oh no, i left my charger cord plugged into an outlet at dollar*
> *general"*
> *"oh no, i forgot my head at the burger king"*
>
> .
>
> *now the same thing is starting all over again.*

I don't know if it was the beer, the stories, the sleep deprivation, or the general misery of every muscle in my body, but everything about this race was starting to strike me as hilarious. It was ridiculous that grown people subjected themselves to it all.

I split another Mich Ultra with Peggy and watched Bill walk up and lower himself in another zero-gravity chair.

Mary Cruse drove up too. It was still her 50th wedding anniversary, but she had just volunteered to crew for Gretchen West (49), who had lost her crew when her friend Selena Ferguson had quit at Mile 57. Selena's mom had been crewing for them both, and Gretchen had been on her own for over 50 miles. She was evidently pretty miserable at a Subway in Parsons, where she sat for a long time. Pam was in there and kept telling her, "You got to go, Girl! You got to move." Mary would pick up the slack and help her keep moving.

Pam Pratt, Bill Page, and Peggy Copous at the storytelling, beer-drinking party before Linden. Oh, to have more hours in a LAVS day!

In a front yard, under a little tent outside of Linden, TN, I was having more fun than I'd had the whole race, and I wanted nothing more than to hang out with Pam and Peggy, drinking Mich Ultra on a hot, late afternoon in the middle of rural Tennessee. But Oprah clickety clicked on her stilettos in the background, and I finally had to force myself to say a sad goodbye and head back to the infernal white line.

I almost understood what Shenoa meant about the bonding with road angels bringing her back every year, but . . . well . . . not quite. As much as I liked Pam and Peggy and Mary, as much as I'd miss them in normal life, I wasn't going to be a repeat Vol Stater.

I felt strong leaving the aid station, but I was pretty sure I'd get shut out of real rest in Linden. Regina had mentioned at Serenity Hill that they had gotten the last room at the Commodore Hotel. There was also supposed to be a community center someplace in the town that was letting Vol State racers hang out, so I was thinking maybe I could get a little sleep there before heading into what I'd heard was an 18-mile desert to Hohenwald. In Vol State terms, a *desert* is a stretch without any commercial places to refuel. I'd rather go through a desert in the night than the day.

I walked the next five or so miles into Linden and checked in just before I got into town.

84-Hour Tracker, comments in italics (Sunday evening, July 16, 2023)

Me: 125 miles--*"Oh, the stories Pam can tell!"* 15 miles ahead of Oprah. It seemed like I was making a break for it, but I would rest tonight, and she wouldn't.

Anonymous: *"Just called Jan. This was a stupid idea. We live or we learn, I'm just not sure what I've learned yet!"*

Anonymous: *"Another day in Satan's vagina where it's always hot and moist, and my feet are on fire."* Graphic but apt.

Sadly, my buddy Paul Heckert was out at 88 miles. He'd had a tough last 24 hours.

On the other end of the Vol State World, Ken Zemach was at 296 miles and Bob Hearn was at 280. Barring some unforeseen catastrophe, both men would be at the Rock before the next check-in, and Ken would be the newest King of the Road. Pretty impressive for a first- (and only) timer.

As I walked down the main drag of Linden, I saw the Commodore, an old-world brick building that looked inviting. I figured it couldn't hurt to walk in and ask if they had any rooms. The lobby, with its red leather chairs, blue carpet, decorative fireplace, and chandelier lighting, made me feel underdressed and under-hygiened. The hotel had been built in

1939 and rescued for renovation in 2007. Regina was already at the front desk, which made me feel a little better about my sweaty self. She had run ahead of Bill to get everything ready for him because he was having such a rough time.

I asked if they had any rooms available and the young man said that they did have a room in their other building for $99, which sounded perfect to me. Cheaper than the Days Inn and no doubt more interesting—even if "interesting" wasn't a big deal at this point. Quiet with a bed and bathroom was more than sufficient.

Regina and I grilled the front desk guy about where to eat on a Sunday night. The café at the hotel was closed. "Are there any restaurants open?" I asked.

"No. Well, there is a Sonic and a Subway." They were each about half a mile away, and I was starting to realize why Paul Heckert had told me the first rule of Vol State is you never walk extra miles to anything.

"How about pizza?" I asked.

"Well, yeah, there's Mongos Pizza right over there," he pointed.

"Is it open on Sunday?"

"No."

Helpful. We were looking up other places on our phone. "How about Village Pizza?"

"Village Pizza might be open. I'm not sure."

"And how long is the grocery store open?"

"Well, it's open till 10, but I would get there early because everything closes early in Linden."

At least the Food Giant Grocery Store was across the street. I wouldn't starve.

I walked down the street to the Commodore's other building, the former "Miss Berdie's Boarding House." Erin Dupey was outside, explaining the race to two local guys sitting on a bench. I joined in and asked about places to eat. They said the Village Pizza was closed, so that was out.

"Your best bet is to go to the Giant Food Store," one of the guys said.

"The deli was closed, though," Erin said, "because they close even earlier than the store." I dumped my backpack in my enormous room and set off across the street to wander the grocery store before it decided to close early.

I walked up and down the aisles, seeing little of interest. All this daily heat kept my appetite in check, even as I knew how important it was to eat. I settled on a Starbucks French Vanilla Latte, a banana, and some M&Ms for the walk tomorrow, which would seem less like tomorrow and more like tonight. For dinner, I got some Provolone cheese and a pint of Ben & Jerry's Peanut Butter Cup ice cream. I seemed to be gravitating more toward dairy products of late. Vol State was weirdly impacting my nutritional cravings, so it didn't matter too much that the food choices on a Sunday night in Linden were disappointing. The main thing was the luxurious room, which I could've happily stayed in for a week: the bath water babied my sore muscles and washed away the grime of the last 24 hours. I didn't know where an ice machine was, so I couldn't ice my feet, but I gently propped them up on multiple pillows. My legs and feet didn't quite feel like they were attached to my body—more like two limbs that had been entrusted to my care, so I had to carry them around—or maybe they had to carry me around. The calves and feet were swollen and sore, but they would improve from the miracle drug: sleep. I set my alarm for 2 am.

The desert to Hohenwald

Chris Clemens was a veteran about 45 miles ahead of me, well out of earshot of Oprah's clicks. I was amused by his Facebook post from earlier on Sunday:

> *For what it's worth, quitting this race is a challenge. Early this morning, I was sure I'd had enough. I was trudging into Parsons being battered by a storm. My feet were wrecked (much like the majority of the field). I convinced myself I had nothing to prove and didn't want to be out here anymore. I texted Carl Laniak. He said he was at the rock. Text Jan Redmond Walker. So I did. I came across Zack Lever and Terry Winston Bonnett in parsons. Told them I was done. Zack laughed and reminded me I tried to do the same at hots 2022. And... they said they saw Carl drive past them earlier. As I was moving w Zack, Jan does a slow drive by. She gives me an up and down look. Gives me a thumbs up and drives away.*
> *So... I'm still in this damn race.*

I laughed out loud. *And so was I*, I thought while getting ready to leave that luscious room in Linden.

I was less amused by Laz's email late Sunday night. It started with a photo of bags of trash on a table.

the above mess was left at an aid station.
right next to a litter barrel.
we talked about trash at the last supper.
but apparently you were not listening.
all along the course you are being treated with kindness.
do not repay it by acting like entitled brats.
PICK UP AFTER YOURSELF.

It went on haranguing us from there and ended with,

if any of us see you throw trash on the ground
you will be summarily removed from the course and dis-
qualified.
act like grownups.
laz (and staff)

I didn't think I'd left trash anyplace it wasn't supposed to go, but I would have an all-night slog into Hohenwald to think about it. I was more interested in thinking about a good breakfast when the desert ended.

The night was "close," as the British say—hot, stifling, humid—as if the British could really know about hot, stifling, and humid. At least the sun wasn't shining. I liked the night, even if the only moon was the light of my chest lamp. The darkness wrapped around me like an old friend. Not many distractions, nothing open to tempt you into stopping and resting. Maybe I was meant to be nocturnal.

Not far out of Linden, I came up on Tony. He was looking good. Slower than usual but so much better off than he had been and making good progress. He stopped at a little road-angel tent to get some ice, and I kept walking.

Eighteen miles to Hohenwald seemed an awfully long way. I peed five times on the side of Highway 412. I didn't know why I was peeing so much, but I'd gotten a lot better at it, especially at night. It worked like this: I'd find a little stretch of road that was dark—not difficult on this stretch—turn off my light, pull down my pants on the grass verge and go. I couldn't find my Kleenex the first time, which was when I realized, heck, I can do without and not be in a world of trouble. Guys have been just shaking their penises for eons. True, we're not as efficient, but in a pinch, TP is overrated. I didn't always remember the last step, though: turn my light back on. After I went to the bathroom the last time, my eyes must have quickly adjusted to the dark. At one point a big truck was heading toward me, and it wasn't moving over like most vehicles did. Suddenly, I realized that he couldn't see me. I turned the light back on, and he moved over a bit. All was well.

During the daytime, peeing gets trickier. Bridges were my favorite spots. There's usually a point where the ground dips on the other side of the guard rail from the road, so you can often squat down in the dip, use the rail as a shield, and do your business. Even if cars are passing by, they can't see you....at least, I don't *think* they can.

I'd been talking to Chris in the middle-of-the-night march to Hohenwald. The time difference with England meant that I could chat with him to help stay awake and get advice on the upcoming town while sensible Americans slept.

Eventually, I noticed the subtle shift in the dark. Sunrise was at 5:45 am, but the darkness started lifting quite a bit earlier. I loved the barely perceptible shift from pitch black to black to nearly black. Then I heard barking, and down the road, I saw Terrie and someone else encountering three dogs, all off leashes, making a lot of racket. The dogs were holding their ground and, I suspect, just policing their territory until the interlopers left. Terrie stayed there, though. When I got up to them, she said, "I saw you coming and couldn't tell whether you had sticks or not, and I wanted to keep the dogs off you." Very thoughtful of her.

Angela Rhea (41) and Chrissy Engh (48) were with her, and I walked with them for a while. They were the two women I'd heard about who were helicopter pilots, part of the fun crowd. Actually, Chrissy was a pilot, and Angela worked on the flight crew; they were in the same helicopter crew in Iraq in the mid-aughts and had immediately hit it off as the best of friends. Chrissy had done a tour in Iraq and a tour in Afghanistan, and Angela had done two tours in Iraq. They weren't having much fun that morning because Angela had a terrible shin problem and was worried she had a stress fracture.

Chrissy was in the National Guard. I asked how she felt about being called up for active duty from the Guard. Turns out, she desperately wanted to be in combat. "If I die at war, I want to go down in a blaze of glory." She did not die and now was walking the backroads to Hohenwald, Tennessee. I didn't know if she was finding any glory in Vol

State. I certainly was not. I asked if this race was easy after two tours in the Middle East. Chrissy said, "No, I think this is the hardest thing I've ever done." Angela agreed.

It wasn't long before we looked across the street and saw a brick house with an angel station set up in the carport: all kinds of chairs, lounge chairs, towels, and coolers.

Ruby and Herbert Hinson had been delighting Vol State runners for years with their homegrown tomatoes and cucumbers. They even made their own pickles. Delicious! And it wasn't too early for them to welcome us in person with their hospitality.

I was starting to see the power of pickles during an ultra race. All that salt and cold. And I'm a sucker for real tomatoes. Getting to eat such fresh produce was a huge surprise for me, although the veterans look forward to the Hinsons' place every year.

Herbert and Ruby Hinson plus grandkids take good care of the Vol Staters.

Chrissy tucked Angela into a lounge chair with towels, and Terrie promptly laid down and closed her eyes as well. Terrie had a no-nonsense approach to rest stops: fuel, sleep, and then move on as quickly as possible. She was a marvel.

On the other hand, I was almost always looking for connections at rest stops. I loved chatting with the Hinson family.

Ruby told me that her son Jeff had gotten married yesterday, and they were taking care of some of their grandkids. Two little girls came out of the house. It must've been awfully early for them, but I'm sure it was tough to sleep with all that activity in their grandparents' carport.

I asked them if they had any interest in doing Vol State down the road. They looked at each other. The smaller girl said, "I can see the exercise part of it, but walking in the rain, walking in the heat—I don't think so."

Before I left, I asked the girls, "What do you think of all these smelly people hanging out in your grandparents' carport?"

They just giggled; they'd thought about that before but were too Southern and polite to answer.

I thanked the Hinsons for their hospitality and waved goodbye to all.

Chrissy said, "I hope we won't ever see you again."

I laughed. "Well, there's a lot of crisscrossing."

"I hope for your sake we don't see you again," she said.

I shrugged. I likely would see them again.

My goal was Hohenwald in time for breakfast. The air seemed cloudy in a strange sort of way. Laz had said something about it in his last update, but I figured that was just hyperbole:

> *worse than the heat and humidity is the air quality.*
> *with the rain out of the picture*
> *there was a slight haze this morning.*
> *smoke from the canadian wildfires gradually obliterated*
> *the view of surrounding hills as the day went on.*

I hadn't noticed it yesterday, but I sure did this morning. I checked my weather app: the Tennessee Department of Environment and Conservation had issued a "Code Orange Air Quality Alert for Particulate matter" from midnight last night until 1:00 am Tuesday. The Canadian fires had made their way down after all. My favorite part of the alert was this: "Active children and adults, and people with a respiratory disease such as Asthma, should limit prolonged outdoor exertion." Fat chance.

Chapter 9

A HUMAN AVATAR

"It's not always rainbows and unicorns."
—Lazarus Lake

The moment I realized I was an avatar in a Laz-made reality-video game

I t dawned on me as I walked into Hohenwald after check-in that this race is a lot like a real-life video game. You start with an adventure. Any Laz race is the product of a madman's mind. You're in a Laz-chosen reality-video game landscape with idiosyncratic rules that you must obey or you forfeit the game.

The Vol State Reality-Video Game works this way: you start with a generic avatar with no experience plunked into a foreign landscape, mostly resembling the Deep South, mostly happening in the great state of Tennessee. You get to decide what you want to carry—the more, the harder physically, but the less, the less safety and comfort. There will be places along the way for you to gather trinkets. There will be special road-angel guides along the way who will pop up and help you. The game has a silly, nonsensical goal: getting to Castle Rock in NW Georgia. The Rock gets invested with all this supposed meaning and power. Why do we even care about Castle Rock? Where is it? Never been there. Never heard of it before the game. But it's like any video game. The goal is set, it becomes important, and you get sucked into believing that it matters.

Like any video game, there are levels. Tony got to one level last year—185, the Bench of Despair. Now he's back, playing the game again, trying for a new level. You gobble up miles/points and register those miles/points every 12 hours, where you can see your score against all the others in this massively multiplayer offline role-playing game (MMORPG). OK, maybe it's not *massively* multiplayer. Let's call it a multiplayer offline role-playing game (MORPG) where we each take on a role: for example, ultrarunner or ultra walker or filthy person who hasn't had a shower in days or person temporarily experiencing home-lessness or person temporarily experiencing hallucinations. Whatever the role, it's temporary, but in Laz's game, it often feels like it's forever. I couldn't even think about what ten days means so early in the race.

I thought only of the next angel stop, the next cold water, the next country-ham biscuit, the next Payday bar, the next zero chair or bed. The food, the cold drinks, the chairs to sit in, the occasional motel—these are the energy nuggets that we follow and yearn for to help accumulate miles in the game.

The evil villain in the game is obviously Laz, who makes us adhere to wacky routes and rules and who delights in a significant drop percentage. Other villains may also be *dangerous people* in Tennessee, psychotic rubes who mean to do us harm. That's one of the things that gets spectators so fascinated with the game. In *Demon Copperhead*, Barbara Kingsolver's title character says, "People love to believe in danger as long as it's you in harm's way and them saying bless your heart." The fact that those deranged folks rarely pop up in the game is immaterial. They *could* jump out of the bushes anywhere along the course. The more common *dangerous people* are drivers of cars. They don't generally mean to do us harm, but they can be perilous anyway, relentlessly barreling toward us in vehicles of destruction, just like in a video game where you're constantly dodging obstacles flying toward you. When we're on the odd sidewalks through towns, we can breathe easier, but the vast majority of the time, we're walking on roads, so we have to stay vigilant in the game.

As in any good video game, plenty of other obstacles await—amoral, impersonal impediments like weather (e.g., thunderstorms, heat and humidity, wildfire smoke). Many racers think that Laz has control over Mother Nature's obstacles. Conspiracy theorists suggest Faustian pacts to attract thunderstorms and/or heat indexes over 100. Throw in a little hail, some flooding, and you've amped up the gamesmanship—the more the merrier for Lazarus Lake.

Other obstacles include deserts (those are mostly Laz's doing; he chose the route) and night (the dark is a relief because of the unbusy roads and relatively cooler temperatures, but it's also a torment because of the biorhythms lulling the body to sleep). Let's also include no-vacancy motels, towns with no motels at all, shops and restaurants that close just before we get there or will only open after we wander through.

Besides all these torments, Laz's game offers lots of good witches, sweet fairies, and sage guides, a.k.a. veterans and road angels. They offer succor whenever they can and smooth the way. Other veterans who've played the game before will give us tips ahead of time and along the way on gear, training, strategies, and hazards, maybe even where we can find stashes of goodies. Laz pointedly tells road angels not to announce their mile markers on the Facebook site so that newbies like me can be surprised when they come across a road angel with homemade pickles or cold, wet cloths. Surprises are nice, but when you're hungry, thirsty, and exhausted, it's even nicer to be able to plan where to get provisions or sleep. Still, sometimes the veterans will tell you what mile markers have aid stations, and the road angels themselves delight in foiling Laz. Their only allegiance is to the Vol State racers, so they'll happily tell you in person where the next road-angel stops are. But just because you come across a road-angel stop doesn't mean a road angel will be there. Most of the stops are un-humanned—just a tent in a yard or maybe a Styrofoam cooler with a folding chair next to it. Sounds minimal, but you cannot imagine how welcome a cold water or folding chair might be in a game where folks have been walking continuously in the heat for as long as we have.

The road angels seem to immediately grasp the game and enjoy playing their part as guides and helpers. It's dizzying to be a real avatar in this game, and in road-angel circles, you're treated like a minor celebrity. The angels can end up washing out your bra, for goodness' sake!

And there's more. Tony told me first, "You feel like a 10-year-old again!" Imaginations run wild as children—we star in our own adventures over and over. And here we are in the Vol State game, finding our way for real through these Laz-inspired trials. Is that the fun of it? It doesn't really feel fun. But it does feel much different from normal life. It feels like adventure. Not the vicarious adventure of video games, but a manufactured real one.

Do we give this up as the American Dream seduces us? What happens when we get our house, two-car garage, and insurance to cover mayhem—our Nest thermostat set always to comfortable? Tempur-pedic beds, Nespresso coffee makers, oversized refrigerators, and as many square feet as we can mortgage? Comfort and convenience are a national obsession. And what do many of us choose for vacation? A cruise where all our entertainment and food choices are crammed onto one giant boat that will take us to exotic places where we can snorkel or walk around for an afternoon. Or we pick a foreign resort where we can while away the hours by fresh-water pools or on sandy beaches near a tiki hut where

Raphael will make us Bajan Rum Punches. We need these vacations to help us relax and recuperate from the stressful lives we lead so we can have comfortable, safe houses and cars, and pay for the next vacation. And the loop continues.

Maybe Vol State is just a way to jump out of the loop and play an adventure game. We'll follow the cool kid—Lazarus Lake—and do what he tells us. When we were children, the cool kid who got us into jams was charismatic, mischievous, reckless—and made us feel alive. Maybe we just miss following that kid, and we know Fortnite can't get us far enough outside the Great American Loop.

I keep thinking about all these liberal snowflakes walking through rural Tennessee, being helped by all these right-wing conservatives. Why can't we design more of these reality-video-game scenarios to bring conservatives and liberals together in some common adventure? Vol State is a totally contrived, ridiculous race, but just the idea that everybody pitches in together—not everybody, but LOTS of people—makes it unusual in the U.S. in 2023. Some people think the Trumpers are destroying the country; others think the woke liberals are destroying the country. Maybe we all love the country; we just come at it from different perspectives.

I remembered my time in Belfast, Northern Ireland, last year, walking the historically Catholic and then the historically Protestant streets with American students. We saw the murals of martyrs and warriors on both sides. Our guide Dan grew up in one of the Catholic neighborhoods in Belfast. He was trying to show both sides of the conflict, but, not surprisingly, he wasn't very good at the Protestant side. As an outsider, it was easier to see both sides, but it's difficult for any super-polarized group to accommodate an alternative narrative.

Before we parted ways, Dan cautioned me and the students: "And this is what's gonna happen in America if you keep digging trenches and not talking to each other. Nobody gets out of a trench. If you keep it up in America, our past is gonna be your future."

I thought a lot about Dan's ominous forecast on the Tennessee backroads. We're not likely to give up our political opinions, but periodically, and much more frequently than we do, we should move out of our trenches, away from our partisan politics, culture wars, and echo chambers, so we can remember the other side's humanity, enjoy the community of our United States, and admire the best parts of people, regardless of their political persuasions. When we forget the other side is human, it's all too easy to fall into the traps set for us by the biased media and politically divisive leaders. Maybe we need more reality-video games.

And the race is over . . . for some

> **96-Hour Tracker, comments in italics** (Monday morning, July 17, 2023)
>
> Me: 137 miles--*"Love them Vermont boys! Ben and Jerry'll help with whatever ails ya!"* Oprah was 11 miles behind.
>
> Anonymous: *"I don't understand why people keep coming back for this."* You and me both!
>
> Anonymous: *"Slept on a mattress last night - fucked up my hip. I clearly wasn't built for such luxury. Also.. Wasn't sure if I was going the right way. Then realized it was uphill, against heavy traffic in the fucking hot sun. Must be."*
>
> On the fast end of the Vol State World, the new King of the Road, Ken Zemach, finished in 3 days, 17 hours, 3 minutes, and 22 seconds. The course-record-holding King of the Road Bob Hearn finished in 3 days, 22 hours, 53 minutes, and 51seconds. Congratulations to them both! Who knew that the humble guy I met on the walk from my car to the bus the day before the race would be the new King? At this check-in, The Honey Man, Addison Hendricks was in a distant third place at 270 miles.

Boy, was this race different for Ken and Bob and Addison than for the back-of-the-packers. First, they were racing for speed, not for survival. Or maybe *survival at speed* is a better way to say it. This meant they used up a lot more energy each minute than I did, and they sweated a lot more too. They had even more incentive to sleep as little as possible, which meant they were more sleep-deprived, at least at this point. Likely their Default Mode Networks were much more melted than mine.

And I still had 177 miles to go. This made me laugh. One of those absurd, slightly insane wa-ha-ha-ha laughs. If I made it, I'd be part of the Vol State family, but, oh, what a difference between the front of the family and the back!

Love and grief in Hohenwald

I didn't realize until later that morning that Terrie had put out an all-call on Facebook, looking for a place to stay in Hohenwald:

I was just told there are no rooms available at the Embassy Inn in Hohenwald. Normally in any other town I would just consider going on.....but as you all know the next stretch is murder on someone as slow as me.
Does anyone have any ideas? I don't want to have to drop because I can't get any rest before tackling hampshire and pre-Columbia
I am really bummed out.

This hit Hohenwald like a call to arms. You wouldn't believe the offers and advice from the town's residents. Miz Terrie wasn't going to drop out of Vol State in their town! Ruby started things off: "You can rest on Hinson carport if nothing else is available." Then other offers came pouring in:

Walmart is just down the road and I think there are a few places close to Walmart set up for y'all.

The Howards have a porch you can rest on if nothing else is available.

Please message me if you still need space.

The outpouring of love and support went on and on.

I made it into Hohenwald by about 10:00 that morning. Just as I entered the town, an old guy in a pickup truck was parked ahead. He rolled down the window and shouted, "Are you Terrie?"

"Uh, no. Terrie's behind me a little ways. Can I help you?"

"I just saw the Facebook post she left and wanted her to know about a B & B up ahead who would be fine letting her stay out back. I just figured I'd wait for her here so that she would know."

These folks were unbelievable. This man was waiting in his truck for a person he couldn't recognize just to make sure she had a place to lay her head. If only Mary and Joseph had had such support!

I stopped at one more angel station to sit down for a few minutes, then headed for the Southern Skillet, though not in time for breakfast. I had mediocre chicken strips and fries with a side of delicious air conditioning. While there, I discovered Regina's FB post about Bill: "Don't tell him I said this because he lost his phone but we might need someone to come back and crew bill." Oh, my gosh. Poor guy. Weird things start to happen the more sleep-deprived and exhausted people get.

I would eventually hear different versions of the fuller story: Between Pam and Peggy's aid stop (where I'd last seen Bill lying in a zero-gravity chair) and Linden (where he was to meet Regina at the Commodore), he had stopped to rest at a guard rail beside the road and had dropped either his hiking stick or his phone over the guardrail, and when he went down into the steep ravine to retrieve it, he couldn't get back up to the road. Kendra and Terra had passed by and tried to help, but it finally took two Linden police officers to rope Bill in and pull him back up. The phone was still apparently at large. Not something you want to lose ever, but especially not in this race. What an unfun adventure!

I pried myself from the Southern Skillet air conditioning just about high noon. The heat, as usual, was enough to make me grumpy. Add in the Canadian smoke particles, and I was mega miserable. *Why was I continually surprised at how much the hot temperatures and sun affected my mood?* I walked through downtown Hohenwald and passed a shop called Faith & Fashions where I could buy a "Let me tell you about my Jesus" shirt. Farther still was the Elephant Sanctuary Discovery Center. Hohenwald has one of the most famous elephant sanctuaries in the country. The sanctuary itself is closed to the public, and I was bummed that the Discovery Center wasn't open on Mondays.

The main thing, though, was to find rubber tips for my hiking poles. I was sure Hohenwald would be the place. They had an Ace Hardware, just off the route, and although the Ace folks looked all over, they had no tips small enough to fit my poles.

Next stop, Walmart. Vol Staters thrill at Dollar General stores, but Walmart is even better. Unfortunately, they still didn't have any tips by themselves, but they did again have hiking poles with tips. Because I knew Tony was coming there to get hiking poles to replace his broom handles, I thought, *This is silly. I should just buy the hiking poles, take the tips off them, and leave the poles for Tony at the customer service desk. He's been walking with broom handles, for goodness' sake. Free hiking poles without rubber tips will still be a big step forward.*

Audra at the customer service desk was super helpful. She kept the poles in a bag for Tony, and I wrote his name on the outside. I gave him a call. He was on his way to Walmart and was happy to take the poles. He didn't care about the tips like I did.

As I left Walmart, Tony called me back. He was walking with Terrie, and she wanted to tell me that a church was opening up for us—the Central Christian Fellowship—and if I wanted to stay there, I could. She wanted to make sure I knew because I was ahead of them and would get to it first and might pass it. I hoped I hadn't passed it already. I checked my Apple map, and it was still about a mile up the route. Seemed like a worthy interim goal, especially on a day when I was so hot and grouchy. I called Chris and vented to him about how lousy I felt, sweaty and exhausted and disheartened.

On the way to the church, I passed a house with a half-American/half-Confederate flag flying proudly out front. Vol State necessarily subjected me to many more triggers than my life in England, but Vol State also hammered home the generosity and kindness in the South. It's a weird incongruity, but it's essential, I think, to hold both parts of the South simultaneously. In my normal life, it was much easier to fixate on the radical politics and not remember the radical hospitality.

Just before I got to the Central Christian Fellowship, a pickup truck pulled into the cross street in front of me and stopped. Out of the cab jumped a guy named Robert Brewer, wearing a "Mammoth March Finisher" t-shirt and a gray "High Forest Outdoors" baseball hat with deer antlers in the front and stars and stripes wrapped around the back. He had big coolers in the bed of his truck as well as padded chairs. He pulled one out for me, set it up, and said, "What can I get you? I've got water, Gatorade, beer." Wow, I liked the guy already. I told Chris I'd call him back.

"I'd love a water first, but I'll take a beer after if I can."

"Sure. What else? I've got bananas, candy bars." He told me it was his first year as a road angel, but he was a natural. I gladly took a banana and a cold Reese's Peanut Butter Cup.

I sat down, never so grateful for a pad in a folding chair, and Robert pulled out a chair too. He was good friends with the Pastor and his wife at the Central Christian Fellowship. They had asked him to help open up the church, and he had cleared that it was OK to drink beer on the street next to the church. I doubted it was exactly legal, but the main thing was that he didn't want to offend his friends or the church.

I asked Robert how he came to be a road angel, and he told me he was doing it as a tribute to his son Ethan, a 23-year-old who had died tragically in a nearby truck accident in October 2021. "He was probably fooling around with a friend of his who was on a motorcycle," said Robert. "They were weaving in and out. Something happened. We don't really know what happened, but he lost control of the vehicle and hit a tree. The truck exploded. Ethan died instantly. The tree still has the burn marks on it, and we set up a memorial there with all his favorite stuff. Ethan loved America. Everything was red, white, and blue. He used to run around in these little red, white, and blue shorts. So we planted a red, white, and blue flower bed by the burnt Pine. We've got a cross in the heart-shaped flower bed. He loved the flag. We put up an American flag with a baseball and mitt on it. He loved his baseball."

When Robert's wife Regina came up, Robert walked over to make sure everything was OK at the church. I told Regina how sorry I was about her son. What a thing to lose a child. It happens to too many parents. It had happened to my mother when we lost my little brother John to cancer. It had happened to my cousin when we lost Buck earlier that spring. All that creation and love and nurturing and investment and energy, and then part of you suddenly gone.

Regina was particularly mournful that day because she was getting ready to go to a wake for another mother's son— "a 17-year-old I had taught, who had just graduated" and who had died in a tragic accident. The young man was from Hampshire, the next little hamlet I was walking toward. I remembered reading about his death the second day of the race on Facebook. The boy's family were road angels.

It seemed especially awful that we would be straggling through Hampshire on our frivolous mission at such a grave time. Barring some mishap, I would be there late tonight, in between the wake and the funeral of a young man beloved by a tiny community with a flock of road angels.

Regina left to get ready for the wake, and Robert came back and drank a Corona with me. He said he'd often rather just stay at home with his grief, but it wasn't good for him. "I've lost my attention span since Ethan's death, so I try to keep really busy because when I'm not busy, I start thinking about things, and it's too much."

He told me what a great cook Ethan was, what a great baseball player he was, how kind he was to other people. "He'd loan his friends money, sometimes a lot of money, and I'd give him a hard time, but he was always like, 'I'll get it back, Dad. Don't worry.' He was chill and really liked helping people. A lot of people wrote after his death to say how important he had been—when they were the youngest on the baseball team and he had taken them under his wing or bought a meal for someone on the team who didn't have any money. Just on and on. He was a giver."

I heard about how Ethan had shot his first buck, a 15-point deer, bigger than anybody in the family had ever gotten. Robert introduced his sons and his daughter to hunting. When the kids were little, he'd let them sleep in the tree stand until he saw a deer; then he'd wake them up and let them shoot it. And that's how Ethan got his 15-point deer. They eat everything they kill: squirrels, rabbits, deer. And Robert is also a birder. He's got a bunch of hummingbird feeders, and he showed me a video of hummingbirds coming in on his porch.

I have friends who are anti-hunting, but the few times I've gone hunting—twice for dove and once for deer—it was the closest I've ever felt to nature, way closer than my many hikes. I think it's because with hunting there's so much stillness and quiet, so much waiting in the woods. You become one with the forest. Hiking in the woods doesn't impact me the same way as I move toward some destination. I didn't get a deer the day I went hunting for them, but I did shoot doves, and there was this weird disconnect. I loved the sport of waiting, targeting, and shooting the birds, but I was ashamed and repulsed by the birds I had killed. I didn't want to kill birds when I was faced with the birds on the ground, but when they were in the sky, I loved the challenge of hitting them.

I also loved the sense of community out in the woods with hunters: the food on a propane stove, the stories around the campfire, the sounds of the night while snuggled into sleeping bags. This is true of camping too, but growing up, I was always envious of my friends whose parents had hunting camps. During the season, they'd all go to the camps and hang out with the same folks in the woods every weekend, communing with nature and each other.

Despite my own squeamishness in the face of what I've killed, I'm *for* responsible hunting like the Brewers do. I don't have a lot of patience for hypocritical meat-eaters who are anti-hunting. Hunting is way more humane than factory farming, even considering the times that things go wrong for an animal. I had a feeling I'd have a great time hunting with the Brewers.

Robert and Regina had been hiking in the Grand Canyon when they got the news about Ethan's death. They flew home immediately and had to start learning to live life without him. They were still learning. By the time Robert and I finished our beers, I felt like I knew Ethan and had been friends with the Brewers for years.

At one point in the conversation, Robert asked me what kind of shoes I was wearing.

"Hokas," I said.

He glanced down at his own shoes. "I like my Brooks, but I just wish it wasn't such a liberal company."

I looked surprised because I was. "I didn't know it was a liberal company."

He nodded. "Yeah, yeah."

I had totally forgotten about the gulf between us until that comment. Here was a guy who was a stranger an hour ago, who'd taken amazingly good care of me when I was in a bad place. I liked him a lot. I liked Regina and the rest of the Brewer family I'd heard about— three boys, including Ethan, and a girl. I could imagine going hiking or hunting with them. They're good people. Interesting people. Generous people. Deep people. And almost certainly Trump supporters. I decided that the U.S. needed a lot more excuses for rightwing and leftwing people to sit behind a pickup truck, drink beer, tell each other their problems, and enjoy each other's company. I don't think we'd change each other's minds about politics, but I do think we could blur the fault lines that separate us, the ones threatening an American seismic catastrophe. Like Robert Frost, I don't believe that "good fences make good neighbors."

> *Before I built a wall I'd ask to know*
> *What I was walling in or walling out,*
> *And to whom I was like to give offense.*
> *Something there is that doesn't love a wall,*
> *That wants it down.*

Maybe chipping at the walls between us is as much as we can aspire to in this current political environment.

More Vol State folks were arriving, so I thanked Robert sincerely, and we headed into the church hall. I wasn't quite sure what Robert's connection to the church was—I didn't think he was a member, but he was a friend and was helping out Chris and Delana Bean, the pastor and his wife. We walked into a big room with tables, chairs, and one cot, which Terrie was already setting her stuff on. Robert told me that there was a room in the back with a couch that we could use, and I offered it to Terrie since all this was her doing. She preferred the cot, so I got the sofa just down the hall past the kitchen. I assumed they held church services in the back of the building, but I never saw that part.

"Delana said to help yourself to whatever you find in the kitchen," said Robert, "and there's a bathroom with a shower just off it." Amazing.

I got a little cleaned up, then checked out the kitchen and what was in the refrigerator. Lots of juice bottles and water. I opened the freezer and saw a big blue ice block. That could be useful.

I headed back to the little room with the couch, spread a ground cloth over it, and laid down with my feet on the blue ice block. My traumatized soles loved the cold. I couldn't sleep, though. There had been too much going on emotionally with the stories of Ethan and the boy from Hampshire. I was thinking too much. I texted with my Aunt Fran and Chris, and Chrissy kept coming in and asking me questions. Can we use the shower? She had a card with some money it in for the church. She wanted me to sign it. She wanted to know if I had left a headlamp back at Ruby's carport.

Then suddenly, Delana Bean, the young pastor's wife, was there in person. She was beside herself, worrying about how to take care of all these walkers who had now descended on the church. It had started out as just Terrie; then we grew like loaves and fishes. Delana was genuinely distraught about how to be as hospitable as possible.

"We want everyone here. We want to open it up next year and do a really good job with lots of cots and food, etc. I went to Walmart and bought some more towels for the shower and peanut butter crackers and tuna and Band-Aids. We'll be ready next year. We only just realized there were people in need, and we want to help. That's what we do!"

"Don't worry at all," I told her. "We're just grateful for anything. It's wonderful to have a place to rest. You've already gone above and beyond." They truly had.

On its website, the church calls itself "A haven for lost souls." That sounded pretty perfect for a bunch of Vol State racers. The church's "creed is 'To Enlist-To Arm-To Occupy!'" This sounded scarier to me, although, at the moment, I wouldn't begrudge anyone their creed who had air conditioning, a couch, and indoor plumbing. The website explained further: "Our desire is to not only see souls saved but to arm them with the word of God so that they may occupy the land." I wondered what Jesus would think about the militaristic lingo, but I was sure He would be well pleased with all they were doing for the Vol State community.

People could not have been kinder to us at the Central Christian Fellowship, but really, it was too much drama for my sleep-deprived half-mind. I did rest for a little while with my feet on the ice block, but I gave up pretty quickly and offered the couch and little room to Angela, who was seriously in a bad way with her possible stress fracture.

When I walked back into the big room, more folks had arrived. Tara was on the floor by the wall, softly crying. I asked if she wanted the ice block for her feet. She shook her head, and I patted her knee. What was there to say? I suspected she just needed to cry. There was plenty to cry about. And plenty to be grateful for.

I eventually got out of there. Chrissy was the pilot in charge of the place, getting everything done. If I had to fly in a combat zone, I'd be happy to have her piloting my helicopter. She was sitting on the front stoop of the church when I left and asked me for the third time if I had signed the card. I had. Now it was back to the white line.

I didn't have to walk far before I saw Ethan's Memorial up ahead on the left, just as Robert described, by the pine tree burnt from the explosion. In front of it, the red, white, and blue flowers surrounding a cross made of 4 x 4's inside a stone-paver heart, and stuck in the little memorial garden was an American flag with a graphic of an old baseball mitt and ball on it. Another cross hung on the tree, and a sign that said ETHAN with a cross for the "t" leaned up against it. I took a picture of the memorial and posted it on the Vol State FB page with the message, "Thinking of Ethan" and a little angel emoji. I'd come to feel the loss of a young man I never knew, but somehow I also felt his presence. Maybe Tony was right: "This race has angels all over the place."

Thinking of Ethan Brewer: July 2, 1998
– Oct. 8, 2021.

Chapter 10

A BRAIN-DAMAGED STRAY DOG RELYING ON THE GOODNESS OF STRANGERS

"A smile and a wave works the same in every neighborhood.
So, if you want to renew your faith in humanity,
and you want to renew your faith in the country,
walk across it and put yourself dependent
on the kindness of strangers."
—Lazarus Lake (*Conversations with Tyler* podcast)

Yet more road-angel magic

The walk into Hampshire seemed longer than 15 miles, but at least Highway 412 had a good shoulder. While it was still light, a blue hatchback pulled over, and the passenger window rolled down. A woman asked if I'd like a cold drink. Definitely! I was pretty sure I'd seen this woman before, but it wasn't until she, her mother, and her daughter got out that I remembered I'd met them at Pam Pratt's second angel stop. They were the trio getting ready to drive in one direction on the Vol State route to help runners, then spend the night and drive back the same route. I can't explain how lovely it is to be walking a long, lonely highway in the middle of nowhere, sleep-deprived and hot, and have some friendly faces stop and offer you cold drinks. Just having someone to talk to for a few minutes is also great. I can't quite imagine HOTS, where the road angels are much fewer and farther between. I loved that these three generations of women were bonding with each other in this selfless mission. And I liked that the little girl was getting to see what mad adventures were possible in this life.

I realized how messed up my mind was when I asked their names so I could write them down in my notes. "Leanna, Amy, and Amelia," Leanna said.

And when I went to write them down, all I could remember was Leanna. "I'm sorry. Can I ask again your names?" "Leanna, Amy, and Amelia."

I got down Amy, but I couldn't remember the last name. "One more time, please. I'm sorry. The sleep deprivation has messed up my short-term memory. What's your name?" I asked the little girl.

"Amelia."

There. I got all three names in three tries. I felt like I was brain-damaged. I suppose I was. It was strange how the sleep deprivation worked. I could keep walking and carry on coherent conversations when called for, but my short-term memory shriveled, and my math skills went into hibernation. It was crazy how difficult it was for me to do simple math problems, like figuring out how many miles I had to go before I could sleep if I was at Mile 152 and Hampshire was at Mile 161. The gap between 152 and 161 seemed like some sort of riddle that I'd try to puzzle it out in various ways. I understood how easy this would be in my normal life, but it took me a long time to figure out on the road. And my degree of confidence when I finally landed on a number? *Somewhat.*

Leanna, Amy, and Amelia, the youngest road angel.

I thanked the road angels and got back to walking. It was check-in time.

108-Hour Tracker, comments in italics (Monday evening, July 17, 2023)

Me: 153 miles—*"Day drinking a road-angel beer definitely led to a favorable attitude adjustment!"* A dozen miles ahead of Oprah.

Anonymous: *"Nearly had an orgasm massaging my feet."* Vol State sex talk.

Anonymous: *"Just outside Columbia, I grabbed one of the popsicles. As I was struggling to open it, a lady pulled up to see if we needed anything. I said only if you have scissors in your pocket. Well she reached in her pocket and there they were."*

Sadly, Bill dropped out between Linden and Hohenwald. Regina continued. Similarly, Angela bowed out of the race at the church, and Chrissy went on without her.

Soon it was twilight. Mercifully, the sun would give me a break from its relentless 10-hour beating.

Suddenly a dark blur startled me, jumping out of the woods on my left. I could tell by the movement that it was a deer. A fawn! And it was heading out onto the road. I realized our kinship. We were both trying not to get hit by a car, but I had slightly more common sense.

The fawn was trying to get across the road. *Oh, my gosh. Don't go. He's going. He's going. I think he's going to make it. Yes, but now he's standing around in the far lane.* "GO ON!!!" I screamed. "GET OUT OF HERE! JUMP OVER. YOU CAN DO IT! ATTABOY!" There. He bounded up the hill on the other side of the highway while I was still down with the traffic, only smart enough to stay on the shoulder and not veer onto the lane. In normal life, I was the one in the car, trying not to hit the deer. At Vol State, I *was* the deer.

In another moment, a bigger deer crashed out of the woods and across the highway—a doe chasing her runaway fawn. I yelled at her too. "GO! GET ACROSS! KEEP GOING!" She made it more easily. I'd done my good deeds for the day.

And then the fireflies started blinking their luminous greetings. I'd hoped to see them on this trek, and now they were out in fairy armies as if a Disney set designer had popped them into the trees to add magical whimsy. Despite all my whining, Vol State did have its moments.

It was a little after 9:00 and dark when I saw in the distance the silhouette of something on the side of the road. It looked like a giant snowman's hat, no doubt my distorted mind.

As I got closer, I realized that it was a vehicle. I wondered if this was the beginning of a *Deliverance* story, some local yokels waiting to scare the stupid woman wandering the highway alone after dark. Why would a truck be on the side of the road at night? Probably lots of reasons, but I could only think of the nefarious ones. A drug deal? A drunk driver taking a nap? A sadistic psychopath lying in wait?

No civilization was around.

Then a light went on in the truck. Two people stepped out of either side of the cab. Unbelievable.

I recognized them: Robert and Regina. They drove all the way here?

And they'd been waiting patiently. "We could see your lamp for a long way off down the road, but it took you a long time to get here," said Robert.

I grinned. It was so great to see them. Most of the time, you only see road angels once at Vol State, but running into what felt like old friends was special.

They had chairs out behind the truck. I got a water with a Propel and a Mandarin Orange. We chatted about Regina's teaching job. She teaches math to seventh and eighth graders, at the tiny Hampshire Unit School, a PK-12 public school with only 36 people in the eighth-grade class. Eighteen seniors graduated that summer. "They're all together," she said, "and the older ones take care of the little ones." She had taught 6th grade for years and loved middle-school-aged kids. Thank goodness teachers are called to all different ages of students. Middle school seemed like the most challenging age to me.

Robert talked more about the Mammoth March, a popular 20-mile walk on Shelby Farms Park trails in Memphis, as well as some other hikes and runs they'd done. He kept mentioning how much he enjoyed a beer at the end of a long hike till finally I said, "You know, you've been talking so much about beer. I think I'd like one." So, he popped open a couple of Coronas for us, we clinked bottles, and once again, I pretended that I was drinking behind a pickup truck with old friends out on a highway and didn't have 165-odd miles to walk over the next five days or so.

"You guys have some really great coolers in Tennessee," I told Robert. Folks here are serious about coolers. They can be the size of a couch. In England, you're lucky to see a soft-sided shoulder-strap cooler that holds a six-pack and a cucumber sandwich.

"Yeah," he said, "people always want to borrow your cooler. You've got to put your name on it. Then, when they forget that they borrowed it from you, you can show them with the name."

In Tennessee, people know how to keep things cold because in July, it's still hot, even at night. Not hot like it was in the afternoon but still plenty sweltering. Tennessee folks value cold.

I asked what sort of insect music I was listening to in the dark—crickets? cicadas?

"Probably katydids," said Regina.

"And the occasional bullfrog?" I asked.

"Probably tree frogs," she said. I had no doubt she knew what she was talking about.

I finally had to get back into race mode and say my goodbyes to the Brewers—no doubt they needed to get back home and go to bed. What a sacrifice they'd made coming out to wait for me! And I needed to get to Hampshire.

I thanked them profusely. It was great to sit here and chat and pretend like life was normal, pretend that I didn't have to hike back into the darkness. They climbed into their truck and drove back down the highway toward Hohenwald.

Predictably, it wasn't long before I had to pee and managed to find a little place behind a guard rail. I turned off my light, and it was totally dark except for a hint of ambient light over the distant hills. When I pulled my shorts back up, they felt wet. I must've missed some of the ground and hit the shorts instead. Unbelievably gross in normal life. As a stray dog at Vol State, I figured they'd dry in a few miles . . . maybe.

I stopped off at a tent beside the road that had chairs and a cooler. I got water and signed the guestbook on a box of medical supplies. Plenty of folks expressed their gratitude, but I couldn't believe the number of Vol Staters who had just put their name and the city they were from in the guestbook without even saying thanks. It made me wonder how entitled we had gotten with so many people taking care of us. That's just what Republicans say happens if the government gives too many handouts. People become ungrateful and entitled. I was still full of thanks, but I could see what the rightwing meant.

I didn't think I was ever going to get to Hampshire. I walked and walked. At one point, I saw a cooler on the side of the road lit by an outdoor spotlight in the grass. A mirage? No, the real thing. Written in marker on the top of the Igloo cooler: "LAVS Good Luck [heart shape] The Mayberrys." Anyone could've come along and stolen the cooler or the outdoor spotlight, but they hadn't. *Thank you, Mayberrys!*

Highway 412 narrowed into two lanes at one point, and I knew Hampshire Pike had a big lefthand turn coming up, but I accidentally took a left on Ridgetop Rd just before it. I walked up a hill for a couple hundred yards before realizing my error and heading back down to the route. I was just glad I hadn't gone farther off course. Hampshire itself was up on a hill, so there was still plenty of climbing. At night, though, figuring out the road's contours is harder because all you know is the white circle in front of you.

After midnight, I was looking for the firehouse in Hampshire, which I'd heard was up on a hill just before the town and was open for Vol Staters. By the time I got to the quaint residential part of Hampshire—a *Mayberry R.F.D.* kind of town—I knew I must've missed it. Still, I'd heard that someone named Holly Anderson had a house with tents and air mattresses in the front yard, and suddenly, there they were. She'd left her porch light on and had a portable refrigerator with drinks, a charging station with USB ports, snacks, medical supplies, and an air mattress on the porch, along with a couple of fans with extension cords. A sign on the porch told me I could take one of the fans into a tent. That was an innovative idea, and I decided to try it.

A Hampshire godsend on a hot night.

The sign on the porch also said, "The post office is open. It has air conditioning. You can use an air mattress to sleep on there. Just bring it back and be out by 7 am." Wow. This was the kind of hospitality that made me want to cry. I didn't have the energy to take an air mattress to the post office, but I loved the idea and the trust.

First, though, I had to pee and couldn't figure out where to do it. The sign on the porch and another one on the mailbox said, "There are bathrooms past the bridge in behind the church on right by school." I hadn't the slightest idea where any of that was, so I walked down the street a bit farther. I didn't see the bridge, so I was looking for any dark place with a tree that I could hide behind and pee, but it was all houses and mostly lit ones. I walked back to the Holly's house. They had a dark side yard with a hedge, and I thought, well, I'll head for that. I got about 15 feet before the neighbor's motion-detector light came on and flooded the whole area. Damn! I felt like I was in some crazy comedy sketch.

The only place I could find that seemed dark, secluded, and close was between the tent and the plants that grew up on the lot line. So, that's where I peed, which seemed lousy to do at a house that's so unbelievably hospitable to Vol State. But by then, I HAD to go. I didn't have an alternative except to pee in my pants or under a streetlight. Desperate times call for desperate measures.

I pulled the fan into one of the tents and had it on for a little while until it got too cold, even though it wasn't cold out—maybe 70 degrees in the middle of the night—My skin was clammy and salty and gross—a film of filth over it. I got into my little faux-silk sleeping liner and set my alarm for 4:30. Somehow, I faded off for a few hours and woke up on my own. My watch had gone flat, but my phone told me it was 4:20 am. I took the watch up to plug into a charger on the porch while I got my belongings repacked into my running vest so that I could leave. Tony had come in at some point and was fast asleep on his back, fully clothed on the air mattress under the bright light of the porch. I tried to be as quiet as I could.

As I was packing up in the tent, I heard an alarm go off on the porch. Tony must've set it for himself. But the alarm kept going, and I kept wondering why Tony hadn't turned it off. Surely he could hear it.

Suddenly, it dawned on me—that was MY alarm! Like Lazarus, my dead watch had come to life with the charge and sounded the alarm I had programmed earlier to make sure I didn't oversleep. I was truly the Vol State house guest from hell. I rushed out of the tent and back up to the porch.

Poor Tony was by now fully awake and ready to go. I apologized profusely. Zombie-like, he waved me off and hit the road again. I felt terrible.

It took me forever to get all my stuff packed in the tent with just my little light. In a parallel universe somewhere, I am an organized, efficient packer. I was heading back to the porch to write a thank-you note to the homeowner in the guest book when a woman pulled up in the driveway and carried a toddler up to the door.

I assumed it was the woman who owned the place. "Do you live here?" I asked.

"No, I'm the babysitter."

The woman who answered the door and took the boy said to me, "Well, did you get any sleep?"

"I got a little bit. I was just about to write you a note. I felt like a stray dog today who had been adopted by a really nice family, but then at 4:30 am, my former owner, Laz, sent out an alarm and told me I had to keep going."

She said, "Really?"

Clearly my analogy made no sense at all to her. It made perfect sense to me in my brain-addled state. "No, no no. I'm just kidding about Laz, but my alarm went off, and unfortunately, I've got to get moving again. You have such a great place. Thank you so much."

She was very kind to the idiot I was.

"Are you a newbie?" she asked.

"I am."

"I'll pray for you."

"Thanks."

I'm not much on petitionary prayers—I trust God to take care of things or not on His or Her or Their own, without being petty enough to make decisions after tallying up the prayers for and against—but by this point, if somebody wanted to pray for my discombobulated self, I was fine with it. Couldn't hurt.

And then I was back on the road, just as scummy and filthy as I had been when I got in the tent last night. Probably more so. I didn't brush my teeth. I hadn't even found the running water that was outside the house. So, yeah, a terrible night, but a really sweet angel stop in a town filled with so much real, as opposed to conjured-up, hardship and heartache. God knows why I'm doing this.

Ed Masouka, the retired NASA guy, had walked by in his bee-keeper's costume while I was getting ready. *How in the world did he keep those white clothes looking mostly clean after four days of this nonsense?* And poor Tony was up ahead somewhere too. Still mortified that I'd ruined what little sleep he was getting in the early morning, I knew I had to let it go. I couldn't fix it. All I could do was put in more miles before check-in.

Walking downhill from Hampshire, I had to say that miraculously, even after a terrible sleep by almost any measure, my body had rebounded. I felt so much better. My feet felt better. My legs felt better. Everything felt better. That's one of the most amazing things about these goofy ultra races. With a journey race like this, you get to pay money on purpose to see how quickly the body can rejuvenate itself from an abyss. This is so much easier than learning the lesson through war or urgent emigration or the apocalypse. You think you need a lot more to replenish yourself than you actually do. Once it realizes what hardship is happening, the body can be miraculously efficient at getting its act together quickly and taking what little it can—nutrition, liquid, sleep—and magically turning it into something like normality, something like health. But the body doesn't do it when you first abuse it. At the initial signs of too much physical activity, the muscles and joints get sore and demand a good night's sleep and a square meal. It's only after you repeatedly deny the body these basic repair functions and subject it to ever more tough love and misery that it finally understands that normal recovery help isn't possible. Then it starts bucking up, taking what scraps it can get, and going into overdrive repair. This is fortunate, or people like me, undertrained newbies, would never be able to keep going in this race. It's also why everyone says not to drop out during the first three days. The body wants you to think that things will never get better until you properly rest, but it's lying to you.

On the multiple uses of a frozen water bottle

About 6:30 am, I met up with Gina Kimrey, a 53-year-old from Greensboro. We were doing our stray dog thing, scrounging for food and drink at an angel station under a couple of trees in the front yard of an otherwise tidy home, owned by the Butters according to their welcome sign. Just then, a sleepy guy came out the front door and gave us each a frozen water. We thanked him. He added a couple more to the cooler and walked back into the house.

I had no idea there were so many uses for frozen water. First of all, I put it on my neck. That was pretty great! Then I stuck it in my cleavage. Oooo! Then under my hoodie, across my shoulders, held up by my running vest. Ahhhhh. This was just fabulous. These are the things that the veterans forget to tell you. I'd seen frozen waters before, but I was never sure what to do with them except wait until they melted enough to drink.

I saw Ed up ahead, walking slower than usual, and I knew he couldn't have gotten a frozen water bottle from the sleepy angel, so I gave him mine as I passed. I hoped he would enjoy it as much as I had.

Gina Kimrey and Ed Masuoka take a rest between Hampshire and Columbia. The veteran has gravitated to shade.

I don't know if it was karma, but shortly after I gave Ed the frozen water, I came upon a random cooler by the road. I looked in, sad to find a number of melted popsicles. Just then a road-angel woman walked over from her house with a new supply of frozen ones. These folks wake up in the morning and first thing, come out to replenish their angel supplies?

There is no doubt—happiness is a frozen purple popsicle.

Columbia is 15 miles from Hampshire, and when I finally got to the outskirts, I stopped at a Fast Stop Convenience Store, my only commercial stop since Hohenwald, and got to sit with Tony for a few minutes. He was still speaking to me despite my watch alarm waking him up.

Top of my agenda was brushing my teeth for the first time in 30 hours. I'm not sure if ever in my life, including lots of primitive backpacking, I'd gone that long without brushing my teeth. Why hadn't I brushed them at the church in Hohenwald? Maybe I forgot. Besides, stray dogs don't brush their teeth--why should I? Because brushing my teeth in that gas station bathroom felt like the ultimate luxury—like Louis Vuitton, Dom

Perignon, Rolex, and Lamborghini all rolled up into one sumptuous, cleansing experience.

120-Hour Tracker, comments in italics (Tuesday morning, July 18, 2023)

Me: 167 miles--*"Early this morning, I officially morphed from a human to a stray dog. I got adopted by a sweet family in Hampshire. Unfortunately, my abusive former owner (whose name rhymes with Razz) found out where I was, set an alarm for 4:30 am, and screamed, 'You get on home!!' The family was nice while they lasted."* I was determined to milk this story. Maybe it would work better in print. I was 10 miles ahead of Oprah.

Anonymous: *"Don't do drugs kids. Hope the guy who ODed in the hotel room next door in Columbia made it another day. Wish I was kidding."*

Anonymous: *"I miss my family. Today's soundtrack is 'Just Breathe' by Pearl Jam."*

I finally reached the "Welcome to Columbia / Old South Charm / New South Progress" sign. It always seemed like a long time between the welcome sign for a town and the town itself, but eventually, I got to some commercial civilization. I would have to walk through Columbia to get to the Richland Inn on the other end of the city where I'd booked a room. I wasn't very far into civilization before I heard a woman yell from behind me, "Hey, are you in that Vol State race?"

I guess I had that look. I turned around. "Yep."

"My husband and I have been following it. How are you're doing?"

I told her I was OK but was looking for a place to eat lunch. "You know anything about the Red 7 Pizza Co. I just passed?"

"It's good," she said. "I'm meeting my husband there now for lunch."

"Would you mind if I joined you?" Perhaps a bit unseemly to invite myself to eat with folks who regularly showered, but having just brushed my teeth, I was brimming with social confidence, and besides, she was the one who'd started the conversation.

"Not at all," she said.

Red 7 Pizza was one of those fast-casual, create-your-own pizza places with a hotter-than-hell oven that cooked your customized pizza in a nanosecond. We sat at a 6-top, and I put an empty chair between me and my new friend Christy and apologized for smelling bad. I didn't want to put her off her lunch—her husband sat on the other side. The two of them had been following the race, but all they knew about was the tracker. They didn't know about the comments on the tracker or the FB page with all the behind-the-scenes stuff. Christy was totally interested; her husband was kind of quiet, probably wondering how Christy landed this smelly, dirty woman at their table. They said grace before the meal. I waited, then gratefully tucked into my pepperoni-mushroom-sausage-extra cheese-and-pesto pizza just as a major thunderstorm blew in. *It must be my lucky day!* Christy and her husband had to leave to get back to work before the rain let up, but I was content to have another diet Coke and wait it out.

"Thanks for letting me join you and for saving me from the storm," I said.

"Good luck to you," said Christy. I could use plenty of that.

When I got back on the road, the sun was busy evaporating all the water the storm had dumped. Laz says we get a chance to go through rain twice: once when it's coming down and once with humidity as it heads back up. It was 91 degrees, but the mugginess made it feel much worse. Still, air conditioning, a bath, and sleep were in my very near future, so I couldn't complain. Up ahead was the Maury County Courthouse, an imposing limestone Neoclassical building with a cupula clock tower watching over Vol State racers as they turn right and head down Columbia's Main Street. Farther along the town square, I noticed Hattie Jane's Creamery and couldn't resist stopping in for a chocolate malted milkshake.

While waiting in line, a guy asked me if I was doing Vol State. It turned out to be Chris Roach, who'd done the race in 2021. "Did you enjoy it?" I asked.

"Yeah, I enjoyed it . . .well, no, I didn't actually enjoy it, but I'm thinking about doing another one. When I did it, I was like, one and done. I'm never doing it again. But now I'm gearing up again and trying to figure out if I can get some time off to do it."

I had to laugh. I don't know what overcomes people, why they want to do this infernal race more than once, but something seems to. It had not bitten me yet, whatever it was. I will thoroughly enjoy following the race from England next year and seeing who does what, and maybe I'll have just a little FOMO while they're doing it, but then I'll remember days like this.

The Richland Inn was over two miles from Red 7 Pizza, and it felt all of that and more, even with the milkshake chaser. I opened the lobby door at 2:30 pm and hit a blessed wall of air conditioning. I walked past a woman in tie-dyed spandex pants and wondered for a second if she could be a Vol State racer, but who would wear spandex pants past their knees for this event? I told the front-desk clerk my name and said I had a reservation through Booking.com. I had already booked the room and paid for it. She looked up my reservation and told me I'd have to pay for it again and get the money back from Booking.com because the "virtual card" (whatever that was!) wasn't coming through. That sounded fishy and way more trouble than I wanted to go through to get money back from anybody, so I called the support number for Booking.com and talked to a very nice lady in India.

I sat in the lobby while all the logistics were being worked out, and the next thing I knew, the woman in spandex was lying on the floor in the back of the lobby, and the front desk clerk was yelling, "You can't lie down in here! You can't lie down on the floor of the lobby!"

The woman ignored her. The front-desk clerk lowered her voice and boomed again in slow time: "You ... cannot ..... lie down...on the floor... of the lobby... in *my* hotel!" Hmmm. She was very proprietary. I wondered if it really was her hotel. The woman on the floor was evidently a vagrant, looking for a way to get out of the heat and a place to rest, and she was happy enough to ignore the desk clerk.

The front-desk woman kept giving her a hard time from behind the safety of the front desk, and I couldn't help but think just how similar I was to the woman lying on the floor. I'm much more privileged because I can afford to get a hotel room when there is one, and when there's not one, I'm also more privileged because all kinds of people make places available for me just because I'm doing this crazy race. They leave fans and chargers on their front porch and pitch tents in their front yard. This woman was actually trying to live her life, not a game. My guess was that she might have some mental problems—another way in which I was privileged; my mental problems were mainly of the sleep-deprivation-induced kind, and people were willing to feel sorry for me and cut me slack because of the race.

Then again, maybe her problems were drug-induced. That seemed possible too, and somehow that made it seem more like her own fault, but was that really true? What if she'd gotten injured or had surgery and had taken prescribed pain pills until she found herself worshipping the Big-Pharma opioid deity? What if she'd been born into abject poverty and an abusive family and had none of the privileges I'd had growing up? What if she had just been seduced by a little chemical happiness?

As I sat waiting for the world to solve my accommodation problem because I had the money they wanted, I wondered what we should be doing as a country to help people like this woman. I had no clue, but what I did know was that we weren't doing enough. And what I also knew was that *I* wasn't doing enough. I didn't invite the woman to share my hotel room, so I'm obviously part of the majority who will sit back and let someone else figure out how to deal with it.

I was struck by the outpouring of grassroots help for Vol State and this crazy reality-video game we're in. If only there were some way to make the people experiencing homelessness part of some larger game where other people would feel like they had a real stake in their well-being. The problem is as old as human existence, but there must be better ways to deal with it.

I was literally a walking contradiction, wondering why we couldn't all take care of each other at the same time that I was clearly unwilling to take care of this woman and give her a place to rest and get out of the heat, even though I could empathize with her plight much more than the front-desk clerk could.

And why was I so reluctant to help? The biggest reason is that I was kind of scared of her. She didn't seem stable. I had no idea what she might do in my hotel room. Another reason is that I'm selfish. I wanted to make sure I had enough peace to get some rest and do what I needed to do to help myself get ready to continue the race without having to worry about someone worse off than me.

It doesn't seem fair that Vol State racers get SOOO much help. And people LOVE to help us. They do it out of the goodness of their heart, and they do it with such joy. Why aren't we like that with people who need our help much more than the privileged, elective adventurers of Vol State? What does Vol State have that we could transform and put in place for the country itself?

I don't know. I do know that once people figure out that we're in a race—that we have elected to temporarily become tired, hungry, thirsty, and smelly—they're often intrigued by us and rarely scared of us. Something about life or destiny making people tired, hungry, thirsty, or smelly makes people more suspicious, more cautious. People worry that those people might have brought the situation on themselves. They worry that handouts might enable these people to live on the streets and not become productive members of society.

When folks found out we were in a race, they assumed, probably correctly, that we were productive members of society, citizens like them who were paying our dues, but we also seemed to be inspirational because of our feats of fortitude and bravery. Does one need less fortitude to be homeless, less bravery? Are people tougher and more courageous if they choose an adventure of their own free will and pay for it instead of having life thrust it upon them? Or do Vol Staters just seem more familiar and less scary?

Booking.com ended up calling the manager of the Richland Inn, and they got my room all worked out. My problem was solved, but unfortunately, the woman in spandex would have to figure out how to get sleep and cool on her own.

Chapter 11

ON DESPAIR AND LITTERBUGS

—Lazarus Lake email to Vol Staters

Blisters and Kings

My room at the Richland was beautiful, but I didn't get much sleep. I got myself and my clothes cleaned up. Then this HUGE thunderstorm rolled in, *way* bigger than the one I ate pizza through—thunder, lightning, rain driving sideways, the whole bit. I was hoping that nobody I knew was out on the course at that point, but what were the chances? I'm sure lots of folks got caught in it. I wondered where the woman in spandex was spending the storm.

I'd been amazingly lucky at avoiding the worst of the torrents on this trip. How long would my luck last? They were calling for more rain at about 9 that night. My aunt Fran had been checking the weather reports in Columbia and warning me of what was ahead.

I hoped to get to the Nutt House, a famous road-angel stop about 8 miles away. It's run by the Nutt family, who built an outdoor toilet and shower specially for Vol State. The name seemed apt, but they were the best kind of Nutts! First, though, the Bench of Despair was only about five miles away, so that was another thought. I could potentially get some sleep at the Nutt House or wait for the storm to pass at either of those places.

My right inside heel blister that was getting worse and worse. It was about the size of a nickel at that point. It wasn't yet excruciating, but I knew it was only a matter of time. I looked through *Fixing Your Feet* on my phone Kindle app but couldn't figure out what I should do, probably because my IQ had dropped severely since this race started, and simple tasks had become confusing. I ended up texting Jan. I told her everything I'd done the few times I'd drained the blister, put Neosporin on it, patched it up, and taped it.

She texted right back with advice: "Stop putting Neosporin on it. Use Desitin. Neosporin won't dry it up. The zinc in Desitin will." This seemed like important information that would've been good to have about 30 years ago. She went on to tell me to cut a "V" in the roof of the blister to keep it draining so it wouldn't close back up (which was what kept happening when I lanced the blister with one prick of a needle. Somewhere in the recesses of what was left of my brain, I remembered reading about this "V" in *Fixing Your Feet).* Jan said to get Desitin to rub on it and in it. A dab on top would keep a hydrocolloid bandage from sticking. Then she explained how to put the Leukotape K over that from the bottom of my foot to my ankle like a stirrup. "If you have an ENGO patch that will fit where your heel is rubbing, put that in your shoe. When you walk, keep your foot pointed straight. That will help keep your heel from pushing on your shoe."

This was exactly the clear-headed information I needed. Unfortunately, I'd thrown out my Desitin early on because I'd decided it was just duplicating my Squirrel's Nut Butter. And I didn't have any hydrocolloid gel bandages. I'd never had good luck with them because my blister would always fill back up underneath the bandage, and I didn't know about the Desitin dab to keep from tearing off the blister's roof when I removed the bandage. The "V" and the Desitin made sense, and I did have an ENGO patch, which looks like it could be a kid's egg-shaped blue sticker. When you pay $17 for six of those and get them in the mail, you're sure it's a scam, but if Jan believed in them, they've got to be good. I was grateful for her sharp thinking. I knew she wasn't getting a lot of sleep during this race either, having to shuttle the DNFs around and check on Vol Staters along the way.

Just a few blocks away was a Dollar General, and it seemed better to get the footcare stuff while I had a cool, clean place to deal with the blister. The rain had mostly stopped, so I walked up to the DG and found Desitin and a lighter to sterilize the baby scissors I would use to make the "V," but no Hydrocolloid patches. Oh, well. The next town was Lewisburg, 22 long miles away. I'd get the patches there.

> **132-Hour Tracker, comments in italics** (Tuesday evening, July 18, 2023)
>
> Me: 179 miles----*"I'm letting Oprah walk through the raging storms without me."* Oprah was gaining on me, only six miles behind.
>
> Anonymous: *"Just my luck the roofers kept working through the rain and the icing on the cake was their standing outside and talking loudly. So much for a little sleep at the Richland Inn."* Someone else was having trouble sleeping at the Richland.
>
> Anonymous: *"The road to Shelbyville was blazing hot today. Until the clouds. Getting blacker. Bringing heavy humidity and elevating the feels-like temp even without any sun. Then suddenly the wind blew up, leaves went flying, the temperature dropped about 20°, and the thunderstorm hit. What a day! Tennessee is awesome!!"*

The Richland Inn ended up being more of a base for clean-up, patch-up, and communications, and in the end, I only got about 2 hours of sleep. Still, I couldn't overestimate the value of having a hotel room during that dreadful storm. Photos started popping up on Facebook, showing the damage to various angel stops. The Bailey's spectacular tent at Mile 230, complete with running lights leading up to it, was in tatters. Other tents had suffered a similar fate, and Laz and Carl had apparently been battling the elements at the Rock. Laz's 132-hour update included,

> *today featured heat.*
> *tonight featured a huge storm that swept the field.*
> *including the finish line.*
>
> .
>
> *a small victory on the day was keeping the tents standing at*
> *the finish.*

I left Columbia about 11:30 pm. I wasn't very happy to be on the road, but it didn't really matter. My preferences were immaterial, and even though I had a beautiful hotel room that would've been great to spend the night in, sleeping through whatever rain was heading our way, maybe watching a little TV if I woke up . . . but no. Laz and Oprah still owned my life for four and a half more days minus four hours. So, I kept walking. I only had six miles on Oprah now, but I wouldn't have wanted to be out in that storm, so I was happy enough to concede the miles. She was impervious to storms, heat, sleep deprivation. *Click click click.*

Meanwhile, in the front of the pack, it was all fun and games. Ken Zemach and Bob Hearn, respectively the new King of the Road and the course-record-holding King of the Road, must've gotten a little sleep after their Day-4 finishes and then gone full doolally. Their first Facebook post was in front of the Mountain Mart, near Jasper, each wearing a Burger King crown and singing (a cappella) this parody of Roger Miller's "King of the Road," complete with finger snapping and dance moves you'd expect from MIT PhD's. In the video, Addison Hendricks sits on the asphalt behind them, fixing his feet and trying not to laugh.

> *Fast drivin' pick-up trucks*
> *Sketch hotel, 50 bucks*
> *No crew, no hope, regrets*
> *While Laz smokes his cigarettes*
>
> *Two AM it kinda sucks*
> *Hallucination Peking Ducks*
> *Running man of means by no means*
> *King of the Road*
>
> *Got chafing on my cock*
> *Destination kiss the Rock*
> *This race will make ya' hard*
> *Just lost my credit card*
>
> *Road angel awesome shock*
> *No toilet paper, lose a sock*
> *Running man of means by no means*
> *King of the Road!*

Music video complete, these two embarked on what Ken called the "Vagrants on the Highway" tour. Ever in their Burger King crowns, they drove backward along the course and stopped to applaud and have their pictures made with amused Vol Staters still in the race. Somewhere along the way, the kings separated to encourage more sleep-deprived subjects.

Bob posted "More Vagrants on the Highway," then Ken posted "Vagants III: Rise of the Unwashed." Lots of fun photos and captions of the kings and surprised participants. All this silliness cheered up those still suffering, in person and on Facebook. I was so far back in the pack that we would've needed Vagrants V or VI for them to make it all the way to us. No doubt the Royal Guards stopped the kings from traveling too far afield.

You can see how Facebook gives a skewed idea of how fun this race is. Those guys, instead of just sleeping and recuperating, were out giving hugs and kudos to others in the pack, spurring them on—incredibly generous. It certainly gave the race a family feel—and to think that they'd just spent three-plus days competing with each other under horrible conditions! So many ways to blur the lines of division in this world.

It was barely sprinkling when I left the Richland Inn. Lots of puddles, but the sky was calm-ish and the earth was sated for the moment. I wore my Walmart emergency rain poncho and carried my expensive umbrella, which was a pain because I could only use one hiking stick, making me feel lopsided. Preferences. Preferences. They just don't matter as much as we think they do. This was one of the things I loved most about long-distance endurance trips. In the normal world, I spend a lot of time trying to align life with my preferences. *Do I feel like tacos or a tuna roll? Do I want to do yoga before work or after? Which Netflix movie best matches my mood?* Hours, days, years fill up with catering to our preferences or, if we're generous or people pleasing or have small children, other people's preferences. The more privileged we are, the more time we spend catering to preferences, and when we can't manage them, we whine and whinge. Some of us, anyway.

Me, I mean.

All this reverence for preferences works even less well on Vol State. One's preferences are foiled at almost every moment, and feeling whiny just makes everything worse. Which is not to say I didn't whine a lot, especially to Chris, but at my best, I just did what I had to do to get to the next town, road-angel stop, convenience store, check-in, or motel. I don't know that he puts it this way, but Lazarus Lake is a big believer in dismantling people's preferences, except for the preference to majorly challenge oneself. His Vol State game makes moving beyond preferences easier or at least a lot more likely.

On the way out of Columbia, I ran into Paul and Gretchen. She was getting something out of the cooler in the back of his car. Mary Cruse had passed the crewing baton to Paul now that he was out of the race. I said hello to them both, but there's an invisible wall between crewed and screwed runners. It's like being the poor kids watching the rich kids get ready for the cotillion. Neither group really has much to say to the other. The wall is woven with embarrassment, desire, envy, and privilege. A classic haves-and-have-nots story. It's not just that we sort of resent them for having so much help. It's also them realizing that they shouldn't flaunt the help they're getting and maybe should be a little sheepish about it. To the rest of the world, it doesn't matter much whether you're crewed or screwed—it's still an insane race where everyone has to go 314 miles on their own two feet. But the racers feel the difference keenly. I didn't wish I were crewed, but I sort of wished the crewed category didn't exist. Besides seeing normal people all day long focused as best they can on comfort, I also had to see Vol State competitors who have someone whose whole job is catering to their preferences. Maybe this is just another great way for Laz to add misery to a screwed journey run. I take back my wish that the crewed category didn't exist. Still, I missed my preferences mattering to anyone except the road angels. But *wishing* and *missing* are just more preferences. Sigh.

This must be a little the way HOTS runners look at Vol State runners, except they're not together in time and space. Everyone at HOTS is truly screwed because the route is secret. It's announced to the runners the night before it starts, but they aren't allowed to disseminate the route, so spectators only figure out the route when the frontrunners have passed through that area. The screwed HOTS runners still get help, which is, after all, the way the human condition works—we all get help along the way, just some of us more than others, some of us a lot more than others. At HOTS, random road angels start to figure things out as they meet up with the competitors, so the back-of-the-packers tend to get more help from generous folks who've met runners up front and decided to help. Even so, HOTS is nothing like Vol State, where there's a veritable army of angels trying to cater to our preferences. As in life, there are always people better off than you and always people worse off than you, so I shouldn't judge. Even if they get more chairs, ice, and popsicles, crewed runners still have to walk 314 miles in 10 days, and it's actually harder for them mentally because they can quit anytime they want. Plus, they end up worrying about their crew, whose job is boring, selfless, and sleep-deprived.

I asked Paul how he was doing. I felt more kinship for a screwed runner who had dropped than a crewed runner who was still in.

"I'm disappointed that I had to quit," he said. "I got to a point where I was just too wobbly and dangerous, and the motel was across the street. I decided it was time to pull the plug."

I felt bad for him, but it was great of him to stay in the game by crewing. Clearly, Mary and Paul had been doing good work. Gretchen was making great time. "She walks really well at night," said Paul.

I walked on. At some point, I saw Laz's updated Facebook post: "Just so you know, we've had the first trash DQ." Like me, many people wondered what sort of Blizzard he was talking about from Dairy Queen. But no, apparently, somebody had gotten disqualified for littering, which I'm totally for. I'm even more radical than that. I'm for jail time for purposeful litterers. Let everybody out for marijuana use, and sub in all the litterbugs. Still, I wondered who it was. It would be pretty terrible to do all this work and not get a sticker.

It had quit sprinkling, so I happily took off my emergency poncho, which was plenty hot despite its flimsiness. I was about five miles outside of Columbia with only my chest lamp and the katydids for company when I saw the silhouette of a car parked up ahead on my side of the road. The dark alone wasn't scary to me, but random parked vehicles in the middle of the night spooked me. Still, there was nothing to do if someone in the car had villainous intentions. Was I going to turn around? Hell no, I'd just have to walk the same route again. Was I going to call 911 and say *Uh, I'm out on the New Lewisburg Highway by myself in the middle of the night, and there's a car parked beside the road?*

And is anyone in the car?

Well, I don't know because I'm not up to it yet.

There's no law about parking on the side of the New Lewisburg Highway, Ma'am. Call us back if you get there and have any trouble. Maybe you shouldn't be walking by yourself on roads in the middle of the night.

Yeah, maybe.

You can't call 911 because you're scared. Well, you can, but they're not going to do anything. I just kept walking. I considered crossing to the other side of the street, but what good would that do? Might as well look tough and confident and hope it was an abandoned car or a road angel with insomnia.

It was neither.

It was Paul, waiting for Gretchen to make sure she didn't miss the righthand turn just ahead.

"It's an easy turn to miss," he said. And I didn't doubt it. You can get into a sort of trance at night, just following the white line in the circle of light. Sometimes the white line went the wrong way. I thanked him for the reminder.

"Hey, do you know who the trash DQ was?" I asked him.

"No, I don't. Jan was talking about it and couldn't believe that people were still littering. Or littering to start with."

"Me either. See you down the road."

I made the right onto Culleoka Highway and came up to the old Glendale Market, which was closed, of course. Outside, was the famous red bench with faded black block lettering: THE BENCH OF DESPAIR. Black signatures and '23s were all over it—a Vol State tradition. Somebody must've painted it before this year to give room for the current crop of racers. I took the Sharpie marker that had been left on the bench and squeezed my name and "7-18-23" under Ryan Lemp and next to Todd and Allison Barcelona. It seemed only fair to give the date since Bob Hearn had marked his with "7-15-23," *three whole days* before me.

(Only later did I realize that I'd signed it just after midnight, and the date had already ticked over to the 19th. Bob had been there *four* days before me!) The bench gave another tangible reminder of how *many* people were ahead of me. Lots! I'd been looking forward to the BENCH OF DESPAIR. Now that I was there, it seemed anticlimactic but still tribal. I was signing as part of a weird family. This was as far as Tony had gotten last year. Almost to mile 185. He'd be through here soon.

Might as well keep walking and try to get a break at the Nutt House, a few miles up ahead.

Aptly named bench.

Perversely, I enjoyed watching the effects of sleep deprivation: freaky but fascinating. Besides math and short-term memory problems, I was also getting confused about whether the cars should drive on the left-hand side or the right-hand side of the road. This happens to me regularly when I travel from the States to England, but almost never when I travel back to the States where my default directional sense developed. My mind was no longer compartmentalizing as it should. But I didn't *feel* sleepy all the time. Oddly, I felt reasonably energized and ready to go.

The plan now was to do a big day through Lewisburg in the morning and then walk all the way to Shelbyville and get a room there. Chris texted me about a couple of hotels a mile off the route. *A MILE off the route??! What was he thinking?* I was hoping he meant a ½ mile off the route and a mile total to get back, but I would worry about that later because if I didn't make it to Shelbyville and I only made it to Lewisburg, then Oprah would pass me, and I'd be scrambling to stay in this race. Best to walk a long way, then fall into a bed in Shelbyville, which will not be at the Magnolia Motel, the place I'd heard all the horror stories about. Maybe I *would* be willing to walk a little extra to get to decent room.

No use lingering at the Bench of Despair. Seemed like bad juju somehow, playing with fire. As I walked along the two-lane Culleoka Highway, I saw my first and second live armadillos. They were doing what armadillos (and chickens) do, but fortunately, it was close to 1 am on a Wednesday. Sensible people were asleep with their cars parked, so both the armadillos made it across fine. I'd seen so many of their compatriots in shambles. Their shells get all broken up and blown around, so you'd see one little piece of a shell and then another piece and then another, ad nauseum down the road. It was good to see these two still moving as complete, lively units.

In three miles, I was at the Nutt House where I found Paul sitting by the big tent with strings of red fairy lights, which gave it an eerie feel. So did the way I kept seeing Paul, without noticing that he had passed me. *Twilight* episode meets Shirley Jackson short story. He just kept popping up. We whispered to each other, so as not to wake the three racers in zero-gravity chairs with beach towels over them. He told me about a 24-hour convenience store open at the intersection of I-65, still about eight miles down the road. Eight miles was about four hours at the rate I was walking and stopping.

The Nutts were asleep, which made them seem like sensible people, but they had added an outdoor toilet and shower to their house for Vol Staters, so I wasn't sure "sensible" really applied. It was a fantastic setup. It didn't seem worth taking a shower at that time of night, but I availed myself of their toilet under the stars—kind of cool—and I tried to rest in a zero-gravity chair for a few minutes, but I couldn't sleep, so I said goodbye to Paul and took off again.

Farther down the road, at another angel stop, I ran into Terrie, who said she was worried about Tony. He had passed her before the turn toward the Bench of Despair and said he would meet her there. Only he wasn't at the Bench. "I thought he would be at the Nutt House," she told me, "but he wasn't there either, and I'm wondering if he missed the turn."

I texted him immediately. "Hey, Tony. Terrie is worried about you. What mile are you at?"

He texted right back: "I got lost. Back on track almost at bench of despair."

Oh, no! "Ugh! Very sorry. Terrie was afraid of that. Keep the faith. Stay tough."

"Tell her to move on. I will catch up," Tony texted.

"Sounds good. She is at 190."

I felt terrible for Tony. It was bad enough to walk every mile of this course. To walk more and then have to backtrack must be unbelievably demoralizing. Tony had come through worse last year, though, and he knew the drill. He was a pro and incredibly tough.

I kept walking and found my eyes distorting things. I'd see a road-angel station that wasn't there. A grill under a pavilion would turn into a couple. A rocking chair on a porch would be an old man in a hat. The people weren't scary or anything. But they also weren't there, and I would figure that out as I passed.

I walked through Culleoka with its ancient post office and Sinclair Gas Station with the dinosaur logo. Talking to Chris on WhatsApp helped me stay awake.

The luxury of a bench nap

Just before mile 194, I got to the Mooresville Market. It was closed, of course, but the porch was lit up. There were bars on the windows and doors, and they had a bench outside that was calling my name. I sat down on it, told Chris I would rest, and said goodbye. I took off my shoes, then curled up on the bench with my pack as a pillow. It was unimaginably comfortable. I set my alarm for 10 minutes and fell asleep immediately. You'd be amazed at how much 10 minutes of sleep can do for someone in my state. When the alarm went off, I sat up and started putting my shoes on just as a car pulled up next to the porch.

It was about 4:30, and they didn't open till 6, but the woman who got out of the car was there to get things ready. "You don't have to get up," she told me. "You're alright. It's been a long night." Clearly, she'd seen other Vol Staters show up on her porch.

"Yeah, it has," I agreed. "But I gotta get up. I'd like to sleep for about three hours on your bench, but I can't do it."

"Well, do you want to go to the bathroom or anything?"

"Can I?!"

"Yeah, sure. Come on in. Just close the gate when you leave." What an angel!

The sleeping benches at the Mooresville Market.

It was hard to leave that hospitable bench, but I knew I was getting close to Lewisburg and civilization. I walked on.

Just before the I-65 overpass, I saw a giant astronaut in the distance, maybe 30-feet tall. He soon morphed into an angel; then the angel broke in half: the lower half turned into a pair of white jeans, and the top half of the angel flew away. A lovely hallucination. By the time I got to I-65, I didn't see any strange astronauts or angels. I wondered if they were sent to carry me away to unearthly realms? Better than hallucinations was the 24-hour BP Station Paul had told me about. The sun was just starting to rise as I ate my country ham biscuit in front of the station.

For bio-rhythmic reasons I don't understand, the sun gives all kinds of energy to the body just by eliminating the darkness. I could use the sunny jolt if not the increased heat it would bring. Everything is a tradeoff. That's when a woman named Jessica came up to me and became my check-in comment.

144-Hour Tracker, comments in italics (Wednesday morning, July 19, 2023)

Me: 200 miles. *"So, I'm sitting on an upside-down milk carton in front of the BP store, eating a country-ham biscuit. A woman comes by, gives me $3, and says, 'This is for you to buy a drink.' I assumed she thought I was homeless, but I was grateful for the 3 bucks in any case. But no, she thought I was a Vol State walker and wanted to help. I think when people ask what we're doing this for, and we tell them it's for a sticker, they figure we need help. Thanks, Jessica!"* I was 12 miles ahead of Oprah. If we were both walking at the same time, I could walk faster in Hokas than she could in heels.

Anonymous: *"Want to experience killer hallucinations, but need to pass a urinalysis? Run LAVS."* I get that.

Anonymous: *"Waiting out storm on a horse barn."* "In" the barn might have been better, but pronouns go the way of addition and subtraction as the race takes its toll on the brain.

After 7:30, I checked the tracker to see where Tony was. By 8, he still hadn't checked in. I texted him again: "You OK, Tony? I didn't see your check in."

He texted back right away: "Omg I forgot been stressing trying to make up."

"Don't stress. It sucks to do extra miles, but you got this! Plenty of time to make up for it."

"Thank you."

Chapter 12

DONUTS AND STORMS AND CHICKEN-KILL HIGHWAY

*"In a world whose absurdity appears to be so impenetrable,
we simply must reach a greater degree of understanding among
men, a greater sincerity. We must achieve this or perish."*
--Albert Camus

On the joy of bespoke donuts

After a biscuit at the BP, I walked further into Lewisburg and saw a free-standing Donut Shop across the street. I love a good donut, and Lewisburg Donut Shop turned out to be world-class. The woman serving them may or may not have been Korean. She had unfilled donuts in the case, including one topped with chocolate, and I got to pick the filling—vanilla crème for me, not Bavarian crème and chocolate crème. I watched her fill my donut! Hallelujah! I also got a chocolate-covered raised donut with sprinkles.

I'd seen a documentary about how one man (Ted Ngoy) had started a Korean donut dynasty all over California. I wondered if she knew *The Donut King*? The last time I'd had world-class donuts was on a spring road trip in Alpine, Texas, at Baker's Dozen Donuts, run by a man who may or may not have been Korean. By now, in true ignorant, racist fashion, I'd decided that people who at least might be Korean definitely make the best American donuts. I took my bespoke donuts to a table far in the back, past a table of Lewisburg's finest. I'm always a bit uncomfortable around police officers, even if I haven't done anything wrong, and this was especially true now that I was a vagrant, roaming the roads at all hours of the day and night. The policemen ignored me, though, and I got to eat my delectable donuts in peace.

If anything were going to make me want to go back and do Vol State, it might be the Lewisburg Donut Shop. Since the heat had suppressed my appetite, I could eat only two, but I wish I could've tried the sweet potato cake or avocado cake donuts. Donut artistry! Apparently at lunch, the theme changes, and they sell fried rice, noodle soup, and egg rolls. I could only imagine how good these would be. If not for Oprah, I'd stay here all day, feasting and reading the Kindle app on my phone. But no.

I ran into Terrie further along into Lewisburg. She was a little miracle of persistence, keeping at her slow pace, unable to lollygag as I did at donut shops because every minute meant more to her if she was going to beat Oprah to the Rock. By Vol State standards, I was a dawdler, but when Terrie stopped, it was for a quick bite, sit, or sleep. I walked with her in search of hydrocolloid patches for my blister. We stopped at one pharmacy across from the Marshall County Courthouse. No patches, but the mayor of Lewisburg chatted us up outside. He was justifiably proud of his town, although he didn't mention the spectacular donuts.

Terrie insisted I take a couple of her hydrocolloidal pads, which I was grateful for, but I still wanted bigger ones, so we stopped off at a Walgreens on the route out of town. As we went into the store, I noticed a wall of black sky heading our way from the northwest. Terrie was going to the nearby Celebration Inn, so she would be fine. While paying for my hydrocolloid patches, I asked the cashier if there was a place I could sit and hang out till the storm passed. She and a local guy started thinking about places nearby, but the Dairy Queen wasn't open and neither were the Mexican or Japanese restaurants.

"There's no coffee shop around here?" I asked.

They shook their heads. I thought maybe I'd see if I could sit in the lobby of Terrie's motel, but as we walked further, I noticed a laundromat on the right. Perfect! I could take refuge from the storm and wash all my clothes at the same time. I changed into my boxer shorts and lightweight jacket in the bathroom and washed everything else. The clothes were on the soak cycle when the storm hit, lashes of rain and thunder pummeling all who walked the streets. I couldn't help thinking how lucky I had been so far on this journey. I'd only been stuck in one big rain shower, which hadn't compared to the two I'd avoided in Columbia and the one I was sitting out here in Lewisburg. I checked in with Tony to see if he'd found a place to avoid the storm. He texted back, "I've walked through it so far. I train in hurricanes lol."

I told him that was an excellent way to gain ground on Oprah and wimps like me in a laundromat.

The storm had largely passed by the time my clothes were ready. Truly clean clothes seemed incredibly decadent, so I decided to dawdle some more. I walked back to the Walgreens and treated myself to a better emergency poncho that would cover more of me; then I went to the Japanese restaurant next door, sat in a big booth, and ate a three-roll combo special. Tony texted to say that he'd stopped by the laundromat, but I wasn't there. I was sorry to miss him and told him I was now lollygagging with sushi. The sushi was OK, not great, but it was all I needed. Well, that and a fortune cookie that said, "In life, it's good not to get too comfortable." No doubt a warning from Oprah . . . or Laz.

A kick-in-the-butt message for me at the Yamato Steakhouse in Lewisburg.

Time to end my many comfortable hours in Lewisburg and finally get back to walking. For some reason, I had the idea that this 21-mile stretch to Shelbyville was going to be relatively easy. Resting in a bed seemed just around the corner. The break had revived me, and my good attitude would last about five miles to the Dollar General in Farmington, where I turned right onto Chicken-Kill Highway, also known as State Road 64. I remembered Jim Halsey mentioning it on the bus ride: "This is the road where you get passed from behind by big trucks filled with chickens, and the same big trucks with no chickens pass you on the way back." Hence the name.

It didn't take long to see my first load of chickens. The 16 miles along that road were exposed, hot, humid, and generally miserable, but the chicken trucks were the least of my problems. Finding a place to go to the bathroom was the big one. A daytime walk on an exposed road with fields, farms, and houses but few trees made finding a place to pull down one's pants no minor issue. My bladder was becoming increasingly uncomfortable.

Thankfully, before anything untoward happened, I spotted a food bank on the right side of the road with a porta-potty outside. I've never in my life been so thankful for an unlocked porta-potty.

The more bleak life became along Chicken Kill Highway, the more amenable I became to spending too much money on a room in Shelbyville. Chris had been researching places to stay. The infamous Magnolia Motel was the only one directly on the route. I could see why people succumbed to its expedient charms, but I wasn't quite that desperate yet. The Microtel Inn & Suites was over a mile off the route, and that wasn't going to happen. The solution turned out to be the Belmont Inn, a lovely, restored antebellum B&B just a long block off the course. Hotels that charged by the hour would be much more economical during Vol State, but those places would probably be more like the Magnolia Motel. The Belmont Inn was one of those destination lodgings you'd love to linger in for a romantic weekend getaway. What a concept! The $134 seemed well worth it.

I could feel my feet swelling as I slogged along the scorching asphalt. I wasn't usually a prima donna when it came to lodgings, but I texted the Belmont Innkeeper to see if there was access to ice anywhere on the premises.

She wrote back to say there was ice for breakfast drinks but not for coolers.

Hmmm. I think I'll try playing the Vol State card. I wrote back and said, "OK. I'm walking from Columbia last night into town, and I won't get in till late. I was hoping to put my feet on some ice."

"Oh.... you're on the Vol State Road Race?" she asked. *Bingo!* "You're all set. Big gallon bag of ice in your mini-fridge room freezer and some Epsom Salt. Safe travels. Thank you for visiting." Wow! I'd never be an influencer, but I appreciated my tiny window of celebrity as a sore-footed zombie.

I drank some Gatorade and took time off my feet at the Pit Stop Convenience Store, still about nine miles from the Inn. I was feeling sorry for myself and checked the Vol State Facebook page. Glenn Kasper had posted a picture of his legs, sprawled out on a road with all his stuff next to him.

> It doesn't get bad until it gets bad...Pity party starts at mile 221.1 in ten minutes!! BYOB!

I commented back,

> Hey, Glenn. Just think how pitiful it would be to be at 214 and still have to walk another seven just to get to a pity party that started two hours ago and has probably already moved up the line. Some folks envy your progress. I'm at the Pit Stop. I could buy beer, but I can't carry it. Hang tough.

Misery that loved company must be a big reason Vol State folks think of each other as family.

156-Hour Tracker, comments in italics (Wednesday evening, July 19, 2023)

Me: 217 miles—*"Whose idea was this?"* I was 13 miles ahead of Oprah.

Anonymous: *"Yesterday when I had ran out of water when it was hot, I put it out in the universe that I could use some water. I should have been more specific."*

Anonymous: *"Random lady at Walgreens: 'So what're you walking for?' Me: 'We're part of a doomsday cult. We're on a mission to buy Kool-Aid for our next gathering.'"*

My Martin savior Steven Godfrey finished the race in a blazing 6 days, 1 hour, 47 minutes, and 10 seconds. I knew he'd slam this course. Congratulations, Steven! He found another way back to Florida. It would be a long time before I got there.

Another few miles up the road, it was getting dark, and I caught up with Edward in his bee suit. He wanted to know if I was planning to stop in Shelbyville and where. I told him about the Belmont, and he called and got a room there too. Ed, a veteran of many of these stupid journey races, was excellent company and helped make the grueling last five miles into Shelbyville a little less painful. He had just run HOTS the month before and had been planning to enter Laz's inaugural Last

Annual Third Circle of Hell the next month, but he was having second thoughts about the feasibility of that. He said he liked HOTS because the competitors worked together much more. They were all in the same boat since they got the race route at the last minute. I don't remember what else we talked about, but I remember walking like I was drunk. I kept stumbling into the grass next to the shoulder, and by the time we got on the sidewalks of town, I couldn't walk next to Ed but had to walk in the very center of the sidewalk to keep from falling off it.

In Shelbyville, we passed the aptly named "Never Rest Park" shortly before the infamous Magnolia Motel, whose parking lot was mostly full, but I saw no humans. I couldn't see any bedbugs from the road, but I could imagine why so many Vol Staters had ended up there despite the warnings. It's a long stretch of nothing from Lewisburg to Shelbyville, and 223 miles into this race, a bed was a bed was a bed, or so it might have seemed.

The Belmont wasn't much farther along, and in contrast to the seedy motel, it had beautiful columns out in front and a massive porch where sensible people were meant to sit, rest, and drink sweet tea. When I got to King Room #1 about 11:15 pm, I felt like Cinderella crashing the ball still in her cinder clothes. The room was filled with antiques and Americana on the walls, including the Declaration of Independence and the Constitution, but all I cared about was the bathroom, the four-poster king-sized bed, the ice in the freezer, and the tub of Epsom salt in front of a leather chair. Thank you, Belmont Inn!

Cinderella arrives at the Belmont Inn!

By Shelbyville, I officially hated this race. I mean really hated it. My feet were just SO sore. Jan's advice had improved my big blister majorly, but all 26 bones, 33 joints, and more than 100 muscles, tendons, and ligaments in each foot screamed at me that this race was a terrible idea. One of my worst! And for the first time, a shower and a scandalous 5 ½ hours of sleep did nothing to change my mind about how awful this race was. I went out to the self-serve breakfast room at 6 that morning and tried to put my phone in my shorts, but there was no pocket. I wondered if, perchance, I had brought a backup pair that didn't have pockets. Why would I do that?

But no, I just had my shorts on inside out. I returned to my room to rectify the error, then came back and ravenously dug into English muffins, apple sauce, yogurt, and orange juice before heading back out to the route. At least I was well fed. When I signed the guest book, I saw that Ed had already left and Glenn had been there the night before, at least for a while. He'd posted on Facebook that he'd gone out for a Mexican meal in Shelbyville, and they'd felt so sorry for him that they upgraded his margarita to a large. He might be fun to complain with if I ever caught up to him.

168-Hour Tracker, comments in italics (Thursday morning, July 20, 2023)

Me: Mile 223--- *"Looking for fun in all the wrong places..."* Oprah was only 3 miles behind me. That's what a beautiful B&B can mean for a Vol Stater.

Anonymous: *"All my body parts are screaming at each other. Can't we just learn to get along? Just for 94 more miles?"*

Anonymous: *"Extreme dislike for Chicken-Kill Highway. Extreme dislike."* (On the bus, it was hard to imagine why some parts of the course were so terrible when they looked so innocuous. Chicken-Kill Highway was like that.)

Gretchen tapped out at Mile 211. I felt bad for her, despite her crewed status. I was sorry for Paul too, but at least they both could get some much-needed rest. So could Chris Clemens who finished the race in 6 days, 16 hours, and 45 minutes. Good thing Carl and Jan didn't let him quit when he tried to. This race is funny like that. People want to quit, even decide to quit, but if they're just given some time, many of them start moving again toward the Rock and end up making it.

Can a Froster change the world?

On the way out of Shelbyville, I stopped at Circle K to go to the bathroom at about Mile 225, and I got a Slurpee-like drink called a Froster. When I went up to the young cashier to pay, I said, "I'm sure a Froster will make my day better."

She looked me over. "It's on me," she said.

"Really?! Well, that makes my day better too. Thank you!" The way random strangers took care of us never failed to amaze me. And it made a big difference in my disposition that morning. I didn't *need* her to buy my Froster, but it made me feel so much better that some stranger cared about how miserable I was. How many miserable people had I passed in my life and showed that I didn't care at all about their misery?

The long stretch of nothing over nine miles between Shelbyville and Wartrace gave me plenty of time to think about my relative inhumanity in the face of other people's suffering. When something so small as buying me a Froster could lift my spirits, why don't I do more for people I see who are in bad shape?

Today wasn't supposed to be quite as hot as yesterday, but it was already oppressive by check-in time. I was still hoping to catch up to some fun people.

Only five people were behind me on the tracker. I had worked my butt off yesterday, but my Lewisburg dawdling and my collapse in Shelbyville took way too long. Oprah clicked behind me, wielding a stick, and potentially fun people ahead of me had imaginary carrots dangling off their packs next to their flags. The end of this mad race was still days away, so that didn't yet count as a carrot. My extrinsic motivation was all carrots and sticks. I wasn't sure what sort of intrinsic motivation I had left, probably just the desire not to fail. So many people in the world were having real problems while I was doing this ridiculous race. I had a friend in dire shape in the hospital and another one in and out of doctors' offices, trying to figure out what was wrong. Sometimes, this elective misery felt like a mockery of folks forced into real misery.

At Mile 230, I got to a lovely house with an aid station on the porch. Terrie was already sitting down when I arrived. Holy gamoly! She looked like she'd taken a right cross from Tyson Fury.

She told me the story of her fall, shortly after I last saw her, in front of Celebration Inn in Lewisburg. She had cracked her glasses, cut herself above her eye, and ended up with a black eye and a skinned knee for her trouble. If Laz had a tracker for toughness, Terrie would be a front-of-the-packer instead of back with me. Besides being 74, she'd had kidney issues, macular degeneration, epilepsy, and the residual problems from her band surgery, not to mention overuse problems she'd had in past races with stress fractures and plantar fasciitis. And now this!

Caron Lovvorn, the road angel with the great porch, came out to talk to us. We took pictures and chatted.

Me, Terrie Wurzbacher, and road angel Caron Lovvorn

I got to talk to my cousin Karen Gentry on the way to Wartrace. Despite my protests, before the race, she had insisted on Venmo-ing me money for a hotel room. Walking the roads at night tends to be the scariest thing of all for people not in the race, but really, the night walking was my favorite time. Well, except for the hotel rooms. Those were my very favorite times. Talking to my cousin reminded me of my cozy life and family beyond the white line. They seemed like some far-away dream.

In Wartrace, I stopped off at Chabi's, a little Southern-hipster bakery and café. I ordered a chicken-fried steak sandwich with a side of jambalaya—real-people food!

While waiting, I checked the Vol State Facebook page and learned that Addison, the Honey Boy, was the "trash DQ." He wrote a heartfelt mea culpa to the group on Facebook. I was impressed. It must have been devastating to get disqualified after a third-place finish and his first sub-five-day time, but he was humble and contrite, took full responsibility, and didn't hold it against Laz. I was proud of Laz for making an example of Addison and showing how serious he is about littering, and I was proud of Addison for maturely stepping up to the DQ.

The whole thing reminded me why Laz is so special as a race director. He's not just putting on a race; he's coaching people to be better than their normal selves.

Was my Vol State self really better than my normal self?

I bought a cookie for the road and headed past the Big Creek Winery Tasting room, which, thankfully, was closed for another 20 minutes. I could imagine wasting a whole afternoon there; in retrospect, that might not have been such a terrible idea. The Bailey's House was at 240, only seven miles away. How bad could seven miles be?

Coming out of Wartrace, I was talking to Chris.

"You seem energetic and rested," he said.

"No, no. What I sound like is chill. I feel pretty chill. Sort of a post-food coma."

A few minutes later when I was signing off, frustrated by the poor reception. I said, "Now, I'm grouchy."

"You didn't sound grouchy a minute ago," he said.

"No, I'm grouchy now." I was walking in what Terrie had called the Swamp: a valley with no breeze, hot and sticky. Even though the temperature wasn't terrible—only 85 degrees—I felt like I was in a hot pot. So now I was grumpy. My emotions were just below the surface these days. Like a quick-change circus clown in a room full of *Snow White and the Seven Dwarfs* costumes, I could go from Happy to Dopey to Grumpy in a millisecond. Uber exhaustion and walking on scorching asphalt in the dismal Swamp were getting to me. I was a toddler who could laugh and then scream in almost the same breath, but I knew this was just emotional weather—it would keep shifting, and it didn't really matter.

But soon, I'd be at the Baileys' and sit on their porch for a while, and all will be well in the world. At the start of the race, the Baileys had the coolest tent setup. They'd posted a picture of it on Facebook, complete with running lights leading up to the tent. It was a thing of beauty until it got mutilated in the storm I sheltered through at the Richland Inn in Columbia. Moving immediately to Plan B, they'd hauled all the cots and zero-gravity chairs onto their porch. It sounded like paradise to me.

Up ahead in the swamp, I noticed a blob of white in a driveway turn-in and hoped it was a Vol State cooler. I could really go for a cold drink. More distorted vision. When I got closer, I realized it was just a sign saying, "Acts continuing pray and worship entrance." Oh, well.

Not too much farther, a big SUV stopped next to me. A woman drove with a teenage girl in the passenger's seat.

"Would you like a water?" the teenager asked.

"Oh, would I ever like a water! Yes, please."

So, she handed me a water bottle. I plastered on a smile and said, "Aw, thank you! That's so great. Thank you very much!"

They drove off. Only it was warm water, so now I had two separate warm waters, plus my soft bottles that I had to drag along. It was very kind of them, and if they'd said, "Would you like a warm water?" I still would've said yes because I'm keeping to my rule of never saying no to a generous offer, but really, I did not want a warm water. Then it dawned on me that I could pour it out! Wasteful, yes, but at least I wouldn't have to carry a full bottle, and the crushed bottle would fit in my shirt pocket. Much better.

It didn't take long to realize why the air was so humid in the swamp. Thunder first, then flashes of lightning, then the rain came. A canopy of trees sheltered the road a bit at first, and the showers brought down the temperature as I started climbing out of the swamp. I felt hotter, though, once I put on my fancy Walgreens emergency rain poncho. Nothing to be done about any of this because my preferences didn't make a damn bit of difference. The goal was just to get to the Bailey house.

At one point, I thought I was seeing a deer up ahead, but I knew it could be a mirage. I didn't trust my eyes or my brain anymore. It might just be a log. The deer could be a bear, but it wasn't moving. Probably a log.

Then, the storm ramped up its crescendo. The rain slashed down as I climbed up the road. Lightning cracked right next to me—BOOM!—the thunder a split second later. I had hoped to keep my shoes dry with my umbrella. That was my main objective because I didn't want to get Chris Haas-sized blisters across the bottom of my feet. Thor laughed at my umbrella plan. It almost worked when it was raining normally, but not in this torrent. I kept hoping I would get to the Baileys in the middle of it, but I was farther away than I thought. Where was it?

More crackling thunder. My feet were soaked. Then suddenly I started crying, sobbing that couldn't be heard in the storm. *I hate this freaking race. Hate it. Why am I here? Stupid stupid stupid.* I plodded on, my tears merged into the deluge. And then, quite suddenly, the rain let up.

I called Chris again—poor guy, having to listen to me whine and cry from so far away. He really is an angel. I tried to explain. "I'm not crying because I'm going to quit. I'm crying because I'm miserable, and I hate this. I'm not getting any of the fun parts of it. I don't know what the fun parts are. I'm finding no spiritual enlightenment, very little beer, very few fun people to hang with. Lots of nice road angels, but none since Caron at 230. When I get to the Baileys' house at 240, I'll have another 74 miles. Not that long. I'm sure I'll be able to crank it out. But it just sucks. Sucks sucks sucks. I think that's all I've got to say. It's starting to rain again, so I better go." Poor Chris could barely get a word in edgewise. He was stuck being my sounding board and then not knowing what was happening to me.

I clicked off the call as the storm entered a new phase. The rain belted down, more thunder, more lightning, then the wind shifted into a higher gear and whipped up to horizontal. I pointed my sun umbrella into the gusts. My emergency poncho blew all over the place, and I was drenched. All my worry about soaked feet and blisters went by the wayside as finding shelter took priority. I was wading as fast as I could upstream through a river of water now washing down the road. Lots of trees on both sides, and I passed houses along the way, but I didn't see any that looked inviting. One tempting covered carport had two signs on a tree by the road: "**SMILE YOU'RE ON CAMERA**" and '**WARNING GUARD DOGS.**" Tennessee has more sweet people than you can imagine, and it also has plenty of scared people with guns. I figured I was better off braving the lightning striking all around me and the wind that worried me almost as much. I imagined a gust blowing me into a tree or into some guy's yard, past his DON'T TREAD ON ME flag. *Was this stupid race ever going to end*? I splashed onward as fast as I could.

I could barely see through sheets of rain and my water-streaked glasses, but up ahead I thought I spied a contorted structure by the side of the road. As I got closer, I decided it had to be the Baileys' torn-up road-angel station. The house was set back and up from the road, and there was a long driveway before I could get to the house. I wasn't totally sure it was the Baileys', but I figured I'd give it a go. This neighborhood had fancier houses, and if I wound up on one of their neighbor's porches, at least I'd be under shelter. I could hope they wouldn't shoot me because they'd heard about the Vol State nonsense from the Baileys.

I bent forward, aimed my head and umbrella at the porch 50 yards away, and ran as fast as I could into the wind across the sodden front yard. When I got to the porch, Robin Bailey and Erin Dupey were standing there watching. "Boy, am I glad to be here!" I said to Robin, an attractive middle-aged woman with glasses and a blonde bob. Her wrap-around porch was big enough for two cots with quilts and several zero-gravity chairs. I took off my emergency poncho and pointed to the large fern by the door. "Is it OK if I put it here?" I asked, hoping to allow it to dry a bit.

"Actually, I'm going to put it over here," Robin said, taking the poncho and moving it to the other side of the front door. "See," she said, pulling back the foliage and pointing to a bird's nest with eggs in it. Naturally, any intelligent bird would choose Robin Bailey's front porch to lay her eggs. "You just get into bed and pull the quilt up around you," she told me. "Don't worry about getting the bedding wet."

I haven't been sent to bed since I was in single digits, but I must've looked as shattered as I felt. At that moment, Robin truly seemed like an angel sent from heaven. Normally, I would protest in the name of manners—a stinky, drenched person wrapping up in some stranger's quilts? But I was way past social graces. I took off my soggy shoes and socks, crawled on the cot in my wet clothes, pulled the quilt over me, and pretended like I was at home instead of this ludicrous race. I hovered back and forth on the edge of sleep for about 45 minutes. When I finally woke up, things were hopping on the L-shaped porch. Tara and Erin were resting in the zero-gravity chairs, Gina had arrived, and Terrie came up. Everyone was sopping wet, and Robin moved around like a M*A*S*H unit nurse, giving food, drink, medical supplies, good cheer, and advice to the wounded. I heard her offer to dry Erin's clothes.

"I'm just worried," moaned Erin, "about Laz disqualifying me if you dry my clothes."

"Laz is not going to disqualify you," I piped up. "Robin offered to dry your clothes." I turned to Robin. "And now that you mention it, is there any chance you could dry this sun hoodie for me?"

"Of course," she said. What a luxury—to start back on the course in a dry shirt! Even a smelly, dry shirt.

The cot and quilts had brought me back to myself enough to actually carry on a conversation with Robin and her tall husband Vincent, who'd come out on the porch in his work clothes: navy pants and a button-down shirt with a Nissan logo over the pocket. I could imagine a case where a nurturing wife would take on the herculean task of spending days and nights caring for all these stray Vol State sub-humans, and her grumpy husband would resent the heck out of it, but not so with the Baileys. Vincent was every bit as charming and generous as his wife. They were in it as a couple. And they couldn't have been in a better place at a better time for me. . . well, unless their house had been a couple of miles west.

Robin worked in the school system as a counselor who helped challenged kids stay mainstream instead of getting sent to special-ed schools. "No wonder you're so great at keeping people in this race," I told her. "You're professionally trained!"

I would've liked to stay on the Baileys' porch for hours, but plenty of other Vol State drowned rats needed the cots and chairs, and Oprah called, as did my bladder. That was an urgent issue that the Baileys couldn't help with, thanks to Laz's rule that we couldn't go in houses. There was wide-open road for as far as I could see. No hidey-hole spots anywhere and lots of folks on the front porch looking out. I wondered if the mangled tent could give me some shelter.

After thanking Robin and Vincent profusely, I headed down their lawn to check out the big tent that had folded in on itself. Inside there was a table over a grass area that was surrounded on two sides by a tarp and one side by a plastic trash bag. I thought if I crawled over some folded chairs to get under the table, I wouldn't be seen and could pee to my heart's content. Folding my body so that it would fit under the table was no easy task, given how stiff I was, and it was more than a bit awkward getting my shorts and underwear down and then back up in a deep squat. Desperate times call for desperate body positions.

When I came out of the tent, there was Vincent walking down toward it. *OMG! He knows I was peeing on his grass under his table, and he's coming down to reprimand me!* I took a deep breath. Once I thought about it, I couldn't quite imagine Vincent reprimanding any of the runners. He seemed more like the kind of guy who could make you feel terrible just by putting on his disappointed face, but at the moment, he just looked concerned. He probably saw me go in the tent and wondered if I'd passed out or something. I didn't mention the peeing (and I apologize to the Baileys in case they read or hear about this—so embarrassing—and after all their unbelievable hospitality!) but I did ask him why they go to so much trouble and expense for a group of crazy strangers.

"We just like helping people get to the Rock," he said. "If we can give hope to the hopeless, that's enough for us."

They certainly did a version of that for me. I asked him for their address so I could send a thank-you note if I ever made it back to normal life. The Bailey House was exactly the quick-time rehabilitation I needed after those brutal storms. It was hard to believe that Robin and Vincent are real people instead of another angelic hallucination.

Next it was on to Manchester.

The Bailey Rehabilitation Center.

Chapter 13

ON GANGS AND BILLBOARDS AND QUITTING

"Nonsense and beauty have close connections."
—E.M. Forster

I know why kids join gangs

Whispering Oaks Campground was just a few miles from the Baileys' house and had a barn where they'd set up cots, chairs, and snacks for Vol State runners. They also had showers and real bathrooms, but they didn't have the Baileys' quilts or gentle caretaking.

When I got there, I found a whole raft of Vol State folks who had been holed up there during and after the storms, including Carmel, Jarrod, Terra, Kendra, and Kurt Phillips. The water had apparently gotten calf-deep in the parking lot of the campground during the worst of the storm but had drained off by the time I got there. Carmel's shin was in bad shape, and he was worried that he had a stress fracture. He and Jerrod were keeping on, though.

I had spent so much time miserable and alone on this trek that it was starting to get to me. I envied all these folks who had people to hang out with, so I took a quick pee break in a proper toilet, changed into my Bedrock sandals with socks, hung my Hokas on the back of my pack to give them a chance to dry out, and joined up with Terra, Kendra, and Kurt on the road to Manchester. Kurt was only 34, a tall, trail-running ultra guy from Tennessee. They were a good trio, though, and I was comfortable keeping up with them. I had a feeling this could be an entirely different race if you were hanging out with a simpatico group.

180-Hour Tracker, comments in italics (Thursday evening, July 20, 2023)

Me: 246 miles--*"Thank heaven for the Baileys! A perfect port in a storm!"* Ten miles ahead of Oprah.

Anonymous: *"Oprah ordering up storms just to cause chaos."* (nb: Was it Oprah or Laz?)

Anonymous: *"I've never worked this hard in my life. Not to sprint uphill to shelter from a monsoon, not to poop and not be caught on camera, not to sleep inside a gas station on a hard cold cement floor, only to decide to haul a$$ in the heat to the next cut off so I can sleep on some random stranger's driveway and start over in a few hours. I'd cry, but that's SO yesterday."*

Congratulations to Vicky Halsey, who finished in 7 days, 14 hours, 23 minutes, and 48 seconds. She and her husband Jim sure gave me good advice before this race started.

It turned out that Tony checked in at 246 miles too, but I didn't see him. I'd found a cheap Scottish Inn on the other end of Manchester at 252. He texted that he was tired and was staying someplace in Manchester too. In the meantime, I was thrilled to be walking with company.

Shortly before Manchester, Kurt yelled, "OPRAH!" *Oprah?* We all looked where he was pointing. And there she was, the real Oprah, fresh and glamorous, up on a billboard next to a car repair shop while we derelicts gaped below. Naturally, we had to have our pictures made with Oprah. At first, we could only see the right side of the billboard with her picture on it. The rest of the billboard, mostly obscured by the trees, said, "Be a force for good. Encouragement. PassItOn.com The Foundation for a better life." Seriously...Oprah was offering me *encouragement?* Hmm . . . I suppose she'd been offering me that the entire race.

I wondered: were we a force for good or just a bunch of crazy masochists siphoning off the generosity of Tennessee folks? What even counted as being a force for good in the U.S. in 2023? Did it mean taking up the cause and becoming an advocate for justice? Or being a peacemaker, trying to bridge the gaps? Or being an inspirational distraction for people? Or just trying to be kind and ignoring the news? So many questions and so few answers.

Kendra, Terra, and Kurt, cheered on by Oprah.

On the outskirts of Manchester, we stopped off at a convenience store, picked up some beers, and had a small party around a trashcan outside the store. This was the most fun I'd had since Pam Pratt's bra story. I got about halfway through my Kona Big Wave before Kurt said, "Well, we better keep moving." This was precisely why having fun in this race was hard: Oprah kept encouraging us.

We walked on through the dark into Manchester proper and (of course) past the Coffee County Courthouse. I was getting blisters from my sandals, but I didn't want to make the whole group stop, and I knew I would be getting a chance to fix my feet at the Scottish Inn. They had decided on Taco Bell for a late dinner.

Before we got there, we passed a classic car lot. "Whenever we go past someplace like this," said Terra, "Kendra always has us choose our favorite. Which one do you like best?"

I picked a baby blue Mustang from the 60s. While we were standing there gawking and choosing our favs, the folks working at the place sat outside with their Friday night, post-closing-time beers. One gray-bearded guy came over to talk to us and ask what we were doing. He and Kurt exchanged car talk. I can't explain why this seemed precisely the kind of thing I'd been looking for this entire trip. We were engaging with the world around us—childishly, curiously, open—and talking to a local in a city I'd never been to. This race doesn't get much better than that, but we had to keep going. Taco Bell wasn't far up ahead. Their choice, not mine, but again, I just liked being in a fun little gang. On the Camino de Santiago, we would've called it the start of a "Camino family," a road family, even though we'd been together for less than 10 miles.

Just before Taco Bell, Terra and Kendra stopped off at a Dunkin Donuts to get something for later, and Kurt stopped off at the Mobil station for some snacks. I figured I'd go ahead on to Taco Bell and order. I sat down with my taco and quesadilla and looked out the window to see Kurt—cartoon like—frantically waving and miming that he was locked out. I was the last person they'd let in the restaurant before closing the place to only drive-thru traffic. Great. I was finally going to sit down with a gang to eat a meal, and they couldn't get in. I waved sadly and went back to finish my quesadilla. Only later did I find out they'd gone across the street to eat at the Waffle House. I could've had the breakfast I'd been craving. It hadn't dawned on me to carry my food outside and follow them. I was heading for the motel anyway, and they were walking on. It was fun while it lasted.

At the Scottish Inn, just past the I-24 overpass, I took a bath, babied my new blisters from the sandals, and put my Hokas in front of the air conditioning in hopes that they would dry out. I got about four hours of sleep and was back on the road by 3:30 in the morning.

A few truckers were out and about, but it was mostly that early morning sleepy, deserted darkness, even by a major interstate. I started on the 15-mile slog along Hillsboro Highway toward Pelham at Mile 267. Soon after would be the climb up to Monteagle. For the first time, I could actually envision the end of this race, and it couldn't come soon enough. With 60 miles to go, all thoughts of finding out more about America in the summer of '23 had moved well down the priority list. All I wanted to do was get to the Rock so I could stop. Nothing sounded better than stopping. Nothing. I could sleep as long as I wanted in a real bed. I could lollygag through life to my heart's content. Oprah would be just another insightful talk show host again.

Who am I kidding? Oprah would *never* be just an insightful talk show host again. A DG store would never be just a Dollar General. I would never think of Tennessee in the same way again. But 60 miles was still 60 miles—a long way with the two biggest climbs of the race still left to go.

> **192-Hour Tracker, comments in italics** (Friday morning, July 21, 2024)
>
> Me: 260 miles-- *"Creepy! The Oprah billboard outside Manchester reminded me of "the eyes of Doctor T. J. Eckleburg" billboard in* The Great Gatsby. *"*
>
> Anonymous: *"I farted real loud after leaving the Baileys road side Angel station and I heard Mrs. Bailey mention how loud the bullfrogs were...those weren't bullfrogs"* I guess the Baileys had to put up with a lot of bodily functions. Bless them.
>
> Anonymous: *"Yesterday went off the rails when I realized my Bible must've fallen out of my pocket during a roadside pit stop. When I backtracked in an effort to recover it, I found a bag of weed. I found comfort in knowing I wasn't the only one to lose my higher power."*

Glenn Kasper was late checking in. I thought maybe he had dropped, but finally he came up on the tracker at 266 miles. I might catch up with him after all.

Wonder Cave Spelunking

Between the Scottish Inn and Pelham, Hillsboro Highway took me past lots of red barns, green fields, and black-and-white cows. Pretty country, but a long hike on a cloudy morning. Near the tiny hamlet of Hillsboro, I passed a white barn with a faded red roof that had the words "WONDER CAVE" across the top in red relief. I wondered what had happened in that barn-cave, and I wondered about this race. I wondered why so many people invested in it—to run it or to help others run it. I wondered about ultrarunners in general. Was there a neuron or two loose in ultrarunner brains that kept them grasping for the next sticker, the next buckle, the next adventure?

Wondering . . . .

Ultrarunners themselves throw around pop psychology ideas of childhood traumas that spur people into this masochism. Various scientific studies have linked ultrarunning to an increase in eating disorders, exercise addiction, depression, and sleep disturbance. No surprises there, but it brings up the chicken-egg issue: does UER (ultra-endurance running) foster an environment that exacerbates mental-health issues, or does it attract more people with mental-health issues?

Then there are the physical problems with ultrarunning. Everyone agrees that physical activity generally helps stave off mortality for a while, but multiple studies are starting to question the adverse effects of ultrarunning on the cardiovascular and renal systems. And if you spend any time talking to ultrarunners, you'll discover that managing injuries is a major part of staying in the sport. Neuropathy, stress fractures, and other overuse injuries to joints, muscles, and backs is normal. Of course, many sports are risky in terms of the musculoskeletal system—I'd heard about an orthopedist who makes a living from pickleball injuries—but most sports don't have adverse effects on internal organ systems.

The idea that ultrarunning may be bad for us physically doesn't take a mad scientist to figure out. The mental-health issues are more interesting, though. I err on the side of thinking that ultrarunning is quite good for people mentally, but that doesn't mean that the crazy sport doesn't draw more people than other sports who already have mental-health issues. I really don't know about any of this, but I wonder.

I called my sister-in-law Jude to pass the time on the Hillsboro Highway. Like my Aunt Fran, Jude had been sucked into the wackiness of the race and had started following other racers as well as me. Always inquisitive, she had plenty of questions about people and logistics.

Just before Pelham, I came across a long gravel road off to the left with tents lined up. A total surprise for me: Bobby Brown's legendary angel stop. It's Mar-A-Lago for Vol State racers. He's got three coolers marked Gatorade, Water, and Sundrop/Dr. Pepper. He's got Subway sandwiches in a portable fridge. He's got cots, electrical outlets, a porta-potty (with an electric fan rigged up in it), a shower tent, medical supplies, zero-gravity chairs—in other words, paradise. Had I known where his stop was, I might have tried to push on through Manchester with the gang.

Bobby, a blond guy about my age in a sleeveless yellow t-shirt, khaki cargo pants, and camo Crocks, was sitting by the tents with his white poodle when I arrived mid-morning. I picked out a Gatorade and sat down to chat with him for a while. He was justifiably proud of his palatial digs, including his shower tent, which could easily have fit ten runners, although it had only one jury-rigged hose and showerhead. He'd even built a way to properly close the tent from the inside, "so that women would feel comfortable."

"This place is amazing. Why do you do all this for us?"

"I like to meet the people and hear their stories," he said. And he's obviously a storyteller himself. Just that morning, he told me, Glenn Kasper had been there. "He'd dropped his phone in that storm yesterday, and the rushing water just swept it away. I had to help him check in with Laz." Losing your phone would be terrible in the best of times, but in this race, catastrophic. It was a map as well as a communication device. You couldn't even get a hold of someone to help you, maybe crew you till the end of the race. I don't know what I'd do if I lost my phone. I suppose I'd latch on to the next Vol State runner I found and follow them lockstep. At least Glenn was only 48 miles from the end.

I asked Bobby where to eat in Pelham, and he said there were two main places, but he was biased because his daughter ran one: Tess's Kitchen Café. Unfortunately it wasn't going to be open when I got to Pelham, and by this point in the race, I was more interested in finishing than dawdling. Bobby offered me a free sub a couple of times, but I was jonesing for a more substantial meal. If I'd only known where Bobby's place was, I would've programmed it in for a long stop. Rookie ignorance.

Sadly, I bid farewell to Bobby and his amazing set-up and headed on to Pelham. The Simply Southern Café, looked like a house and served Southern favorites like fried catfish, fried bologna and cheese melt, country fried steak, and the long-cooked vegetables my Granny Booth made when I was as a child. I could've sworn I heard the waitress repeat back to a customer, "Oprah, mac 'n cheese, and turnip greens." She probably said "okra," but I couldn't be sure.

Departing from the Southern theme for reasons even I can't fathom—my stomach had a life of its own these day—I got the California Fried Chicken Salad. It hit the spot.

Bobby Brown and just a portion of his amazing setup.

I had hoped some real food would refresh me, but it didn't work that way. On the way out of town, I was still just exhausted. The roads were not much traveled, but the sun was getting to me like it always seemed to in the middle of the day. I saw a deserted Methodist Church with benches on a shaded porch, and I decided that would be just the ticket. I was getting twinges of plantar fasciitis in both feet, and I thought some stretching and resting would do me good. I'd been hobbled by plantar fasciitis on my first trip Camino de Santiago and had ended up hiking the last two weeks as a cripple. I didn't want to take any chances in the homestretch of this race. The concrete of the church porch and a gentle breeze blowing through it were a welcome respite. I lay down on my ground cloth, put my feet up on the bench, and set my watch for 15 minutes. Temporary bliss.

Surprisingly, I've grown quite fond of country churches in the South and how they provide sanctuary for transients. It reminded me of medieval Europe when criminals would claim sanctuary in churches—sacred spaces where weapons and arrests were verboten. Even on the backroads of Tennessee, I felt safe at churches and figured that none of the folks there would shoot me if I climbed up on their porch and fell asleep for a while. It was bad optics if nothing else, plus something about the church itself seemed to remind people of their Christian duty to the down-and-out. Commercial places seemed semi-safe too, but I was pretty sure some would call the police first and ask questions later if they found you sleeping on the premises. People's houses—not including road angels—seemed the most dangerous. I wasn't worried about a random violent person; I was worried about homeowners who were afraid. Scared people are the most dangerous—except for garden-variety psychopaths, I mean. I have to say, though, I hadn't met anyone dangerous on this journey, despite passing by plenty of houses that looked ominous with their confederate flags and aggressive signage. But I had a newfound appreciation for the Christian ethos that frowned upon churchgoers being mean to stinky, exhausted people trespassing on church property.

The respite had been good, but back on the road, I was still not a happy bunny. It felt like the minor breaking points were hitting more frequently as I got nearer to the Rock—no doubt, the accumulation of sleep deprivation and pain and wanting more than ever to be done. For many days, I hadn't been able to envision the Rock. It was too depressing to think about how far away it was, so I'd just compartmentalized and tried to think about the next thing. Now that I *could* imagine the Rock, the mental grasping was making me more miserable.

Farther along, Valley Home Community Church's sign reminded me that "SIN BURN IS PREVENTED BY SON SCREEN."

Maybe I should just think about Monteagle, my next stop, but that didn't really interest me. Only the Rock interested me. Well, maybe the Clarion Inn was kind of interesting before the Rock. I just kept thinking about why road angels were so good to us and why we have such a hard time in this country being good to poor people? Republicans rightly worry a lot about people gaming the system, taking advantage of it. Democrats should probably worry more about that too. It seems like human nature to become entitled when we get handouts. Vol State runners are susceptible to this too. On the bus before I started this race, I asked if road angels had a collection box to help them pay for goodies. I was gobsmacked that they did it all for free. Now I'm quite used to getting free handouts, and I would think it odd if some road angels put out a set of prices for various treats they were offering. How did I so quickly get used to strangers offering me free stuff? How did I come to feel entitled to free stuff? For their part, the road angels didn't seem bothered in the least that we might be taking advantage of them. They didn't ask us if we had money for a hotel before they offered us a tent in their yard. They didn't ask if we could afford to pay for the Gatorade in their cooler. They didn't try to figure out if we were taking advantage of their generosity. They just helped us. They just loved us.

Bobby Brown said he did it to hear people's stories. But in a diverse country like this, we have *so* many stories. And immigrants have even *more* stories with *more* peril and *more* perseverance for way bigger stakes than getting to the Rock. I wondered how much the Vol State tracker has to do with all this interest and largess. What if the immigrants coming to the U.S. were all on a tracker? We'd know their name, age, and the country they were from. Some algorhythmic AI type thingy would figure out their mileage. They might have trouble getting wi-fi to check-in every 12 hours. Maybe we'd give them a tracker so they wouldn't have to bother. And we could watch their progress. We'd need a Laz-like figure to be writing poems twice a day about how the race to the border was going. Maybe we'd take the media folks who could speak Spanish or Haitian Creole off the Trump-Biden-Swift stories and send them to Central America and Haiti to get the stories of these racers.

We wouldn't talk about open or closed borders. We'd have a grassroots movement to actually start trying to figure out which people should cross the border or not and why. We'd see why they were seeking asylum and think for ourselves about whether they deserved it. The stories would all be posted on a special website, and we'd get to know Juan and Teresa and Jean and Fabienne and their children. We'd hear about how far they walked each day and what trains they managed to get on and what sort of crummy places they found to sleep, eat, and go to the bathroom. We'd hear all their scary stories and hope for their safe passage to the Texas border or not. The most intrepid of road angels could cross the border into Mexico and set up angel stops with free Gatorade and water and zero-gravity chairs. Others could just have angel stations along the road in Texas or California or outside airports where immigrants might get sent. There must be some way to infuse all this American goodness into more worthy endeavors than helping pseudo-pilgrims like us, running and walking 500K across Tennessee and a few other bits of states to a "mythical" place called Castle Rock.

We all act like Vol State matters. Laz acts like it matters. Jan acts like it matters. The road angels act like it matters. People along the way wish us good luck. Cars get out of our way. Our lives matter enough that they don't want to hit us. I can't help but wonder, though, why does this race matter to all these people more than the life-and death journeys of "others"? Why do we matter more than immigrants fleeing for their lives? Is it because we have American flags on our packs, because we won the uterus lottery and were born here, because we either ARE Americans or we're foreigners who aren't planning to live here? Even here in the U.S., there are so many poor people who need real help, who are struggling to put food on the table. Instead of them working three jobs, if we put them in some Vol State-like game and got them to walk across Tennessee in the heat, would we cheer them on then? Would we donate to their cause?

I was losing it—hot and tearful on my way up to Monteagle. Chris had told me that Michelle Chauvin had quit at 250. I just kept thinking about patching up her back at God knows what that was—Mile 75 maybe—and she carried on another 175 miles with that bra digging into her back or without a bra and trying to navigate it that way. Pam Pratt's story wasn't so funny now. It was all funny if you made it to the Rock, and if you didn't....

Besides crying about immigrants and poor people and DNFs, I kept taking pictures of roadkill, which are everywhere if you happen to be walking Southern backroads. It must have been some contemplation on death. I could just as easily be roadkill as one of these armadillos or deer or possums or raccoons or birds or turtles or whatever. And I will be some day, some version of roadkill, felled by an accident or a disease or old age or heat stroke. Every picture of some flattened animal, I thought, *there but for the grace of God go I.* We'll all be roadkill sooner or later, but for now, we're in this fraught, beautiful, kooky life game together. Why can't we get along like we do at Vol State?

People always think that the important part of Vol State is the hardening: the toughness and grit that you either bring with you or develop along the way so you can finish. The race will almost certainly harden determination and calf muscles. The hardening isn't the main thing, though. The main thing is the softening—the softening of the mind, the softening of the harsh lenses through which we see others' suffering. It's the breaking down that matters more than the toughening.

On mountain goats and quitting

Tony sent me a picture of his Flying Pig sandwich with the Mountain Goat Market sign in the background. Three more miles. I climbed up the switchbacks to Monteagle. I've climbed lots of hills, and 1000 feet at a reasonable grade like this one wasn't daunting, but I'd never done it in the heat of summer with so little sleep. It seemed to go up forever. I periodically stopped to sit on guardrails for breathers. Surely it would be cooler at the top.

Eventually, the climb ended in the lovely little tourist mountain town of Monteagle. I headed to the Mountain Goat Market and walked into mountain-hipster sensory overload. Brightly colored paintings of mountain goats everywhere: mountain goats with mushrooms, mountain goats in black hats and coats, mountain goats in sunglasses, mountain goats eating pizza, mountain goats flying, mountain goats standing on bicycles, mountain goats riding bicycles, mountain goats on picnic blankets drinking wine. And people everywhere: families with little kids running around, gangs of well-dressed teenagers, couples on mountain getaways. Loud colors and noise. My first inclination was to turn right around and leave, but instead, I wandered around, looking at the food. The pizzas looked good. I wasn't sure where I would sit, though. I didn't want to sit too close to anyone because I could only guess how bad I smelled. Surely there was a quieter place to get something to eat. I looked at my map. Up in Smoke BBQ was a block away.

I walked up the road. No cars out front. The BBQ joint was closed. I needed to get food somewhere. I had just walked past the Local Bar and Grill 2 parking lot with a few pick-up trucks out front. Maybe that was the ticket. "WHO HAS MORE FUN THAN US," said a sign out front. A statement, not a question. Only a handful of people at the bar. They all turned to look at me when I opened the door. Suddenly, this didn't look like my kind of place either. I felt like Goldilocks—*this restaurant is too crowded, this restaurant is too quiet, this restaurant is too closed.* I was a beggar; why was I being so choosey? I went back to the

Mountain Goat. A few spaces to sit had opened up, and I ordered one of their herbivore pizzas—pesto, artichokes, spinach, roasted red peppers, mozzarella, and feta. I added pepperoni for good measure and bought a Creature Comforts Tropical IPA to wash it down.

The late lunch crowd was starting to clear out. At another time, this would've been my kind of place. In the bathroom stall, a sign read, "Please do not flush paper towels, tissues & wipes, sanitary products, kittens & puppies, prosthetic limbs, hopes & dreams. Thank you."

To amuse myself while waiting for the pizza, I checked the weather. "Thunderstorms likely around 4:30 p.m. Potential for severe thunderstorms." I had about 45 minutes. And the storms should be over by 9 p.m. Great. The good news was that the temperatures would only be in the 80s.

I finished the beer and a delicious pizza, then headed back out toward Tracy City. I could see the black wall menacing from the north. Tracy City was about six miles away at Mile 280. I was primed for a fun time with the storms approaching and the Friday afternoon mountain traffic heating up. At least I wasn't hungry or thirsty, and the beer had taken the edge off my mental ranting.

I made it almost 2 miles to just outside Summerfield Market before the skies exploded. I ran the last 100 yards in the rain to the convenience store-laundromat duplex. When I bought a Gatorade, the guys at the counter said I was welcome to wait out the rain in the laundromat if I wanted. I sat there for a while, staring out the window and sizing up my predicament. I could wait here for four hours or so and then head out in the dark to Tracy City. There were no hotels on the route, and the ones in Tracy City were crazy expensive anyway because it was summer in the mountains—and that was IF they even had a vacancy anywhere. I was going to have to rough it, one way or the other.

Oh, hell. The Rock was not getting any closer by watching clothes tumble dry. I might as well suck it up and move toward the eventual end to this madness. Forty miles and a lifetime ago, Robin Bailey had suggested the fashionable look of a trash-bag skirt—cut the bottom and use the drawstrings as a belt—to match the ever-chic emergency poncho. I had brought along a trash bag from her for just this sort of glamorous occasion.

I went to one hiking stick and an umbrella and cinched the see-through poncho with a chest-lamp belt so the traffic had a better chance of noticing me. *Are we having fun yet?*

Cars splashed greetings as they passed, and I went into some numb zombie state, a shell of a former human, moving through the sheets of gray wet. *The Rock. Gotta make it to the Rock.*

204-Hour Tracker, comments in italics (Friday evening, July 21, 2023):

Me: 281 miles--*"From a schadenfreude/misery-loves-company point of view, it pleases me a bit that Laz also had to suffer through those crazy storms yesterday. I know that thought comes from a small-minded, mean corner of my personality, but there it is. Loved the tent-poles line, Laz!"* In his 192-hour update, Laz had written,

> *rather than the customary*
> *celebration*
> *arriving finishers*
> *(and their families)*
> *were assigned tent poles to*
> *cling to*
> *so that the entire finish set up*
> *would not*
> *blow off the mountain.*

Oprah was 14 miles back.

Anonymous: *"Great a tornado is coming. Maybe I will get a decent tailwind."*

Anonymous: *"It's all downhill from here! Except for those hills..."*

It was great to see that Regina Sooey finished in 8:01:00:23.

Suddenly, a white sedan pulled into the road right in front of me and stopped. The driver rolled down his window. "Are you in the Vol State Race?"

I nodded, smiled, and quickly calculated that there was nothing in the world this angel could do for me. I was doomed to the drenched life I was in.

"Well, we've got a Vol State walker." He rolled down the back window, and there was Glenn Kasper in the backseat, looking awfully sad. I was shocked. It's hard to explain the horror of seeing a Vol Stater in a car, the finality of it at this late stage in the race. There would be no talking him out of anything. The car made it a done deal. Vol State was over for him.

"I'm out," he said. "I can't do it. I've been dizzy for three days, and it's just too dangerous to be out there walking in this." I looked around: hard rain, small shoulder, heavy traffic. *Couldn't he have just slept under a pavilion someplace or in a laundromat?* Too late for these questions.

"Awww, man, I was trying to catch up with you," I said. "You've had such great posts."

"Well, you would've caught up with me."

"Bummer. We could've had such a good time." No doubt hyperbole—maybe a better time than I was having by myself, maybe a better time than he was having before he quit.

The couple had stopped me because Glenn had lost his phone in the crazy storm yesterday, so he didn't have Laz's or Jan's phone number. He couldn't call and get picked up. They were driving along, figuring they'd eventually run into some dumbass Vol Stater out in the rain. I mean me. I pulled up the numbers on my phone, and the woman in the passenger's seat took a picture of them, so they could get a hold of Jan and get Glenn a ride back to his car, the Clarion, wherever—I didn't really know. But I felt incredibly sorry for him. This was his second time trying, and he blew out at 267 last time. This year he'd made it to 279—amazingly far, both years. The Rock was so close.

Who was I kidding? The Rock was still many miles away. Glenn made me realize that I wasn't out of the woods yet.

"Rest up," I told Glenn as he sat in a dry car with people helping him. Maybe he was not the one to feel sorry for.

Chapter 14

THE LOST KINGDOM OF THE MANGLED RED TENT

> *"Do we need an ironic dystopian-future*
> *race that mimics what's to come?"*
> --my friend Danny Bodiford, musing on Vol State

And the search for a trash can

Tracy City was a wet ghost town at Mile 280. I went into a Save A Lot and picked up some water and candy bars which I consumed in the parking lot. Then, I looked for a trash can to throw the bag away but found none in any of the usual spots there or on the way out of Tracy City. This would be no big deal except that I had to carry the bag. I supposed I could've taken off my vest and tied it to the back, but that seemed too much trouble. I knew there was an aid station somewhere outside Tracy City. They'd have a trash container.

I couldn't envision walking the next 14 miles into Jasper without a rest. Even downhill, it was too far without some sleep. I was wet and exhausted and beyond grouchy; I needed a chair under cover or at least someplace to put my ground cloth out of the rain.

I called Chris and vented to him, yet again, about the unbridled torment. I couldn't imagine the roles being reversed: me being on the other side of the Atlantic, listening to him so miserable on the phone while walking in dark, rainy, rural Tennessee. He was a brick through it all.

The traffic on State Road 150 had slacked off considerably. My chest lamp lit the wet road in front of me and—when I turned my body—the woods to the left or right. It was mountain country, and the next commercial building was the Mountain Mart at Mile 291. I was petrified of missing the aid station because if I did, I'd have to walk all the way to the Mountain Mart, or I'd have to sleep on somebody's driveway, which didn't sound like a great idea. If I missed the angel stop, I wouldn't know it, so there would be no way of going back—just as well because backtracking for any reason was anathema.

I continued for what seemed a long way out of Tracy City. *Where was that tent?*

I tried to call my friend Jane, but I couldn't talk to her because my earbuds weren't working, and I couldn't hold the phone, the umbrella, the hiking stick, and the trash all at the same time. Just as I was trying to juggle all this in the rain and walk at the same time, Chris buzzed in again on WhatsApp.

"What? What do you want?" I yelled at him. "I'm trying to talk to Jane, and nothing is working."

In his calm, charming British voice, he said, "I just wanted to tell you that I found out where the angel station is. It's at Mile 285.5, according to an old Facebook post."

"OK, thanks," I said. He hung up and I immediately felt terrible in a whole new way. It was the middle of the night in England, and he had just been trying to help and make my life a lot better, and I'd screamed at him. My best friend and best help of all on this stupid trip, and I couldn't just be nice to him. Adding guilt to all the rest of my pain about put me over the top.

I sent him a text that he didn't answer: "Love you, Boo. I'm sorry. *Heart emoji.*"

I trudged for another two and a half miles of katydids and frogs—another hour and a bit—until finally, about midnight, I saw a path of solar lights. A car behind me lit up the red tent. I'd found it: the lost kingdom of the mangled red tent. I shined my light on a professionally printed sign by the road: **"LAVS STREET OASIS."** It was certainly that.

I walked up the lit path and saw Terra and Kendra sleeping in two portable chairs just inside a big tent that had once had a high roof on it, which, thanks to one of the pernicious storms, had collapsed inside the tent so it looked like a big "M" with tables, chairs, boxes, and coolers strewn inside. My arrival woke the women up, and we chatted for a while. Terra and I complained like four-year-olds about the "stupid race," "stupid rain," "stupid tent." "Where's Kurt?" I asked.

"He went on ahead."

"Stupid Kurt," I added. (Just kidding, Kurt.) There was something cathartic in all this childish whining. Just beyond the horizon of pain and misery, the whole damn thing was funny. Kendra was much more mature and measured than Terra and me. She didn't complain; she even seemed to know how much she appreciated the race while still in the middle of the awful parts. In a mangled red tent 27.5 miles from the finish, I could appreciate all the people who'd helped us but not the race itself. I could, occasionally, see the humor in it, though.

The girls were getting ready to leave when Ed walked up, still in his whites. Why wasn't that bee suit filthy by now? It didn't look that bad. When the girls left, Ed and I took over the two chairs, and I got to enjoy a motion-detector light that would come on and shine exactly into my eyes every time the wind moved something. (With my problem-solving facilities maxed out, it never occurred to me to turn the chair around to face the other way.) The station mercifully had a box for trash, and I had a Styrofoam cooler in front of me to put my feet on. I got out my lightweight jacket and my ground cloth to cover me up because I was suddenly super cold, almost too cold to stay in one place, thanks to being wet and the wind picking up. I needed some sleep, though, even in fits and starts.

At some point in the night, Gina came up. Another zombie-like figure, she put her ground cloth down, curled into a ball, and passed out on the other side of the cooler. I could only imagine what a rough night she'd had. I looked over at Ed and realized he had his space blanket spread over his bee-keeper clothes. Why hadn't I gotten out my space blanket? That's the mark of a veteran—not only do they bring a space blanket, but they have brain cells enough to use it. He'd worked for NASA—*of course* he'd remembered his space blanket! I'd carried this silver packet the whole race and never used it, even when I was freezing! It was too late now. I'd wake up Ed and Gina both if I went scrambling around in my bag, looking for it, then unfolding it, crinkle by crinkle. I fell asleep again for the 400th time.

A loud crash jolted me awake. I didn't know what it was, but there was a newly collapsed part of the tent between me and Ed. I couldn't see him anymore. I wondered if the whole tent would collapse. *Don't know. Don't care.* I went back to sleep.

About 3:30 am, I decided it was time to get moving again. The body's powers of recovery never ceased to amaze me. Ed had already gone. I gathered my stuff and left Gina on the ground. I peed in the woods behind the tent and suddenly realized I'd forgotten my hiking pole. I went back up to get it and naturally set off the motion-detector light again. Gina woke up. "I'm so sorry," I said, trying to get out of there as quickly as possible.

I left Gina curled up under plastic by the cooler at the Lost Kingdom of the Mangled Red Tent.

Need picnic supplies and an assault rifle?

The walking was much better with a little sleep and no rain and virtually no cars on the road. My plan was to stop at the Mountain Mart if it was open, then head to Steve's place, the road angel I had dinner with at the Supper Before the Last Supper. He had a house at Mile 295. I had no idea if he would be awake, but it would be good to see him if he was. What a life I'd lived since I ate with him 10 days ago and knew almost nothing about anything. If he wasn't awake, I'd rest for a few minutes and write him a note. I'd walk on to the Clarion in Kimball, where it all started, and see how soon they'd let me into a room. Then a shower, a nap, get up, leave most of my pack, and walk the final 14 miles to the Rock with a lighter load. I'd get my sticker, talk to Laz maybe, and that would be about it. It was almost over.

The Mountain Mart was 5.5 miles beyond the red mangled tent, and I was texting with Chris about when it opened. (He had forgiven me for my earlier outburst.) Google had them opening at 6 am, but when I saw the lights on the Mountain Mart's stone façade a little after five, a green pick-up truck was parked outside. A good sign! And the door was open.

The Mountain Mart is one of those rare places where you can get a superb bacon-and-egg biscuit and an assault rifle with plenty of ammunition. One-stop shopping, in fact, for all your grocery, hunting, picnic, and self-defense needs. Top-notch sustenance, including baked goods, plus rifles, handguns, knives, mace, etc. A prominent American flag hung in the corner near the soft drinks, and another American flag, plus a Marine Corps flag and an Air Force flag, hung over the chips. The military-veteran owners had taken advantage of an entrepreneurial gap.

I told the woman at the cash register how great the biscuit was.

"I've got some fresh-baked strawberry muffins here too," she said.

"Yes, please." I wasn't really hungry, but I wanted to try one.

When I walked out of the place, I saw Gina hoofing it down the road in the first light of day. "Hey, Gina. This place is terrific!" I called.

"Gotta keep going. Can't stop."

I filed in next to her. "Do you want a strawberry muffin?" I asked.

"Naw, that's OK. You keep it."

"Really, I just wanted to try it." I tore off a bite. "You have the rest."

She took it and ate it. The muffin was good, but I was stuffed from the biscuit and French Vanilla Frappuccino. I just couldn't eat much these days.

Gina told me what had been happening with her. Before the mangled tent, she'd been walking along that deserted mountain road, having scary hallucinations. She wanted to quit. She called Jan, who talked her down and told her about the mangled tent stop. No wonder she'd looked so rough coming up to the tent.

I walked on ahead of her as the road started its switch-back descent into Jasper.

"Have you seen Facebook this morning?" Chris texted.

"No."

"There is what looks like a card on the table at the hotel where you collect your tracker."

I checked it out. Sure enough. Claus Rasmussen, a Vol State racer from Denmark, had posted, "Waiting for you in Kimball Nancy Barber—we carried it with us since one of your friends gave it to us in Union City." There was a picture of a bamboo plant with a card in front of it that said, "Nancy Barber Hello!"

They carried a plant all the way from Union City?! I checked the tracker and found out that Claus was crewed—thank goodness. I started laughing, thinking of Claus running with a plant and an umbrella! I blew up the photo and saw in the small print on the card that it was from my Aunt Fran's cousin Pamela. She'd left her phone number on it. I called Chris. "Can you believe that Fran's cousin sent a plant for me to Kimball?"

"Are you sure she sent the plant?" he said. "Maybe it was just the card."

"Do you think it's the hotel's plant? I don't know. Pam's Southern. I think she sent it." This landed me in absolute hysterics. A Danish crew brought a bamboo plant from Union City to Kimball, Tennessee, along with a "Hello" card from someone I'd never met?

I commented on the post: "Wow! How sweet!! Thank you, Claus, for the careful transport over the last ten days, and thank you, Fran and Pamela, for the beautiful plant (and for your faith that I would make it back to Kimball!) *heart, smiley face, smiley face with heart eyes.*" (Now that I thought about it, I was likely to make it back to Kimball, one way or the other, even if it was in Jan's van.)

Speaking of Jan, it wasn't too long before she posted, "Nancy Barber, for clarification, the plant in the photo is the property of the Clarion Hotel. The "Hello" placard was what was left for you by Claus Rasmussen." The misunderstanding made me laugh even harder. I was positively giddy as the early-morning mountain miles into Jasper ticked off.

216-Hour Tracker, comments in italics (Saturday morning, July 22, 2023): 294 miles—I was too sleep deprived to remember what I wrote, but of the few remaining comments at 216 hours, the one I might have written was: *"March of the math-challenged zombies . . . ."* A dozen miles ahead of Oprah. With any luck, my last check-in.

Anonymous: *"Party doesn't end until we get there! Leave the light on!"*

Anonymous: *"Somehow this course never ends..."*

Tony was at 302 miles at that check-in. He would be there soon! That made me so happy I could cry.

At the end of his driveway, Steve Smalling had a black trash can with **Mile 295 Vol 2023 State** painted on it in white. He was already sitting in one of his portable chairs next to a cooler with water and a box for trash. Up the drive in his carport, he had a cot set up and more goodies. I sat down for a chat. Steve is smart, interesting, and kind, a diehard UT

Volunteers fan and a passionate Vol State angel. He's the kind of guy Northerners might underestimate because of his gentlemanly Southern accent. I felt like I was seeing an old friend. Soon, a "civilian" woman named Beverly joined us, a friend of Steve's and an ultrarunner in her own right with minimalist sandals; then Gina arrived. I don't remember much about what we talked about there. I was exhausted again, coming down off whatever rejuvenation I'd gotten at the red, mangled tent and the Mountain Mart. And I was feeling the pull of the Rock. It wouldn't be long now. Tara arrived just before I left. Boy, had she come a long way from her blistered start!

We took pictures with Steve, and I set off for Kimball, only five miles away, but it felt like fifty. Mostly commercial, much of it on sidewalks—it wasn't hard, but it went on and on and on.

Gina Kimrey, Steve Smalling, and me at the Mile 295 angel stop. (Photo by Beverly Burton Reed)

Finally, I was at the Clarion Pointe once again. Back into the lobby, I walked, much more battered and seasoned than the last time. Anything familiar felt like home after so many days of new places. In one way, I felt like I'd just been there, ready to go to a party in the parking lot with a bunch of people I didn't know. In another, it seemed like a million years ago. The bamboo plant was on a high table to the left, my "hello" card propped up on one side. I chuckled. I was sorry I'd never gotten to meet Pamela, my aunt's mysterious cousin whose stories kept popping up along the way. She was awfully sweet to try to track me down.

I picked up the card. Next to it was a sign that gave Vol State instructions for picking up the tracker. When we left the hotel and headed for the Rock, we were supposed to pick up a tracker to wear around our neck and text Carl or Laz to let them know we were on our way. This would ensure that someone would be at the Rock when we arrived.

It was late morning when I got to the Clarion, but the front desk clerk kindly let me check in early. I hobbled to my room, which seemed unimaginably wonderful, took a quick shower, napped for an hour, and changed into some relatively clean clothes. I found out Tony had made it to the Rock and dashed off a text: "Awesome job, Tony!! The Rock must have a gravitational pull for you—you've flown the last couple of days!"

One more push

Gary Ferguson and John Price were sitting in the lobby when I arrived, looking clean, relaxed, and happy. "How's it going?" John asked.

"OK," I smiled. "Ready for the last push." They wished me well, and John told me that it was pretty easy until the final climb, which was quite steep. John had finished Vol State many times as well as lots of other ultra journeys. He'd written the first book I bought in preparation for the race, *The Last Annual Vol State Road Race Book, 2nd Edition*, which listed the route, turn by turn, with attention to what sort of facilities were along the way, including hotels, restaurants, convenience stores, vending machines, etc.

Talking to John and Gary in the lobby, I felt, for the first time, that I was in the club. It's hard to explain, but even though I hadn't finished, they treated me like one of the gang instead of a newbie who might or might not make it. By the Clarion, barring something extraordinary, everyone knows you'll finish. It reminded me of the last day of the Tour de France when they ride down the Champs-Élysées: nobody's gaining any time or anything. The leader is taking a glory ride, and the other cyclists are just pedaling to the end of the long journey. (Except the leaders in our race had been clean and home for days!)

The first part of the route through Kimball is all commercial: Walmart, McDonalds, Dunkin Donuts, Wendy's. The route goes along Highway 72/27 and makes a left at the Sonic Drive-In, where you can see the cerulean steel arches of the iconic Blue Bridge, officially known as the Shelby A. Rhinehart Memorial Bridge. The last time I saw it was shortly after dawn on July 12th, in a bus showing us the route backward. Now I'd walked back to the bridge from Missouri in nine and a half days. It didn't seem possible.

I hiked up New Hope Rd. I didn't know if it was part of Sand Mountain or not, but there had already been a lot of *up*, so I figured it had to count toward the 1000+ feet of climbing before the Rock. I called my mother. She'd supported me all along the way. She always said she'd been given special grace with a child like me to allow her not to worry too much when I went off on crazy adventures. We talked about Laz.

"You know, Fran and Chris don't like him," she told me.

I laughed. "Well, I think he's great." And I do. I did even on the last mountain climb at the end of his miserable race. He's brilliant, wise, funny, free-thinking, and innovative—also grumpy, stubborn, and ornery. He dispenses tough love easily. Besides being a poet, Laz is a teacher. He lectures through the structure, routes, rules, emails, and updates of his races. Vol State is set up so you can't possibly miss life lessons about patience, fortitude, compassion, appreciation, and humor. Just because he's the evil villain in this reality-video game doesn't mean I don't appreciate the actor playing the character and how much he adds to the experience.

As I neared the game's finish, I felt OK, better than I had since early on the first day, and I didn't feel so great at the beginning. I remembered panicking about cramps in my feet before I stepped off the ferry, but the Hoka Bondis had held up fine. Unlike many of my compatriots, I hadn't had to cut out any parts of the shoes so that swollen toes and bunions could peek out. I'd had five blisters over 9 ½ days, and they were all in check. Not bad at all. (I would eventually lose five toenails.)

A pick-up truck approached me from the opposite direction. There was Terra, leaning out the passenger window, her hair blowing in the wind. "Way to go! Great to see you! You got this!"

I just grinned as they stopped. She was in the truck with a woman driving and another in the back seat—family, I assumed. They'd been at the Rock to greet her and pick her up. Terra tried to warn me, "This mountain is steep. It's way worse than Monteagle. It goes straight up. It doesn't have switchbacks like Monteagle. And the road lasts a lot longer than you think it's going to last. And the corn lasts a lot longer than you think it's going to last. And the woods last a lot longer than you think they're going to last!"

"Always the voice of sweetness and light and optimism!" I laughed.

The woman in the backseat said, "You want a beer?"

"Oh, I would love a beer, but I better not."

"She can't have a beer," said Terra. "She'd end up being crewed." Which I had forgotten about. Now that Terra was finished, she was no longer one of us. The rules state that a screwed runner can only get help from another runner currently in the race or a road angel on the course, certainly not the relatives of a finished runner.

The woman in the back said, "Well, how about some ice?"

"She can't have ice!" yelled Terra. "She can't have anything from us, or she'll be crewed."

I just laughed. "Terra and Kendra taught me how to drink beer on Vol State," I told the women.

"Not a surprise," said the driver. They all wished me luck and congratulations, and with a wave, they drove off.

Terra and Kendra were terrific. I liked their style—their determined but light-hearted approach to the race—and I enjoyed the one beer I'd actually gotten to have with them at the convenience store.

This was into the home stretch, maybe seven miles left, about halfway to the Rock from the Clarion. Terra had disabused me of the idea that I'd done much of the climb, but it didn't matter. This was all going to be over, and life would be different.

My mom, Aunt Fran, and my friend Danny all thought it was terrible to put a big climb at the end of such a crazy race. I thought it made perfect sense, definitely in Laz's philosophical wheelhouse. You can't have an evil villain in a game without this sort of ending.

I hadn't worried about the climb because I knew I was near the end. How bad could it be? John and Terra had tried to warn me, but I hadn't really paid attention.

People on the roads were so kind this last day. I assumed that folks in the area knew about the race. They yelled out their windows, honked their horns, and waved. It was super sweet and almost made me cry every time as I headed into the last climb. The light was softening in the late afternoon as the road got steeper. Plenty of veterans had written and talked about the misery of Sand Mountain, but I'd brushed it off. What they hadn't mentioned was how beautiful it was—stunning vistas of mountain lakes and barns by ponds. A sign said, "Welcome to Sweet Home Alabama. Governor Kay Ivey." With more energy, I might've put on Lynyrd Skynyrd and videoed myself dancing a jig in front of the sign for the Vol State Facebook page. But energy was at a premium; no need to squander it.

I stopped to rest on several guard rails along the way, called Chris, and texted with my Aunt Fran. Time had been hobbled, as had my walking pace. It's always the way at the end of even just a long day of hiking. The first miles are a polka, and the last few a dirge. Anything I could do to make time pass was helpful. Everyone was encouraging and excited that it was almost over. People I cared about had gotten less sleep these ten days because of me, and I was feeling so appreciative of everyone who had helped me: the road angels, my family, the race staff, my friends, strangers in cars and stores. This last climb belonged to all of us. Except I was the one who wanted to pass out behind a guard rail.

I did not pass out, and the climb eventually, mercifully came to an end. As much as I had been *for*, in theory, a big climb to end this stupid race, in hindsight, I would just as soon Laz had found some idyllic spot by Nickajack Lake, 633 feet above sea level, rather than Castle Rock at 1,378 feet. As usual in this race, my preferences mattered not a whit.

At Mile 311, a guy in a pick-up truck, who lived nearby, stopped to ask me questions about the race. He had heard of it but didn't know how it worked. Three miles from the end!

All I had to do was stay on my feet for three miles, and then I could stop.

I took the lefthand turn onto the street unaffectionately known as Cheese Grater Rd. Officially Castle Rock Road, but bumpy enough on trashed feet for a mile and a half to earn its nickname. My feet were numb to the pain by this point; just staying upright was the challenge. Part way down the road, I saw a young man next to coolers ahead on the right. The road angel, Shane Blevins, also had chairs, which made me quietly thrilled. I took one of his waters, but not an apple, and sat down with him for a chat. Shane had encouraging signs on all his coolers: **"Vol State Runners, here are some apples for a quick snack. Keep up the great work." "Welcome Vol State Runners. Good luck and safe travels on your journey. You're almost there. Keep going."**

We were still in Alabama, but the Georgia line was just up ahead. Shane filled me in on the pit bulls farther down the lane and the accident he had been in that messed up his back. He was a fixture at the end of this race and had gotten to know many of the runners. I was pretty sure he was the last road angel, which made me sad. I would not be sorry to finish this race, but I would miss the road angels. I remembered what Shenoa had said many days ago in the Gleason Fire Station: "For me, I come back to see my friends in the aid stations. I've made so many friends over the years, and we've really bonded." At the time, that seemed like crazy talk. Now I understood. I wasn't coming back to Vol State, but I already missed so many people from the red counties of Tennessee who had taken such good care of me.

We spend so much of our lives trying to be self-sufficient and independent. The connections at Vol State happen because we're vulnerable and needy, and generous people step in to help us. How can we not feel a special bond with them?

From now on, I vowed to encourage people's most generous selves in real life. When someone offers me a hand with my luggage, instead of "No thank you, I've got it," I'm going to let them help. And be appreciative. I'm going to take strangers up on specific offers to be kind. In a world so focused on division, I'll let people make a generous connection—we'll both feel good. It's only my ego that invests in this commitment to independence—to show the world that I'm capable of doing it by myself. I'd rather have the kinship.

The Last Road Angel: Shane Blevins.

One More Mile . . . .

I said goodbye to The Last Road Angel and kept walking down Cheese Grater Road until I had to turn left through a gate. My GPX told me I was at Mile 313, finally in Georgia, in Marjorie Taylor Green's congressional district, where my erstwhile best friend was born and raised and where my father was born and partly raised—which is to say, the congressional district of my roots, at least in part.

From my early childhood, I remember Pa, my great-grandfather, in Shannon, Georgia, retired from the local paper mill. I remember Ma, nearly blind with filmy cataracts on her eyes, still making biscuits from scratch—a handful of this, a pinch of that—and I remember both of them dipping snuff on the front porch and spitting into a coffee can with paper towels in it. My people.

In a way, this is what Stephen Fry and the Greeks might call a *nostos* journey, a homecoming story. Fry says, "The answer is always at home." So many characters in literature and film—Odysseus, Dorothy, Bilbo Baggins, Luke Skywalker, Harry Potter, on and on—embark on their adventures and then try to find their way back home. Joseph Campbell says that the great stories of the world tell us to accept the "call to adventure," go through the "road of trials," and cross "the return threshold," bringing back home what we've learned. Adventurers often have a new appreciation of home. After Vol State, I do too.

There was no sign of Marjorie Taylor Green's crazy-making when I took the first step into her territory, wherever that step was. I didn't remember seeing a sign for Georgia. Instead of drama and demagoguery, white picket fences and canopied trees saluted the road, protecting the fields of corn from . . . what? Less beauty?

By the wrought-iron fence, a welcome sign had a red arrow and said, "TO FINISH only one more mile!" Finally.

Soon, I walked past the field with our cars in it. The field had been chock-full of vehicles the last time I saw it before walking up the lane with the future King of the Road, Ken Zemach, to catch the bus ten and a half days ago. (The only thing Ken and I had in common as competitors was that we were both committed to being one-and-done in this race.) Now there was just a spattering of cars left—the back-of-the-packers—my little red Kia Rio waiting on me. The rest of the racers were home or in the Clarion Pointe, many of them rejuvenated, even back to work, back to their families, back to their lives away from the white line.

Farther on, at a lefthand turn into the cornfield, another red arrow on another white sign: "Finish one mile no kidding." The shenanigans continued. And those who put the signs there had done so many ultras that they understood just how long each of these last legs was.

Finish one mile. No kidding.

I headed into the cornfield like Shoeless Joe Jackson after a game in Iowa, except that I was on a one-lane dirt road between all the stalks. I walked past corn and more corn and more corn. And after still more corn, I came to another white sign with a red arrow on it: "FINISH LAST MILE! (Really) (Trust me!)" Yeah, yeah, yeah.

Finish Last Mile (Really. Trust me.)

The corn road eventually turned into a forest road, and then there was another white sign with a red arrow: "Only 1 more mile! We really mean it this time!" It seemed interminable, but I knew I must be making progress because I was moving through different ecosystems. I walked farther into the forest, feeling a little like Gretel without Hansel. The forest was deserted and a bit eerie as the sun descended. I kept believing that just around the next bend would be the Rock, but each bend brought only more forest.

Until one bend brought me to a white sign with a black arrow on it: "FINISH One Mile! We would never lie to you!!"

I continued down the forest road, and then suddenly, I could hear voices. *I must be close.* I turned a corner, and there it was: two tents with folks sitting in portable chairs and a couple of coolers. Nobody seemed to notice my arrival, so I decided to video the finish scene. "Hey, she's filming us," I heard Laz say, which got a chuckle. I saw the iconic STOP sign on the safety rail and Nickajack Lake in the distance far below, the sun ready to set behind it. Carl had wandered over to the Rock—to make sure I got to the finish? To make sure I didn't fall off the cliff? His back was to me, and I couldn't help but laugh. This was—by a large margin—the most anticlimactic finish of any race I'd ever done in my life, and I had perhaps never been so happy to be at the end. I didn't have that euphoric feeling of achievement that some runners talk about, but boy, was I pleased to heed that STOP sign. Nine days, 11 hours, 23 minutes, and 33 seconds after Dorena Landing.

Stop time. Finally.

Everyone looked incredibly bored, but what they were was incredibly exhausted. Sherry and Ed had recently finished the race (Ed still in his bee suit, and Sherry, the reigning consecutive-finisher champ, draped in the U.S. flag as she had been on the ferry). Laz and Carl were exhausted too; they'd been greeting finishers for the last six days and nights. And Tara's husband Jeff was there, and he was exhausted too because he'd been waiting all day long with Laz and Carl for her to finish.

I touched the Rock with my hand and headed back to the tent. There was supposed to be a "throne" that each finisher sits on, but there were just a few empty chairs. I sat in one.

"So, was it as easy as you thought it would be?" Laz asked, for likely the 84th time, since I was the 84th finisher.

It was the perfect question to start me off: "Well, you know I had read a lot about this race, so I sort of understood the misery, and I really think you do a great job with the misery. I think you've got the misery right on track. It's fantastic. But I think the fun-to-misery ratio could use a little work."

They laughed.

"The most fun I had—well, I had two fun times. One was standing around a garbage can outside a convenience store and having a beer with three other Vol State runners. And I only got half way through the beer before one of them said, 'Don't you think we ought to get going?'

"And the second time I had fun was listening to Pam Pratt tell the bra story."

"My wife is really concerned about that story," said Laz.

"Is she concerned about Michelle and the bra, or is she concerned about the story being told?"

"She's concerned because now the story has brought to light the fact that Vol State women actually have breasts. And people didn't necessarily know that before, but now they do, and this could be a problem."

I laughed. He wanted to get back on track, though: "Did you cry?" he asked. His second perennial question, a sadistic one designed to find out when the race broke you. I remembered the start to Laz's 36-hour report: *they're all gonna cry*. The Rock made you feel like you were in some REI-inspired confessional booth, and you couldn't lie.

"Yes," I admitted. "I cried in the first major thunderstorm I got caught in."

Someone said something about the second one. "Did you cry in the second one?" Laz asked.

"No, I was tough by then." But the other place I cried that I didn't mention was on the road to Monteagle. I only cried when it was sweltering. I never cared to cry in the middle of the night or the morning or evening. But in the middle of the day, that's when I despaired of everything, and the race would get to me. The thunderstorm cry was existential, while the pre-Monteagle cry was more philosophical. I mean, I was plenty miserable before Monteagle, and that's a good enough reason to cry, but I was also crying because it seemed so crazy to me that while playing this mad game, so many people cared so much about us getting farther down the road to finish this thing. They were so willing to help us—and not just willing, but really loved getting involved. They enjoyed being generous to us and had fun getting to feel part of the race. I wish we could have games all over the place—figure out ways to turn our country's inequities into engaging journey games for everybody to play. Meaningful games that made everyone feel part of some larger purpose, some imperative to love one another and tough out the difficult road ahead. Too grandiose, too idealistic, too impractical, I know, but still.

Vol State is like a video game, but it's also like a reality TV race. People get excited about watching *The Greatest Race* or *Jet Lag: The Game* because they get invested in a real-life, goofy race. In some ways, Vol State is better than reality TV because people have access to it in real-time, even if they're far away. If you're in Sunderland, England, like my sister-in-law, you can pay attention to the tracker, and you can write "them walkers" on the Facebook page. You can maybe even talk to one of them on a WhatApp call. Everybody is accessible. They're either accessible in real life because you can find them on the Tennessee backroads, or they're accessible on Facebook to communicate with and encourage. And the competitors appreciate all the encouragement and *feel* encouraged by it. So, Vol State is more personalized, more true, less crafted, and less edited than reality TV or a video game. Somehow, the intimate reality of the game makes participants and spectators feel connected to each other.

Laz asked if I had any stories, and I told him I'd rather use my time on the throne to ask questions. "My first one is about Oprah. How did she end up in the race?"

Edward jumped in: "It started with the story of Oprah finishing her first marathon in like four and a half hours or whatever it was, and then lots of people wanted to beat Oprah's time or get in under Oprah's time, so that's the way it started."

"We support all origin stories about Oprah," said Laz, "but the truth is that one day it just happened. Suddenly Oprah was on the tracker, and nobody really knows how it happened." I laughed.

A little research revealed that she showed up on the tracker in 2015. Before then, her role was known as the "Grim Reaper," who eventually jumped to the HOTS tracker.

We talked about hallucinations, and Laz explained the difference between a hallucination (something that is wholly made up) and a visual distortion (the misperception of something that you see). So, when my brain read shadows in a pergola as people socializing in the middle of the night, that was a visual distortion, but when astronauts and angels started showing up at an overpass, that was a hallucination.

We talked about insurance for his races. He has normal event insurance for his contained races, but the journey runs are impossible to get insurance for because we're moving through so many different venues, so what insurance there is gets spread out all along the course. The bus insurance covers the bus rides; people's car insurance covers things if you get hit on the road; hotels, restaurants, etc., have insurance to cover things there. Mostly, the participants and Laz just hope for the best—refreshing in America's litigious culture.

We talked about the race itself. "I think everyone ought to do a race like this if they're reasonably healthy," said Laz. "I don't think everyone *will* do a race like this, but I think they should." I wondered if droves of Americans doing races like this might engender a shift in a culture so committed to comfort and, increasingly, to division?

We discussed Laz's 2018 transcon, when he averaged 27 miles a day, and his upcoming transcon, where he planned to average 23 miles a day. "And that's center-line miles, not GPS miles," he said. I had never thought about how different center-line miles were from GPS miles, but it explained why my watch never matched the mileage we were supposed to be doing. The Garmin said I'd done 346 miles by the time I got to the Rock. Map miles are center-line miles, but GPS miles more accurately register how far you've actually walked. Over time, with turns and moving on and off the shoulder, and every time you walk off the course into a convenience store or run up the Baileys' yard in the rain, it adds to the GPS miles.

In 2018, Laz said that he "quit staying at people's houses because they always want to cook for you, but they don't want to start cooking until you get there because they want you to eat at the meal's optimum point. I don't really care what I eat. I just need some sleep. Also, when you're staying at someone's house, you need to talk to 'em. They expect you to have some conversation, and if you're putting in that many miles, you don't have extra time. I'd meet people along the way who'd want to ask me questions, and I'd say, 'If you wanna walk with me. I'm happy to have a conversation, but you gotta walk with me. I don't have any time to stop.'"

Hearing him explain his journey-run philosophy, I realized that it was diametrically opposed to many of my endurance-journey hopes. I wanted to talk to people. I wanted to have time to sit and chat. I didn't see why you would want to go as fast as you could across the country when you could go slower and meet more people and take in more sights and do more stuff besides walking. Even Laz admitted, "I did miss a lot of things I would've liked to have seen, but I just didn't have time." You'd still miss a lot, even with a more leisurely pace, but why stress about putting in 27 or 23 miles a day if it meant you didn't have time to really connect with people while walking across this grand country?

On the other hand, although Vol State's race format doesn't give much time, it gives us something else—a game, an urgency, a cause, a specific imperative for leaving a place and moving on. Can you imagine how strung out across Tennessee 120 people would be if they didn't have to finish the race in 10 days? The poor road angels would never get any rest, all so that we could lollygag, hang out with folks, and see the sights.

Besides keeping things moving, the urgency also leads to a much more intense physical and mental challenge, which means more chance for the Default Mode Network to dissolve. I didn't have any enlightenment experiences like Bob Hearn, but I think my brain did start melting in ways it never had before on long-distance journeys. Maybe if I'd dawdled less, my DMN would've faded even more. Urgent purpose, even if it's invented, has its advantages.

Speaking of invented purpose, I had to ask Laz for my sticker. No conveying-of-the-sticker fanfare. It was a white oval with 314 on it in black, just like the ones you see on people's cars that have 13.1 or 26.2 on them. I couldn't quite see putting it on my car, but I did fancy the idea of seeing another 314 sticker out "in the wild."

I also got a patch made by John Fegyveresi, one of the Vol State veterans who started an annual Vol State patch series in 2014. He begins with a humorous photo from the year before that highlights the misery. The 2023 patch is of tall, thin Swedish runner Peter Schröder, the ninth-place finisher in 2022, who is standing in a cut-up black trash bag instead of a shirt, running shorts, sunglasses on his backward baseball cap, carrying snacks and a phone. He looks . . . feral.

Last but not least, I also got my choice of the remaining woodallions that Carl had slaved over in his woodworking shop. Little wooden "metals" with various carvings: the ferry, the Glendale Market, a Styrofoam cooler with a "Vol State" sign on it, the Bench of Despair with someone sleeping on it. I chose the simplest: the Styrofoam cooler. I would never think of them the same way again. The woodallions don't get talked about enough, but they're the coolest swag of all. I liked the idea of hanging mine from my rearview mirror. If you know, you know.

Gina wandered up to the Rock about 13 minutes after I did. I clapped for her and wooted. Seemed like somebody ought to after all she'd been through. Her turn to touch the Rock and sit on the throne.

Waiting at the Rock: (l to r) Gina Kimrey, Jeff Watson, Carl Laniak, Laz Lake, Sherry Meador, and Ed Masuoka.

This book begins with Bob Hearn's insight that Laz is an artist, a poet: "races are his medium and runners are his paints." It's certainly true, but Laz is also a magician, a trickster, a gamester, a conjurer, maybe even a shaman. He's the cool kid on the playground, inventing the next game. He imagines a race, and with a wave of enthusiasm, double-dog dares, and magic words, he turns it into a unifying force, a community. For a little while, he gives us all a sense of purpose and meaning in an absurd world. The fact that the purpose is a ridiculous invention? A petty detail that in no way detracts from its power to move people, literally and figuratively. I suspect these crazy Vol Staters may return year after year for a ritual renewal of the spirit away from the normal world of comfortable living, which, paradoxically, doesn't seem to make us especially comfortable.

With this renewed spirit, have I come to any greater understanding about why good people support Donald Trump? I have not. The late poet Mark Strand once said, "We live with mystery, but we don't like the feeling. I think we should get used to it." Maybe Vol State has helped me get used to it, at least a little. I do think I've come to a greater appreciation for what being American might still mean underneath the heavy blanket of culture wars, and I've found a hopeful glint that we might somehow find a way to wriggle out from under the oppressive covers and greet a new day in a better country for all of us, Trumpers and Never Trumpers alike. Maybe we just need more game nights or beers behind pickup trucks or overnight walks without any moonlight.

Then again, perhaps Laz and his crazy race highlight an inconvenient truth: that purpose in this chaotic world we inhabit is, at best, an invention. We all concoct the purpose that we want, the purpose that we're called to, the purpose that purports to make us our best selves and our best country, the purpose we can best convince ourselves matters—then we point our compass toward it. And when we Americans come together to support other people trying to achieve the purpose they've embraced—assuming that purpose doesn't hurt others—what an amazing country it is.

Maybe that's Lazarus Lake's superpower: he creates scenarios where purpose and support meet. Instead of a Cold Civil War, he gives us a reason to remember what's really made America great, the united Rock that we are or were or can be.

The Rock. Thanks for the memories, Laz. (Photo with my phone by Jeff Watson or Carl Laniak. I don't remember, and I'm pretty sure they don't either.)

EPILOGUE: THE CIGARETTE-SMOKING "UNLIKELIEST VOL STATER"

Remember Tara Watson, sitting by a gas station pump in Union City, Tennessee, having thrown away her sandals and bought a pair of running shoes from Goodwill? Remember, she didn't know what footcare products to buy at Walgreens to patch up her bloody feet? Remember, after 24 hours, Tara had done 32 miles and was DFL (Dead Fucking Last), only one mile ahead of Oprah? Remember when she was wide-eyed and adrenaline-fueled at the Huntingdon Police Department, having made up much ground? Remember her softly crying at the Central Christian Fellowship outside Hohenwald and later sleeping on the Bailey's porch after the storms? It turns out that Tara had never done a race of any kind before Vol State, and in the middle of the race, she even managed to walk past her bed in her hometown of Lewisburg and keep g oing.

She got to the Rock two hours and seven minutes after I did. It was dark, and she didn't at first notice her husband who had used a walker to get from his car, through the corn fields and through the woods, past all those damn signs, to the Rock. He had been waiting with Carl and Laz all day long. He didn't say anything when Tara came in; he just let her mind and eyes focus. She was sitting on a throne answering Laz's gambit: "Was it as easy as you thought it would be?" Then she saw her husband and hobbled over to give him a big hug.

I was up at the Rock for three hours, cold and exhausted but fascinated by the conversation and experience. Laz didn't let people drive themselves back to the hotel after dark. "We've had some bad luck with that in the past," he explained. I had no interest in arguing or walking back to my car. Erin and Chrissy also made it to the Rock while I was there. Eventually, Jan, the Meat-Wagon Lady, gave us all a ride to the Clarion Pointe. On the way down Sand Mountain, we stopped to check on Terrie, Kara, Shenoa, Casey, and Ray. They would all finish soon. I fell asleep in the Meat Wagon.

Laz ends his 2023 Vol State race reports writing about Tara:

> *10 and a half hours before oprah took that last spill in the*
> *mud*
> *tara watson reached the rock.*
>
> .
>
> *what got her there?*
> *the resolve that;"i'm going to do that".*
> *the vol state is;*
> *"ordinary people doing extraordinary things"*
>
> .
>
> *to all who finished vol state in 2023*
> *"the year of the thunderstorm"*
> *i salute you.*
>
> .
>
> *for 10 days in july you were all extraordinary!*

Tara Watson at Mile 76.   (Photo by Alexis Batausa.)

Acknowledgements

A journey race like Vol State and a book like this one take a village to pull off. First, I'm so thankful to my family. To Chris Darby for all his love and support, for listening to me chatter about Vol State for a year before it started, then helping guide me through it, then listening to Vol State stories and the journey of this book for another year. He was the book's first reader. To my mom, Nancy Barber, Sr., for always supporting me and cheering me on when doing these crazy adventures, no matter what she might think of them, and for her generous hotel sponsorship. Like a road angel for life, she always gives me a safe haven. To my aunt Fran Arnold who threw herself totally into this race, who always has an open-door policy, and who spends her life running around to support other people's dreams, all while living a rich, adventurous life herself. To my cousin Karen Gentry for her hotel sponsorship and support. She's been a great role model all my life for how to be a loving, vibrant, fun, creative, adventurous, athletic human.

My sincere appreciation to all the Vol State administration who make this race happen. They work like dogs so that we can live like stray dogs. To Lazarus Lake, the impish genius of all this craziness and the innovative mastermind of new ways to transcend the status quo. To his wife Sandra Cantrell for her tireless work keeping Laz and his projects going. To Jan Redmond Walker for blister help, ultra advice, and for keeping so many people moving forward even when they don't think they can. That might be a good definition of a saint, or at the very least, a great coach. To Carl Laniak for the fabulous woodallions and for keeping so much of Vol State on track in the shadow of the famous impresario. To Mike Dobies for tracking us all and politely texting when we forgot to check in.

Thanks to all the folks who wrote books that prepped me for Vol State, including (in the order that I read them) John Price (*The Last Annual Vol State Road Race Book*), Dallas Smith (*Bench of Despair*)

Terrie Wurzbacher (*It's Not About the Miles*), Marc Frost (*A Blistering Pace*), and John Vonhof (*Fixing Your Feet*). Thanks also to Tim Hardy for organizing the spring webinar to help the newbies and to Bob Hearn and Jim and Vicky Halsey for their journey-running advice.

I'm especially appreciative of all the road angels for taking such great care of me and the rest of the Vol Staters, especially Robin and Vincent Bailey, Robert and Regina Brewer, Pam Pratt, Peggy Copous, Mary Cruse, Lorraine Threlkeld, David and Russell Scott, and Steve Smalling. I wish I could've stayed longer at the Nutt House and Bobby Brown's. Thanks to Pamela Avery Murphy, Aunt Fran's cousin for showering me with attention, despite never getting to meet me, and to Claus Rasmussen and his crew for bringing her card all the way to Kimball.

Thanks to all the Vol Staters who made things more bearable along the way, especially Steven Godfrey for the hand-me-down hotel room in Martin; Terra Turner, Kendra Stallings, and Kurt Phillips for giving me a taste of what it would be like to be in a fun gang for one of these Last Annual journeys; Ed Masuoka for the good company and for watching to make sure I didn't fall off the sidewalk on the way into Shelbyville; Paul Heckert for advice along the way late at night outside McKenzie and Columbia; and last, but certainly not least, Tony Webb for getting me into all this nonsense in the first place and showing me how it's done.

Besides Chris, I want to thank a number of people for helping me with the manuscript for this book. Judith Hudson was my first beta reader after Chris; she gave me early confidence and helped me with edits. Other early readers who helped make it a better book included Andy Dehnart, Jane and Gary Bolding, my aunt Fran, and my mom. Thanks also to Alan Hines for his publishing advice.

The multi-talented Kirk Marsh worked tirelessly and patiently on the cover design as I hemmed and hawed about what I wanted. Nick Gissal also helped me focus on what needed improving.

I send my on-going appreciation to Terri Witek and Stetson University's Sullivan Creative Writing Program for their generous support of my writing through the years.

Finally, thanks to I.Z. IRT and Hooray Rooray for giving the family mountains of cuteness and joy to rally around, so we don't have to talk about politics.

www.ingramcontent.com/pod-product-compliance
Lightning Source LLC
Chambersburg PA
CBHW061436150726
47987CB00001B/230